AFP Code of Ethical Principles and Standards

ETHICAL PRINCIPLES • Adopted 1964; amended Sept. 2007

The Association of Fundraising Professionals (AFP) exists to foster the development and growth of fundraising professionals and the profession, to promote high ethical behavior in the fundraising profession and to preserve and enhance philanthropy and volunteerism. Members of AFP are motivated by an inner drive to improve the quality of life through the causes they serve. They serve the ideal of philanthropy, are committed to the preservation and enhancement of volunteerism; and hold stewardship of these concepts as the overriding direction of their professional life. They recognize their responsibility to ensure that needed resources are vigorously and ethically sought and that the intent of the donor is honestly fulfilled. To these ends, AFP members, both individual and business, embrace certain values that they strive to uphold in performing their responsibilities for generating philanthropic support. AFP business members strive to promote and protect the work and mission of their client organizations.

AFP members both individual and business aspire to:

- practice their profession with integrity, honesty, truthfulness and adherence to the absolute obligation to safeguard the public trust
- act according to the highest goals and visions of their organizations, professions, clients and consciences
- put philanthropic mission above personal gain;
- inspire others through their own sense of dedication and high purpose
- improve their professional knowledge and skills, so that their performance will better serve others
- demonstrate concern for the interests and well-being of individuals affected by their actions
- value the privacy, freedom of choice and interests of all those affected by their actions
- foster cultural diversity and pluralistic values and treat all people with dignity and respect
- affirm, through personal giving, a commitment to philanthropy and its role in society
- adhere to the spirit as well as the letter of all applicable laws and regulations
- advocate within their organizations adherence to all applicable laws and regulations
- avoid even the appearance of any criminal offense or professional misconduct
- bring credit to the fundraising profession by their public demeanor
- encourage colleagues to embrace and practice these ethical principles and standards
- be aware of the codes of ethics promulgated by other professional organizations that serve philanthropy

ETHICAL STANDARDS

Furthermore, while striving to act according to the above values, AFP members, both individual and business, agree to abide (and to ensure, to the best of their ability, that all members of their staff abide) by the AFP standards. Violation of the standards may subject the member to disciplinary sanctions, including expulsion, as provided in the AFP Ethics Enforcement Procedures.

MEMBER OBLIGATIONS

1. Members shall not engage in activities that harm the members' organizations, clients or profession.
2. Members shall not engage in activities that conflict with their fiduciary, ethical and legal obligations to their organizations, clients or profession.
3. Members shall effectively disclose all potential and actual conflicts of interest; such disclosure does not preclude or imply ethical impropriety.
4. Members shall not exploit any relationship with a donor, prospect, volunteer, client or employee for the benefit of the members or the members' organizations.
5. Members shall comply with all applicable local, state, provincial and federal civil and criminal laws.
6. Members recognize their individual boundaries of competence and are forthcoming and truthful about their professional experience and qualifications and will represent their achievements accurately and without exaggeration.
7. Members shall present and supply products and/or services honestly and without misrepresentation and will clearly identify the details of those products, such as availability of the products and/or services and other factors that may affect the suitability of the products and/or services for donors, clients or nonprofit organizations.
8. Members shall establish the nature and purpose of any contractual relationship at the outset and will be responsive and available to organizations and their employing organizations before, during and after any sale of materials and/or services. Members will comply with all fair and reasonable obligations created by the contract.

9. Members shall refrain from knowingly infringing the intellectual property rights of other parties at all times. Members shall address and rectify any inadvertent infringement that may occur.
10. Members shall protect the confidentiality of all privileged information relating to the provider/client relationships.
11. Members shall refrain from any activity designed to disparage competitors untruthfully.

SOLICITATION AND USE OF PHILANTHROPIC FUNDS

12. Members shall take care to ensure that all solicitation and communication materials are accurate and correctly reflect their organizations' mission and use of solicited funds.
13. Members shall take care to ensure that donors receive informed, accurate and ethical advice about the value and tax implications of contributions.
14. Members shall take care to ensure that contributions are used in accordance with donors' intentions.
15. Members shall take care to ensure proper stewardship of all revenue sources, including timely reports on the use and management of such funds.
16. Members shall obtain explicit consent by donors before altering the conditions of financial transactions.

PRESENTATION OF INFORMATION

17. Members shall not disclose privileged or confidential information to unauthorized parties.
18. Members shall adhere to the principle that all donor and prospect information created by, or on behalf of, an organization or a client is the property of that organization or client and shall not be transferred or utilized except on behalf of that organization or client.
19. Members shall give donors and clients the opportunity to have their names removed from lists that are sold to, rented to or exchanged with other organizations.
20. Members shall, when stating fundraising results, use accurate and consistent accounting methods that conform to the appropriate guidelines adopted by the American Institute of Certified Public Accountants (AICPA)* for the type of organization involved. (* In countries outside of the United States, comparable authority should be utilized.)

COMPENSATION AND CONTRACTS

21. Members shall not accept compensation or enter into a contract that is based on a percentage of contributions; nor shall members accept finder's fees or contingent fees. Business members must refrain from receiving compensation from third parties derived from products or services for a client without disclosing that third-party compensation to the client (for example, volume rebates from vendors to business members).
22. Members may accept performance-based compensation, such as bonuses, provided such bonuses are in accord with prevailing practices within the members' own organizations and are not based on a percentage of contributions.
23. Members shall neither offer nor accept payments or special considerations for the purpose of influencing the selection of products or services.
24. Members shall not pay finder's fees, commissions or percentage compensation based on contributions, and shall take care to discourage their organizations from making such payments.
25. Any member receiving funds on behalf of a donor or client must meet the legal requirements for the disbursement of those funds. Any interest or income earned on the funds should be fully disclosed.

A Donor Bill of Rights

PHILANTHROPY is based on voluntary action for the common good. It is a tradition of giving and sharing that is primary to the quality of life. To assure that philanthropy merits the respect and trust of the general public, and that donors and prospective donors can have full confidence in the not-for-profit organizations and causes they are asked to support, we declare that all donors have these rights:

I.

To be informed of the organization's mission, of the way the organization intends to use donated resources, and of its capacity to use donations effectively for their intended purposes.

II.

To be informed of the identity of those serving on the organization's governing board, and to expect the board to exercise prudent judgement in its stewardship responsibilities.

III.

To have access to the organization's most recent financial statements.

IV.

To be assured their gifts will be used for the purposes for which they were given.

V.

To receive appropriate acknowledgement and recognition.

VI.

To be assured that information about their donations is handled with respect and with confidentiality to the extent provided by law.

VII.

To expect that all relationships with individuals representing organizations of interest to the donor will be professional in nature.

VIII.

To be informed whether those seeking donations are volunteers, employees of the organization or hired solicitors.

IX.

To have the opportunity for their names to be deleted from mailing lists that an organization may intend to share.

X.

To feel free to ask questions when making a donation and to receive prompt, truthful and forthright answers.

DEVELOPED BY

Association for Healthcare Philanthropy (AHP)
Association of Fundraising Professionals (AFP)
Council for Advancement and Support of Education (CASE)
Giving Institute: Leading Consultants to Non-Profits

ENDORSED BY

(in formation)
Independent Sector
National Catholic Development Conference (NCDC)
National Committee on Planned Giving (NCPG)
Council for Resource Development (CRD)
United Way of America

Leading the Fundraising
Charge

The AFP Fund Development Series

The AFP Fund Development Series is intended to provide fund development professionals and volunteers, including board members (and others interested in the nonprofit sector), with top-quality publications that help advance philanthropy as voluntary action for the public good. Our goal is to provide practical, timely guidance and information on fundraising, charitable giving, and related subjects. The Association of Fundraising Professionals (AFP) and John Wiley & Sons, Inc. each bring to this innovative collaboration unique and important resources that result in a whole greater than the sum of its parts. For information on other books in the series, please visit:

Association of
Fundraising Professionals

http://www.afpnet.org

The Association of Fundraising Professionals

The Association of Fundraising Professionals (AFP) represents over 30,000 members in more than 207 chapters throughout the United States, Canada, Mexico, and China, working to advance philanthropy through advocacy, research, education, and certification programs.

The association fosters development and growth of fundraising professionals and promotes high ethical standards in the fundraising profession. For more information or to join the world's largest association of fundraising professionals, visit www.afpnet.org.

2012-2013 AFP Publishing Advisory Committee

John Wiley & Sons, Inc.:
Susan McDermott
Senior Editor (Professional/Trade Division)

AFP Staff:
Jacklyn P. Boice
Editor-in-Chief, Advancing Philanthropy
Chris Griffin
Professional Advancement Coordinator
Rhonda Starr
Vice President, Education and Training
Reed Stockman
AFP Staff Support

Leading the Fundraising Charge

Leading the Fundraising Charge

Charge

The Role of the
Nonprofit Executive

KARLA A. WILLIAMS

WILEY

John Wiley & Sons, Inc.

Cover Design: Leiva-Sposato
Cover Image: Christopher Hudson / iStockphoto

Published by John Wiley & Sons, Inc., Hoboken, New Jersey.
Published simultaneously in Canada.

For general information on our other products and services or for technical support, please contact our Customer Care Department within the United States at (800) 762-2974, outside the United States at (317) 572-3993 or fax (317) 572-4002.

Wiley publishes in a variety of print and electronic formats and by print-on-demand. Some material included with standard print versions of this book may not be included in e-books or in print-on-demand. If this book refers to media such as a CD or DVD that is not included in the version you purchased, you may download this material at http://booksupport.wiley.com. For more information about Wiley products, visit www.wiley.com.

Library of Congress Cataloging-in-Publication Data

Williams, Karla A.
  Leading the fundraising charge: the role of the nonprofit executive/Karla A. Williams.
    p. cm.
  Includes bibliographical references and index.
  ISBN 978-0-470-62198-1 (cloth); ISBN 978-1-118-22078-8 (ebk);
   ISBN 978-1-118-23328-3 (ebk); ISBN 978-1-118-25906-1 (ebk)
  1. Nonprofit organizations—Management. 2. Fund raising. 3. Leadership. I. Title.
  HD62.6.W556 2012
  658.15'224—dc23

                                    2012026253

Printed in the United States of America

10 9 8 7 6 5 4 3 2 1

To family, friends, and colleagues, thank you for challenging, inspiring, and encouraging me. You lift me up when I lack confidence, but call my hand when I become too certain. You appreciate me when I do my level best, but remind me that it may not be enough. You have taught me how to balance passion with reason.

To my MOM, thank you for imparting wisdom, curiosity and life-long learning. To my daughters ALLYSON and LINDSEY, thank you for showing that ethics is not a situation, but a way of life. To my grandchildren ALEXA and LUCAS, thank you for asking the questions and questioning the answers. To DON, thank you for showing me that life is a journey not a destination.

Contents

Preface

This book is, more or less, a culmination of my professional experience and academic exchange. Often, I say I am a student first because of my exposure to others peoples' novel ideas and distinct notions—affording me an opportunity to be a better informed teacher, writer, researcher, and consultant. This book is a repository of 40-plus years of learning and practice . . . an attempt to articulate the best practices of organized philanthropy and fundraising leadership.

Philanthropic fundraising is not a technique; it is a perspective and a process that requires a familiarity with psychology, philosophy, anthropology, and sociology. I have had the privilege to immerse myself in this vast universe: defining what has become a worthy profession; defending the edges of purism against commercialism; helping to codify techniques into theory; and advancing the practice through research, curriculum and certification.

Leading the Fundraising Charge is the first of its kind to link the role of organizational leader with the role of fundraising leader. This book demonstrates that leadership in the fundraising context is not didactic; it is a dynamic that emanates from the top of an organization, influencing strategic directions, penetrating cultural dimensions, and inspiring entire communities to be intentionally generous and thoughtfully engaged.

If you are an executive director, or on the way to being one, this book is for you. If you are a development director, this will help clarify your roles and responsibilities. If you are a board member, this will give you insight into the job of nonprofit leader.

Chapter 1, "Leadership Concepts," focuses on what it takes to be a respected and reflective leader in the position of a nonprofit CEO or executive director, as it relates to fundraising. It covers the dynamics of leadership for the person who oversees an organization that desires, depends upon, and seeks community involvement via philanthropic partnerships. It specifically addresses why the executive director's leadership is so essential to the success of fundraising.

Chapter 1 covers the *essence* of personal leadership, the *enigma* of positional leadership, the *energy* of fundraising leadership, and the *effect* of organizational stages. It points out the essential multifaceted ingredients of leadership that causes an organization to resonate with donors, versus donors resisting support for it. As complex as the topic of leadership is, there is one fundamental truth: Fundraising starts and ends with leadership. In the absence of executive director leadership, fundraising will fail.

Chapter 2, "Philanthropy Concepts," explores the similarities between leadership and philanthropy, which are both motivated by peoples' desire to ameliorate problems or advance causes. It points out that "organized philanthropy" exists because worthy organizations provide programs and services that require financial contributions. It validates the notion that if and when a donor's interests and an organization's needs come together, they produce a transformational exchange of values that provides sustenance to a democratic society.

Chapter 2 covers the *principles* of organized philanthropy, the *motivations* of personal philanthropy, the *benefits* of philanthropy, and the *culture* of philanthropy in an organization. This chapter provides insight into the nonprofit sector and why philanthropy is the expression of people's unabated opinions and intrinsic values. Understanding how philanthropic motives drive people's actions to give time, talent, and treasure is paramount to successful fundraising. More important, this chapter explains how a philanthropic culture enables that success and the lack of a philanthropic culture deters it.

Chapter 3, "Development Concepts," focuses on the structure of a fund development program, covering the historic evolution of organized fundraising, in addition to the how-to of developing a program, staffing it, and preparing a development plan. It examines how fundraising became the organized discipline and professional, credentialed business proposition it is today and how fundraising has had tangents and tribulations, various forms of begging, elements of purism and commercialism, criticism and dynamism.

Chapter 3 is about the fund development *profession*, the fundraising *professionals*, the fundraising *department*, and the organization's development *plan*. It discusses how fund development is a much larger business strategy than is generally understood. It is a function that must be organized as a department to serve a specific clientele (donors), replete with all the infrastructure requirements to steward both mission and money. It suggests that fund development must be integrated into the organization and have equal status with all other programs and departments, as well as sufficient resources to be able to produce the anticipated "profits."

Chapter 4, "Relationship Concepts," presents the process associated with developing relationships that are sustainable for the long term, rather than the short term. It points out that a donor's view of a relationship is quite different from an organization's or a fundraiser's view. It demonstrates that true relationships are not just created, they are earned. Earned relationships are the result of mutual values synchronicity. They are not artificially contrived, but authentically evolved, never predicted, but predicated on opportunities found. This perspective is called donor-focused or donor-centered fundraising.

Chapter 4 focuses on *social-exchange* and marketing relationships, alignment of donor interests with need, *cultivation* that are organized and strategic, and *management of methods* that cause donors to give, give again, and give more. This chapter also contains field and academic research on donor segments who have the highest potential. It brings all the philosophical, theoretical, and practical elements of relationship-building in fundraising together. It applies the sensitivities and sensibilities that are integral to respectful relationships.

Chapter 5, "Solicitation Concepts," dives deeper into the best solicitation practices utilized by the most successful fund development programs in the country. It points out that best practices are not nicely configured in black-and-white, replicable formulas; they are some do's and don'ts, a few maybes and shoulds, but no formulaic absolutes. This chapter covers what the executive director needs to know to be able to assess where to apply inspiration, when to make certain demands, what to hold others accountable for, when you need to step up and exhibit leadership, where to best apply resources, and finally, how to minimize risks.

Chapter 5 covers all the components of a successful integrated development program, including the *case* for solicitation, the various *campaigns* for implementation, and the *communications* needed to elicit a response. It confirms the proposition that executive directors need to lead the fundraising charge, if they want to represent the top philanthropic institutions in the country.

Karla A. Williams, ACFRE

Leadership Concepts

ESSENCE, ENIGMA, ENERGY, AND EFFECT

This book begins with a chapter on organizational leadership because it is prerequisite for fundraising to excel. Leadership in the fundraising context is not didactic; it is a dynamic that emanates from the top of an organization, influencing strategic directions, penetrating cultural dimensions, and inspiring entire communities to be intentionally generous and thoughtfully engaged.

INTRODUCTION

The topic of leadership has become a vast economic and intellectual enterprise. Interest in the subject emanates from scholars, practitioners, consultants, and trainers in virtually every thought-discipline and social culture.

So popular is the topic of leadership that 85,743 books with the word *leadership* in the title can be found on the Amazon.com website. Of this number, 2,256 focus on nonprofit leadership. This popularity stems not only from a widespread curiosity about how to become a leader but also from the scores of divergent opinions about what *kind* of leadership is needed today.

Aspiring leaders are left to discern which among the thousands of books, hundreds of seminars, and multitude of scenarios might fit their particular situation and their organization's status. Wouldn't they all? Most certainly not!

Although most leadership books and training sessions present the basic skills, characteristics, and behaviors needed for leadership within organizations, they also tend to generalize and/or cite examples that are impractical or impossible to replicate.

Most authors offer opinions about organizational leadership largely derived from experiential observations, causing them to be presumptive rather than substantiated by replicable evidence. Many authors imply that leadership applications are transferable across sectors, in spite of different cultural dimensions. It goes without saying, that much work is needed before the topic of nonprofit leadership is fully explored and explained.

Leadership books written just for the nonprofit sector have yet one more shortcoming. They do not explore how important the executive director and other organizational leaders are to fundraising. Perhaps it's because leadership can exist without fundraising, but those of us on the front lines of philanthropy have come to know that fundraising cannot exist without leadership!

Since the topic of leadership is so expansive, this first chapter does not attempt to recite what others have written. Instead, it focuses on what it takes to be a respected and reflective leader in the position of nonprofit CEO or executive director . . . as it relates to fundraising.

It covers the dynamics of leadership for someone who oversees an organization that desires, depends upon, and seeks community involvement via philanthropic partnerships. It specifically addresses why the executive director's leadership is so essential to the success of fundraising.

This book is the first of its kind to link the role of organizational leader with the role of fundraising leader.

Chapter 1 covers:

- ESSENCE of Personal Leadership: Necessary Elements and Ingredients
- ENIGMA of Positional Leadership: Pressure of Being at the Top
- ENERGY of Fundraising Leadership: Differences Between Good and Bad
- EFFECT of Organizational Stages: Various Stages Will Alter Strategy

ESSENCE OF PERSONAL LEADERSHIP

Necessary Elements and Ingredients

> Leadership is everybody's business, and the leadership challenge is everyone's challenge. The next time you say to yourself, "Why don't THEY do something about this?" look in the mirror. Ask the person you see, "Why don't YOU do something about this?"
>
> —James Kouzes and Barry Posner

Most of us respond to leadership challenges because we see a situation we want to change or an opportunity we want to seize. Our determination to *do something* is stimulated by a sense of awe and trepidation or exhilaration and risk. Therein lies the complexity of this topic.

Since leadership is often more situational than prescriptive and generally more dynamic than static, very few authors and experts agree on what it takes. Pick up any leadership book (hard copy, handbook, online, or e-book), and observe the tug and pull between leadership positions and propositions.

The prevailing thought seems to be if you read "the right book" you will be on your way to being a great leader. *(No offense intended here to the many authors who have provided valuable information on this abstract subject.)*

Here are a few seemingly sure-fire *formulas* for becoming a leader:

- *The 21 Irrefutable Laws of Leadership*—John C. Maxwell
- *The 7 Habits of Highly Effective People*—Stephen Covey
- *The 4 Obsessions of an Extraordinary Executive*—Patrick Lencioni
- *100 Ways to Motivate Others*—Steve Chandler

If you can't find the right formula, you can pick up one on leadership type:

- *Principle-Centered Leadership*—Stephen R. Covey
- *Servant Leadership*—Robert K. Greenleaf
- *Strengths-Based Leadership*—Tom Rath and Barry Conchie
- *Primal Leadership*—Daniel Goldman, Richard E. Boyatzis, and Annie McKee

Or you might resonate with the more enticing or animated titles:

- *A Whole New Mind: Why Right-Brainers Will Rule the Future*—Daniel H. Pink
- *Tribes: We Need You to Lead Us*—Seth Godif
- *Unleashing the Power of Rubber Bands: Lessons in Non-Linear Leadership*—Nancy Ortberg
- *Leadership for Dummies*—Marshall Loeb and Stephen Kindel

Too many choices? You can purchase one book and get it all: *The 10 Best Leadership Books of All Time,* by Jack Covert and Todd Sattersten.

One caveat: Learning how to be the consummate leader while sitting in the nonprofit executive director's seat will require more than any book can tell you. In this seat, in addition to everything else, you must be the *leader of fundraising* for your organization.

For an executive director, leadership connotes that you will lead your non-profit organization by inspiring a vision and empowering shared values to achieve a meritorious charitable mission, through and with others. This is, very simply, what fundraising is all about—inviting people to join you in your quest to change the world. The notion of fundraising is not as much about money as it is about mission.

Five key ingredients are needed for fundraising leadership; some inherited, some learned:

- SELF-AWARENESS: Perspective of Strengths and Weaknesses
- SENSE OF REALITY: See Through Objective Lenses
- COURAGE TO CHANGE: Create Ideas and Take Risks
- COMPASSION AND PASSION: Persistence to Make Things Right
- ETHICAL CONSCIENCE: Pursuit of Fairness, Integrity, and Honor

SELF-AWARENESS

Perspective of Strengths and Weaknesses

> Becoming a leader is synonymous with becoming yourself. It is precisely that simple, and it is also that difficult.
>
> —Warren G. Bennis

Whatever you call yourself—executive director, CEO, chancellor, president, hospital administrator, or something else—your *position* asserts you are the leader.

When you ask people what they look for in a *positional* leader, they use adjectives like *honest, transparent, authentic* . . . they mean you need to be real, maybe even larger than life. That's where self-awareness comes in meeting others' expectations without compromising yourself.

As executive director/CEO, you are the leader everyone else wants to know. Not being known personally by the executive director is tantamount to not having importance to the organization or the mission. Donors, board members, and employees all want to be on a first-name basis with you; this is how you affirm them as followers. They not only want to relate to you but also expect to have a relationship with you. To do this, you need to be accessible, approachable, and present.

It's not as much about ego (yours or theirs) as much as it is about equity. Gone are the days when followers (donors, board members, employees) expected their leaders to be charismatic or autocratic. Sure, followers want their leaders to be strong willed, wisely informed, and influential with others . . . but they also want their leaders to hold their ego in check and to be fair and reasonable. Self-awareness comes into play when you exhibit confidence not arrogance, and when you display assertiveness not aggressiveness.

Donors in particular are motivated to give to institutions and organizations whose leaders they *know* and *trust*—two key words. Donors may be familiar with your organization, its mission, and its work, but unless they have confidence that you and your leadership team are capable of taking the organization to the next level, they will not be inclined to seriously invest their own resources.

Donors' trust comes from feeling they are part of the organization's inner circle. As such, they have a high need (which grows exponentially with increased gifts) to have regular contact, to be sought out for advice, and to give counsel. That's where you come in. To be successful in fundraising, you must be open to ideas and guidance from your donors, including how you can do an even better job!

To remain self-aware or authentic, leaders resist engaging in self-deception. Robert Terry (1993), author of *Authentic Leadership*, recommended that leaders embark on a continuous quest of being informed in the following areas and by posing questions to ensure they are seeing their real selves. These questions are not just for one's own gratification; they would make great conversations with your closest advisors and investors.

Ask yourself, about yourself:

- *Personality Preference:* What are my strengths and weaknesses?
- *Inclusiveness:* How do I look at or analyze situations?
- *Self-Correction:* Am I able to learn from my experiences?
- *Call to Engagement:* Do I want to participate and be engaged?
- *Directional Orientation:* What does the ideal future hold?
- *Ethical Foundation:* How am I living love, justice, and freedom?

Terry theorized that authenticity is linked to action. He said that authenticity informs and directs action. Without authenticity, action drifts; without action, authenticity remains idle conjecture and wishful thinking.

Leaders who are self-aware know all about action. They seem to sense what and where their place in life is and how to get there. Self-awareness is a realistic perspective of your strengths and your weaknesses.

I believe that most natural leaders have instincts that cause them to seek out their particular path and create their own destiny by selecting a course that will be satisfying and successful. Life for them becomes a series of situations that call for one response or another: leadership action or followership action. They reflect consciously on the decisions they make and the actions they take to ensure that their ego (or self-deception) is held in check.

Make no mistake: self-awareness is a pursuit, not an accomplishment.

When self-awareness is present in the leadership DNA, there is more transparency and responsiveness to outside supporters. A strong sense of self makes executive directors comfortable in any situation and, in particular, with fundraising. With nothing to hide, the authentic executive director can get face time with funders at the drop of a hat, while the phony executive director can't get calls returned. When self-awareness is present, relationships with others are naturally reciprocal.

This notion that leadership stems from self-awareness and authenticity is not a new idea, nor is it a response to the host of highly publicized CEO scandals in both the corporate and the nonprofit world. Those unfortunate indiscretions do, however, reinforce the real risk of slipping over the precipice of authenticity into artificiality and arrogance. Stories of successful leaders who have fallen from grace point out how very fragile that line is between one's strengths and one's weaknesses.

Making mistakes can also enhance our self-awareness. Parker Palmer (2000) points out that people's darkness can become their pathway to the light. It is one's ability to see both sides and to sense the balance point that contributes to self-awareness.

The popular analogy of seeing a glass as half-full or half-empty suggests that positive and negative perspectives require a delicate balance. When McCall and Lombardo (1983) did their behavioral research, they identified four primary traits upon which leaders could succeed or derail:

1. *Emotional Stability and Composure:* calm, confident, and predictable, particularly when admitting error.

2. *Owning Up to Mistakes:* rather than putting energy into covering up.

3. *Good Interpersonal Skills:* able to communicate and persuade others without resorting to negative or coercive tactics.

4. *Intellectual Breadth:* able to understand a wide range of areas, rather than having narrow (and narrow-minded) expertise.

Our strengths can become our weaknesses in a millisecond. How ironic that we learn more from the latter than the former, confirming that the discovery of self is endless questioning: "What is really going on?"

SELF-AWARENESS Checklist

- Do you have the emotional intelligence and psychological fortitude to work through all kinds of situations, with all kinds of people?

- Do you surround yourself with people who know more than you do and are not threatened by them or their ideas?

- Does your strong sense of self keep you from compromising your values, even in the face of adversity?

- Are you eager to learn, challenge, and change the world, but you accept that you must do it through others?

- Are you psychologically open and able to seek out different perspectives from diverse disciplines, functions, and cultures?

- Do you stay on course with your plan, making changes necessary to achieve or adjust your ultimate goal?
- Do you allow yourself to be vulnerable, in ways that lead to personal and professional growth?

SENSE OF REALITY

See Through Objective Lenses

> The first responsibility of a leader is to define reality. The last is to say thank you. In between the two, the leader must become a servant and debtor. That sums up the progress of an artful leader.
>
> —Max De Pree

Quotes attributed to De Pree's 1987 book *Leadership Is an Art* are prolific and powerful. Very few authors have captured the essence of leadership practice with all its complexities without all the academic justification or jargon. He writes to the point, and every point has meaning.

De Pree's concept of artful leadership (define reality first and say thank you last) suggests that leaders have a dual role: to establish a realistic vision, and empower people to follow.

I suspect De Pree would have a hard time drawing a traditional organization chart with a square box at the top for the executive director and below, boxes neatly arranged in layers for subordinates. He might prefer interconnecting circles to describe the roles of leader-follower as a fluid ebb and tide of interactions and partnerships.

Interconnectivity is but one reality in organizational leadership, and essential to fundraising. No one can accomplish something of merit alone; if you think otherwise, you are not being realistic.

What would your organization's chart look like if you described how all your resources related to each other? Would you draw a box for yourself at the top and add more boxes for each constituent group: one for your leadership team, your board members, your committees, your fundraising volunteers, your individual donors, foundations, corporations, and civic organizations? What do you say about your relationship with your constituents? Do you describe them as customers, stakeholders, constituents, or partners?

Defining reality (where are you going) without defining resources (who is going to get you there) would be foolish. In the nonprofit world, we are first and foremost in the people business. Your constituent groups (whatever you call them) are integral to achieving your mission as dynamic overlapping investors; boxes they are not.

A sense of reality is the ability to see the world with objective lenses.

How does the executive director capture or create a sense of reality? You ask questions of others and then collectively question the answers. You become educated, build consensus about what needs to be done to solve the community's problems, and design organizational missions to address them (not vice versa). This implies you will involve more people rather than fewer, since nonprofit missions are about social impact and community benefit.

Reality checking is a *process* that starts informally and internally and extends formally and externally, akin to an internal-external needs assessment but constant.

When great nonprofit leaders ask, "What's going on here?"—they do so to formulate their decisions, not to justify them. They challenge assumptions not because they want to change them but because they want to understand them. They accept that finding reality takes time and resources and is neither an expedient nor inexpensive process. They allocate enough time to discover solutions and do not waste time belaboring the problems.

Realistic leaders are very good at looking for, and at, different sides of an issue; they examine the facts, figures, opinions, outcomes, and, yes, consequences. As such, they don't make arbitrary and capricious decisions, based on immediacy or emotion, and certainly not by themselves. They use discernment; they balance intuition and rational thought (Maxwell 1991).

Leaders are aware of two tough fundraising realities: money and time.

First reality: Your organization's need for money is one thing; the donor's desire and ability to give money is quite another.

This particular reality is often overlooked in preparing budgets and making program decisions. It's much easier to estimate what you will spend and much more difficult to project what you can raise.

The fact that you need money is a given: You will always find a program or project to implement. But the potential for philanthropy has variations and fluctuations. It is not a constant stream of available or entitled funds. You can't convince donors to give just because you have a good idea; the best you can do is to present a compelling, urgent, and relevant case for them to consider investing. And you better have defensible data to prove it!

This means that you can predict your needs, but you can't predict your donors. For philanthropy to occur, the two must match.

Second reality: It takes real time to build a fundraising program; it cannot be rushed and be successful.

This reality is hard to accept when the need for outside funding is so great. We naturally feel that our mission is so worthy that people should give to us and give now.

Without a solid investment of resources and a reasonable time frame to build the required relationships, the investment will be wasted. Not being aware of the time it takes for donors to gain confidence in your organization and your leadership could result in asking too soon or leaving money on the table. Harm done can seldom be undone. Hiring the wrong development staff will waste time and resources, too. Lost potential is a step backward making the next step forward a veritable staircase.

Fundraising is a financial investment that will eventually produce a greater return on investment (ROI) than any other revenue stream in any organization (short of the radiology department in a health care system). It pays to make the investment up front.

In fundraising, a sense of reality and authenticity are paramount. Your organization's vision must be real (relevant) and it must be resourced (achievable). It can't be a whim or a whine; it must be grounded in fact, elevated by confidence.

As executive director, everyone looks to you to say what is and what is not, where you are going or cannot go. Essentially, you provide the philosophical, psychological, theoretical, and practical leadership for all your organization's aspirations.

You will need to be both practical and pragmatic with your realism and recognize that it is the midpoint between optimism and pessimism. Too much optimism can lead to overly ambitious fundraising goals and pressure tactics with donors. Excessive optimism can lead to accepting gifts that cause mission creep. Too much pessimism can result in the rejection of ambitious plans or bold initiatives, focusing instead on the flaws and risks of pursuing them. Excessive pessimism leads to doing it the old way and missing opportunities for change.

SENSE OF REALITY Checklist

- Do you look beyond the obvious two sides and seek all sides of an issue; if something doesn't work one way, do you try another?

- Do you accept complexity and ambiguity, while establishing defensible and ethical rationales for each option?

- Are you stimulated by taking ideas apart and putting them back together, preferring innovative projects that break the status quo?

- Do you want to know where the organization stands with constituents, because you don't take them for granted?

- Do you take time to be fully informed, to think things over, and not rush into something before its time?

- Do you know how to search out the elusive truths rather than adjust to the political versions of them?

- Are you are confident about what you know? Do you see it, and say it, as it is?

COURAGE TO CHANGE

Create Ideas and Take Risks

> The quest for change is an adventure. It tests our skills and abilities. It brings forth talents that have been dormant. It's the training ground for leadership.
>
> —James Kouzes and Barry Posner

If play is the work of children (corroborated by social scientists), then change is the preoccupation of leaders.

Kouzes and Posner say that leaders *challenge the process*; John Gardner says they *release talent and energy*; and Rosabeth Moss Kanter says leaders are *change masters* and *prime movers*.

But the most common term for leader is *change agent*.

As executive director, it is your job is to weave the continuity and values of yesterday with the challenges and visions of tomorrow. As an agent of change, you are expected to alter the course of events. To do so, you will need more than the willingness to change; you must embrace and instill change as a *constant* in your nonprofit organization.

When executive director candidates come from outside the nonprofit sector, they are warned that this sector is not only different but also fraught with uncertainty. They are cautioned that this sector is not a safety net, even if they want to "do good."

Doing good is a concept that is being reconstructed, as a result of many convergences. The nonprofit sector is going through unprecedented change on the heels of an economic downturn. If this is not enough, there are:

- Enormous demographic shifts that are redefining participation

- Exponential technological growth and global access

- Unmitigated demand for transparency and accountability as a justification for why organizations exist

- Unparalleled competition and blurring between nonprofits, for-profits, and government

- An insatiable demand for new solutions, organizational forms, and leadership models.

It is said in many leadership chronicles that people who love breaking new ground go so far as to seek out problems that might be solved. Are you a change agent who goes looking for situations that require a leadership response and move on when the problems are solved? This would be the litmus test for today's transformational leader.

As a transformational leader, you need to feel comfortable and unapologetic for moving things forward, altering the way business has been done, making things better, capturing stronger market positions, raising more money, driving more business, and being better, bigger, and bolder.

As an executive director, you will need a change agenda, a change process, and a mantra of three little words: *challenge, innovate, and collaborate.*

1. ***Challenge.*** Competent leaders are never afraid to challenge the way things are done because they have the skills to navigate complex and ambiguous situations.

   They don't unnecessarily question to prove they are competent. Instead, they inform themselves so they can see precisely what needs to be explored and challenged. They ask, "*How can things be improved, with what I know and what I have yet to know?*" For them, a fully informed change is not resisted; it is welcomed.

   There is a lot to know, these days, about how fundraising is changing. These changes will require your attention and your ability to challenge assumptions.

   During the past 15 years, fundraising theory and practice have made a seismic shift from being institutionally focused to being donor focused. This was not by accident. As research on donor motivations, behaviors, and attitudes became available, practitioners have been integrating this knowledge into their practices. There is more to come as demographic and psychographic shifts are fully realized. Fundraising practices will only be relevant tomorrow if they utilize sophisticated research, segmentation, and targeted messaging and methods.

   How well the fundraising industry addresses the recent and future challenges, remains to be seen.

2. ***Innovate.*** Competent leaders tend to challenge how something could be not just different, but better. This requires a curious, creative mind-set that inspires others to envision new approaches, articulate new ideas, and craft new pathways.

   Innovation in the nonprofit sector is the edge that causes nonprofits to thrive versus survive. Innovation is the bending, molding, tugging, and pulling at what exists, in an effort to make it more effective or more efficient. In the end, innovation is taking apart the box, without throwing out the box; but your box is likely to have some sharpened edges!

In the nonprofit sector, innovation can be found in many forms of service, not products. Goodwill Industries has added external job placement services, going beyond their internal job training program. Girl Scouts has encouraged the formation of viral online troops, augmenting the traditional weekly troop meetings in suburbia. United Ways are expanding their fall workplace campaign to year-round activities for donors in nontraditional jobs. Other forms of innovation in the nonprofit sector include shared buildings and backroom resources, for-profit ventures, and public-private partnerships.

Innovation is not a one-time event; it is a way of life for our nonprofit sector. As executive director, you are key to incorporating a culture of *systematic* innovation in your organization if you want to release human talent and energy. A recent report from the Kellogg Foundation, *Intention and Innovation,* points out that collaboration, culture, change agents, and technology are needed to improve philanthropy, all resulting in social impact.

3. ***Collaborate.*** Instilling and growing competence (not competition) in our ever-changing world demands a higher level of strategic leadership and professional management, and the only way to do it is to collaborate—not because you have to, but because you *want* to.

The call for collaboration is not new; in fact, it became the mandate of most private foundations during the 1990s. Weary of funding the same old problems and solutions, private funders gave the nonprofit sector an edict: collaborate or no grants. Unfortunately, most nonprofits gave collaboration lip service, until now. From trying to collaborate when we didn't want to, we learned it had to be mutually beneficial to succeed.

Today, collaboration is not a tactic; it is a dual strategy that works in tandem with external and internal partners. External collaboration means looking differently at what we term "competitors." Ironically, there are more opportunities with counterparts than there are threats, and besides, it is more economical to trust than to compete.

The key to collaboration is not thinking about winning, but thinking about succeeding. Succeeding is something that is best achieved in concert with others.

Internal collaboration is similar. There should be healthy competition, with rewards, not punishments. Today's followers want their leaders to exhibit new participative leadership, not old hierarchical mandates. They want their leaders to share the agendas, not impose priorities; give them attention, not dictate results; and define problems, not enforce solutions.

COURAGE TO CHANGE Checklist

- Have you mastered specific skills but acknowledge that you cannot be superior at everything. Do you admit when another nonprofit agency does it better?

- Do you encourage new approaches and new methods that meet constituents' needs for a value exchange?

- Do you grow competency throughout the organization, encourage a culture of inquiry and a learning environment?
  - Do you use left-brain and the right-brain thinking, aligning hard facts with gentle expressions and meeting people's needs for both?
  - Are you willing to integrate innovative technology, even when you don't understand how it works?
  - Do you allocate resources for professional training, job development, and internal promotions?
  - Are you more teacher than preacher, enabling others to be challenged in the process?

COMPASSION AND PASSION

Persistence to Make Things Right

> Effective nonprofit organizations are rich savory cultural stews . . . permeating myths about the value of human worth . . . sharing deep abiding assumptions that they are about something important, something vital to society and to the existence of humankind.
>
> —Terrence Deal and Casey Smith Baluss

Today's nonprofit leaders must be more than interesting; they must be interested. As such, they will gravitate toward others, drawing them out. They will not only stir the cultural stew but also bring the ingredients to a boil, releasing the essence of human potential. If compassion and passion are a part of the mix, you have a winning recipe.

As the executive director, your job is to figure out what it takes to appreciate, motivate, validate, and congratulate others so their aspirations are fulfilled as the mission goes to work. Essentially, you need to ignite your organization to attract and retain those with passion in their bellies.

After decades of research, Kouzes and Posner concluded that CEOs and executive directors are at their best when they help people find meaning and faith in their work and help them answer fundamental questions that have confronted humans of every time and place. Their questions are simple but incredibly profound.

Ask yourself and others these questions:

- Who am I as an individual?
- Who are we as a people?
- What is the purpose of my life, of our collective life?
- What ethical principles should we follow?
- What legacy will we leave?

Great servant leaders create organizational soul by offering the gift of significance, rooted in confidence that the work they do is worthy of everyone's effort and that the institution deserves everyone's commitment and loyalty (De Pree 1987).

I do not want to imply here that being a servant leader is about religion, but it is definitely spiritual when it comes to building a caring environment where relationships and human potential are nurtured in your board members, your staff, your volunteers, and your clients and customers. Fervent attention to your organization's soul creates a tight community of converted believers.

Max De Pree agrees: "Leadership is a concept of owing certain things to the institution. It is a way of thinking about institutional heirs, a way of thinking about stewardship as contrasted with ownership."

He implies that leaders need to measure what they leave behind by way of momentum and effectiveness, of civility and values (De Pree, 1987).

Values are those things an organization believes in, that are printed and hung on the walls. Values are the template used by employees, donors, and board members to interpret behaviors and make sense of actions and events. When we resonate with a set of values, we are instinctively motivated to follow.

In this context, leaders are value centered, having compassion for what is right and passion for doing it right, hopefully spelled out in a values proposition that is broadly circulated and widely stated.

What are the cultural values that followers crave? Clues can be found in what is called the human resource theory of leadership, which highlights the interdependent relationships between people and organizations.

> Organizations need people (for their energy, effort and talent), and people need organizations (for the many intrinsic and extrinsic rewards they offer), but their respective needs are not always well-aligned. If the fit between people and organizations is poor, individuals withdraw their efforts or even work against organizational purposes. If the individual finds satisfaction and meaning in work, the organization profits from effective use of individual talent and energy (Bolman and Deal 2003).

As executive director, your actions show up in the quality of your interactions, the depth of your relationships, and the stories you share around mission.

Leadership is the responsibility to sustain and encourage faith in ourselves and to spark that faith in others.

Your challenge is to reach across boundaries and confront superficial unity to tap the richness of deep diversity, which generates amazing passion you have for the work. Passion is the magnet for donors to give their all to a cause. Be deliberate to include donors in the formation of vision and values and establish a proposition that has organization-wide ownership.

As executive director, when you share your compassion with others, you create an empathetic community and an equitable workplace.

Leaders with strong values unleash individual talent and energy and use high-involvement strategies that generate pride for the fundraising work, not apology.

You may not have had servant leadership in mind when you took the job of executive director, but it will be the most glorious and rewarding of all leadership opportunities, regardless of the type of organization you work for.

Each of the various nonprofit subsectors interprets its human compassion and mission passion in unique ways.

- The *education* subsector does so by teaching people to think critically, discover new truths, and find their meaningful role in work.

- The *religious* subsector does it by inspiring people to think beyond themselves as part of a greater universe and to uplift spirits with hope and joy.

- The *arts and culture* subsector does it by stimulating people's ideas and expressions, celebrating diversity in behavior and attitude.

- The *health* subsector does it by addressing the scientific, biological, and physical aspects of both life and death, striving to mitigate the adverse effects of illness and disease.

- The *human services* subsector does it by filling the gaps between what people need, what they can afford, and what our government provides in the way of life's essentials.

COMPASSION AND PASSION Checklist

- Do you dive deep into the lives of others, pushing away the fear of compromise or obligation?

- Do you give and ask for gifts of time, talent, and treasure before asking others to do so?

- Are you building a culture of grace and gratitude by revealing where your own compassion and passion came from?

- Do you craft reasonable, relevant, and achievable goals, making sure that people have the best chance to succeed rather than fail?

- Do you make sure that everyone in the organization has the right fit so they, too, can ascend to a leadership position?

- Are you dedicated, diligent, and determined to get the job done, even when it takes a little longer?

- Do you hire people with a history of drive who have overcome obstacles and can make a difference too?

ETHICAL CONSCIENCE

Pursuit of Fairness, Integrity, and Honor

> Justice is seen in the way leaders distribute resources and results. It shows up in the attention leaders give to those on the margins. It sees leadership as a service not an accomplishment. Justice asks, "What do I as a leader owe?" It is communicated in every behavior, decision, policy and procedure.
>
> —Max De Pree

Research tells us what followers look for in their leaders: *honesty, integrity, conscientiousness*, and *fair-mindedness*. Ironically, they are all tied to behaviors involving ethics; they are standards of behavior that society perceives as right.

Formally defined, *ethics* is a branch of philosophy that considers questions of personal, organizational, and societal judgments. Ethical reflection and ethical statements are central to human experience, informing that experience and making sense of it (Terry 1993).

It takes real courage and keen insight to be ethical; it requires that you not only know what to do but that you also do it. Ethical courage, it seems, is difficult to teach; one must learn it through experience. Experiencing ethical dilemmas gives you the framework and the discipline to know how to approach confusion and ambiguity.

As executive director, you can expect ethical situations to arise, but you will not be able to predict them. They come at you in a spontaneous moment of time, demanding courageous and responsible actions, with multiple options and consequences. Ethical situations are like mazes, being able to discern which path to take requires wisdom and knowledge.

Terry implied that courage is its own generator and that we can recognize it, describe it, and discern it, but we cannot predictably induce it. Courage is the frontier of risk, not the comfort of the familiar (Terry 1993).

In the nonprofit sector and particularly in fundraising, we are challenged regularly with ethical dilemmas that require us to confront or otherwise to

condone. In ethics, you cannot do "nothing." Consider what you would do in each of the following situations:

1. **Board Giving.** A foundation application requires you to have 100 percent board giving to be eligible for a grant. One of your board members did not make a gift this year for confidential reasons. Do you report a 90 percent participation rate and explain why? Do you make a gift yourself on his or her behalf? Do you ask a board member to make a $10 gift so you can count this person in? Do you make the decision not to apply for the grant, knowing you don't meet the criteria?

2. **Bequests.** A large bequest is received by your organization, and it is designated for a program that you are about to phase out. Do you acknowledge that your program will no longer exist and refuse the bequest? Do you keep the program going for another year or so with an infusion of cash and hope the program has a little more life? Do you accept the bequest and bank it, hoping to have a program in the future that will fit the donor's intent?

These are hypothetical situations; the real ones cause greater angst and require more thoughtfulness. When faced with ethical dilemmas, it helps to have personal restraint and ask: What is valuable? What is meaningful? What is appropriate? Where, in your mind, are the edges of generous, lavish, unreasonable, indulgent, excessive, extravagant, and selfishness? Followers expect clear definitions and model behavior from their leaders (De Pree 1997).

In fundraising, ethics and courage go hand in hand. The public holds our nonprofit organizations to a higher level of trust and transparency because we exist for public benefit. Philanthropy is the litmus test of public trust and a belief that an organization merits a voluntary gift of time, talent, and treasure. Philanthropy is not a tax, a payback, or a purchase; it is "voluntary action for the public good."

Ethically speaking, we don't deserve philanthropy; we earn it by being conscientious stewards of our mission and the charitable conscience of community's civility.

Leaders who are grounded in ethical principles are catalysts for excellence, caring, justice, and faith. There is no other reason to do fundraising.

As a nonprofit leader, you will need a finely tuned sense of realism to be open to whatever hand you are dealt and to be able to accept the challenge of political realities, rather than be compromised by them. You must be zealous but never sell your soul. You need the competence to balance principles and politics.

As executive director, you already know that trust and truth are linked. Telling the truth and keeping promises build trust. Truth opens up an

atmosphere that is free of cover-ups. Trust is not given; it is earned. Think of this as cultivating a field of grain: preparing the soil for the seeds, fertilizing and watering the plants, and finally harvesting the crops. Exhibiting responsibility and good judgment demonstrates to followers that you are a reliable and trustworthy leader.

ETHICAL CONSCIENCE Checklist

- Are you are adamant about doing things right while doing the right thing. Do you cultivate a discipline of integrity while not tolerating dishonest behavior?

- Do you openly analyze ethical situations, continuously clarify ethical principles, act with temperance, and avoid unethical temptations? Do you say "no" to individual gain?

- Do you acknowledge that ethical leadership is fraught with complexity and ascribe to both intrinsic and extrinsic applications? Do you awaken, inform, ground, and enrich your community?

- Can you take a bad situation and transform it into a teachable moment? Do you look beyond the moment, seeking permanence and sustainability?

- Are you fair and just in the distribution of your time and organizational resources? Are your values virtuous, intertwined, and aligned? Do you talk about them openly and expect others to do the same?

- Do you express yourself with kindness and caring? Does your organization have a heart, a head, and a soul?

ENIGMA OF POSITIONAL LEADERSHIP

Pressures of Being at the Top

> Leadership is one of the most observed and least understood phenomena on earth.
>
> —James MacGregor Burns

The first section of this chapter addressed the ESSENCE of leadership from the perspective of knowing yourself. This section focuses on the ENIGMA of leadership from the perspective of how others look at you. Here we examine the ironies of positional leadership from the *follower side.*

In the nonprofit world, CEOs and executive directors are the public face of our charitable organizations, our public institutions, and our philanthropic agendas by virtue of their *position.*

Talk about pressure. Just because of your *position,* you are held to higher standards than leaders who are not at the top, subjecting you to both admiration and admonishment, views that may be well founded or ill contrived, at the same time.

Across the nonprofit world, we hear people unabashedly declare: "He's a great leader" or "She's not a leader." So common and sort of flip are these statements. It's clear that the public's views of *positional leadership* are staunchly opinionated, implying there are only two kinds of leaders: good and bad. We don't hear much about those who fall in the middle.

When people make categorical statements about CEOs in leadership positions, they may not even personally know them. They decide who is and who is not a leader based on their own definition of leadership, using a lens that reflects their own experiences.

This harsh reality makes one wonder whether the years and years of for-profit leadership research of people in high-powered positions has inflated the expectations we have of our positional leaders. Have the recent nonprofit leadership studies, focusing on the impending gap of people in line for CEO and executive director positions, uncovered how difficult the job really is?

When you are executive director, everyone's eyes are on you; the board and staff alike will continuously examine your behaviors, reaffirming or questioning them at every turn. Others (all of them, individually and collectively) will determine if your positional leadership has the behaviors, styles, and skills that fit their own personal definitions of the term *leader.*

To readers of this book, it's clear we are in a very precarious position if we declare ourselves the leader just because we happen to be in the *position* of CEO or executive director, and we would be foolish to do so in today's divergently opinionated environment.

Positional leadership is not ours to have; it is ours to earn. Therein lies the ENIGMA concept. Until we earn our leadership stripes, we won't be anything more than a person in the position. The earning never ends.

What do people look for in an organizational leader that causes them to accept or reject someone's leadership behaviors, styles, and skills? We might be able to answer that with one word: *trust* in the leader and the institution.

Public trust is based as often on an organization's leadership as on its mission; at times, the two may be inextricable. When we think of the great organizations, we can name the individual leaders who founded or headed them or were high-profile proponents for a long time; the personality of the person can be inseparable from the organization's official name. There's Jimmy Carter and Habitat for Humanity. There's William Booth and the Salvation Army. There's Father Flanagan and Boys Town.

When we think of great nonprofit leaders, we often attribute a situation or a circumstance to them. The style of leadership may be different in each leader, but the great ones are seldom forgotten. They become a part of the collective history of great organizations.

In this sector, followership also has a deeper meaning. People don't gravitate to nonprofits for work; they do it for meaning. The concept of followership moves up a level from subordinate to partnership, where relationships are voluntary. For followers, purposeful leadership is *in*; iconic leadership is *out*.

When Leslie Crutchfield and Heather McLeod Grant surveyed thousands of nonprofit leaders for their book, *Forces for Good,* they discovered a new kind of positional leadership they didn't expect: *shared leadership.*

> In much of the leadership literature, the individual heroic leader was often exalted. . . . In just the past decade, theories of "collective leadership" have begun to gain traction . . . strong leadership doesn't only exist at the very top of high-impact nonprofits; rather it extends throughout the organization. . . . CEOs of high-impact organizations . . . use their leadership to empower others. (Crutchfield and Grant 2008).

As an executive director, when you empower others, you are not giving away power, you are gaining power. Collective or participative leadership is built on trust between you and your colleagues: trust that you have their back and they have yours, trust that each person has a role in the collective whole and that together you can do more than anyone could do alone.

Trust results from meeting the expectations of others, and, simply put, others expect you (the CEOs or executive director) to create that culture of trust by providing the leadership vision, values, principles, shared decision making, and mutual relationships.

Six key elements are needed for positional leadership.

- VISION: Dream is Meaningful and Achievable
- VALUES: Mandate for Organizational Success
- PRINCIPLES: Assumptions Guide Decision Making
- PARTNERSHIPS: Teamwork that Fits the Situation
- RELATIONSHIPS: Perceptiveness of Boundaries and Obligations

What does trust have to do with fundraising? Everything! If donors, board members, employees, colleagues, vendors, competitors, and all the rest don't trust you, they won't trust your organization. The litmus test is that, when asked, followers say you are one of the community's preeminent leaders.

VISION

Dream is Meaningful and Achievable

> We can teach ourselves to see things the way they are. Only with vision can we begin to see things the way they can be.
>
> —Max De Pree

Followers want their leaders to first establish the organizational vision, then establish trust that the vision has merit and substance, and then inspire them to explore how they can help make the vision a reality.

The concept of vision was not part of the old management lexicon, the word *purpose* was. The larger meaning of vision likely emerged when human potential psychologists pointed out that followers responded better to a pull than to a push.

Today, in spite of the popular acceptance that anything moving forward needs a vision, the concept may be clear, but the explanation remains vague because vision is more of a dream than a precise goal or a purpose statement.

I like to describe it as something that happens when you reflect on what the possibilities might be—futurizing, if you will. On a visit many years ago to a Naples, Florida, beach, I observed the elusive ephemeral green flash at sunset—a phenomenon so seldom observed that people who see it never forget and, with continued amazement, retell the experience to their friends.

To me, vision is created in one of those rare and insightful moments in time. You may be sitting in a beach chair, looking over the horizon, aware of the cloud formations, the light intersections, the water reflections, and the wave movements—stretching your mind between the grains of sand between your toes and the infinite space at the tip of your fingertips. At a moment like this, a vision is imagined, visualized, inspired. It may pass as quickly as it came or form a longing in your head and heart that won't go away. That euphoric idea becomes a concrete commitment to do something, to be something.

Visions are conceptualizations about possibilities and desired futures; they are expressions of optimism and hope. Our visions are unique, setting us apart from everyone else. Kouzes and Posner provide a few questions to serve as catalysts for clarifying your vision:

- How would you like to change the world for yourself and your organization?
- If you could invent the future, what would it look like?
- What mission in life absolutely obsesses you?
- What is the distinctive role of your organization?

Your first job as a new executive director is to imagine and inspire a vision that will bring people together to make the world a better place, through caring and generosity. That vision is the platform for the role that philanthropy will play in your organization.

VALUES

Mandate for Organizational Success

> In vital organizations, those groups whose purpose has both pragmatic and moral dimensions, people reach outward to serve others and inward toward their own potential.
>
> —Max De Pree

Values provide the infrastructure for the vision by giving it definition. Values express what we believe in and substantiate where we are going and on what basis.

Values are deep-seated beliefs that influence every aspect of our lives. According to Kouzes and Posner (1995), "Values constitute our personal 'bottom-line.'"

In the nonprofit sector, the values we espouse and uphold are quite different than those in the for-profit sector or the government sector because they tend to be more charitable, inasmuch as most nonprofit missions are designed to serve.

An examination of values statements from a variety of nonprofits produces similar qualities: *fairness, equity, justice, integrity, honesty,* and *trust.*

As executive director, you must have your own values and then you must create shared values. Values can't be words; they need to actualized. Conflicts arise when leaders say one thing and do another, thus the need to apply values into what is called a common purpose.

John Gardner, founder and chairperson of Common Cause and a preeminent author on leadership, observed:

> A local constituency is won when people, consciously or unconsciously, judge the leader to be capable of solving their problems and meeting their needs, when the leader is seen as symbolizing their norms, when their image of the leader is congruent with their inner environment of myth and legend (Kouzes and Posner 1995).

There is actually a form of leadership called values-based leadership, which even the Harvard Business School aspires to:

> At Harvard Business School we believe that leadership and values are inseparable. The teaching of ethics here is explicit, not implicit, and our Community Values of mutual respect, honesty and integrity, and personal accountability support the HBS learning environment and are at the heart of a School-wide aspiration: to make HBS a model of the highest standards essential to responsible leadership in the modern business world. Our values are a set of guiding principles for all that we do wherever we are and with everyone we meet.

The evidence that shared values do in fact have merit come from Kouzes and Posner (1995), attesting that a correlation between individual and organizational values has a significant payoff.

The research shows that shared values:

- Foster strong feelings of personal effectiveness.
- Promote high levels of company loyalty.
- Facilitate consensus about organizational goals and stakeholders.
- Encourage ethical behavior.
- Promote strong norms about working hard and caring.
- Reduce levels of job stress and tension.

A word of caution: When selecting words to use to describe your organization's values, try not to borrow anyone else's, for they will sound trite and rhetorical. Try for original words that define how your organization is different, not the same.

PRINCIPLES

Assumptions Guide Decision Making

> True-north principles are always pointing the way. And, if we know how to read them, we won't get lost, confused or fooled by conflicting voices or values.
> —Stephen Covey

Having vision and values isn't enough until we say precisely how we will act on them. We need to elucidate how we will act in certain situations so participants perceive how to connect with others.

To some extent, both vision and values are intangible, while principles are tangible behaviors that define our moral compass.

In his book *Principle-Centered Leadership,* Stephen Covey suggests that principles are unlike values because they are objective and external. They are self-evident, self-validating natural laws—they don't change or shift. They serve as our 'true-north' when navigating the 'streams' of our environment.

Values, on the other hand, are like maps. "Maps are not territories," Covey points out, "because they are only subjective attempts to describe or represent the territory. The more closely our values or maps are aligned with correct principles (with the realities of the territory, with things as they really are) the more accurate and useful they will be. When the territory is constantly changing or when markets are constantly shifting, any map is soon obsolete."

In the nonprofit world, we often think of guiding principles as assumptions that provide a backdrop for our decision making. We can find examples of them in strategic plans or on posters that hang throughout the organization, helping to encourage consistency of quality in everything we do.

PARTNERSHIPS

Teamwork that Fits the Situation

> The CEO of a business has formal authority, and can use a more executive style of leadership to compel people to act. By contrast, leaders in the social sector lead through influence, not authority, and must convince others to act by force of their convictions alone.
>
> —Leslie R. Crutchfield and Heather McLeod Grant

Followers trust that they will be included in the decision making, making them feel they are at the very heart of things, not at the periphery. People feel centered when they are included, and that's what gives their work meaning.

Many words describe partnerships between leaders and followers around decision making: engagement, empowerment, joint decision making, power sharing, and consultative. There's even a leadership term for it: participative leadership.

Participative leadership theory involves others in organizational decisions, in contrast to autocratic leadership theory, where others are told what the decisions are. Be assured, participative leadership does not mean all decisions are shared; it means that voices are heard before decisions are made.

The idea of participating or sharing in leadership decisions came out of the Hersey-Blanchard Situational Leadership Model, where task and relationship behavior were divided into four quadrants. Each calls for a different leadership style depending on the risk level. Throughout, the model uses a consultative approach, which first materialized in the management by objectives (MBO) concept.

Participative leadership theory is only as good as the level of *trust* that the leader and the followers have in each other, as well as in their individual competencies. A lack of trust or a lack of competence negates the value of participative decision making.

When applied, participative decision making produces enormous benefits: Followers are more likely to be invested and will work to achieve the goals; they are less competitive and more collaborative. Plus, the collective decisions are often better because they are made from differing points of view.

In today's four-generation work world, involving others in decisions is not only beneficial, it is compulsory.

1. **The Great or Silent Generation** (1925 to 1945) is nearly gone, and with them, the hierarchical layers of bosses and subordinates, replete with lines of command that were rarely crossed. This generation adapted well to autocratic leadership and at the same time welcomed participative leadership.

2. **The Baby Boomers** (1946 to 1964) are currently at the helm and will be for a while if the economy doesn't pick up. Labeled the "me" generation, they are quite comfortable making decisions on their own, while holding a lot of meetings to achieve due process. They are good team players, love social interaction, and are willing to work long hours.

3. **Gen Xers** (1965 to 1980) have a different "me." They are more resistant to those long hours and want a more balanced life. At work, they not only want to be involved in decision making, they feel entitled to it. If they are left out of decisions, they feel that leaders do not respect them.

4. **Gen Yers** (1981 to 1999) are still developing their style of leadership. As we learn more about them, we are discovering they have a more rugged individualism than any preceding generation and not only are more comfortable with ethnic diversity, they demand it.

A recent study by the Centre for Creative Leadership showed that while generational differences do exist, similarities do, too. All the working-age generations want essentially the same things from their jobs: to trust their supervisors, to be paid well, to have interesting work, to get feedback, and to have the opportunity to learn.

The challenge for leadership is appreciating/accepting significant distinctions in how younger generations value, approach, and leverage engagement, transparency, technology, professional development, and work–life balance.

Suggestions for nonprofits leaders come from a recent study (Gowdy et al., 2009):

- Acknowledge and discuss generational differences, diversity, inclusion, and cultural competency—and clarify their relevance to organizational effectiveness and the ability to effect social change.

- Develop new structures and ways of managing both staff and volunteers to meet generational needs, and adapt to changing workplace values and expectations.

- Go beyond generational and representational diversity and focus on developing organizational strategy and leveraging diverse ideas, approaches, and talents in support of the mission.

RELATIONSHIPS

Perceptiveness of Boundaries and Obligations

At the heart of dealing with people is social perceptiveness—the ability to appraise accurately the readiness or reistanc eo ffollowers to move in a given direction, to know when dissension or confusion is undermining the group's will to act, to make the most of the motives that are there, and to understand the sensitivities.

—John W. Gardner

Vision, values, principles, and decision making all depend on trusting relationships. Trusting relationships are the power to create, build, and grow ideas that result in institutions.

In the nonprofit sector, there are a multitude of constituent groups with whom you, as executive director, must have a relationship to achieve leadership status. I am not referring to a relationship here that has a simple description with adjectives attached to it, such as a *personal relationship* or a *long-term relationship*. I mean a relationship that shares space in the same place.

Some believe relationship building is a natural result of liking people, but I think it is the natural result of being interested in people. Liking them is easy; being interested is hard work.

Leaders who have lots of followers are generally those who are really good at following and move between the leadership and followership without pause in building their relationships with the following key groups.

1. **Board of Directors.** The more effort you make as executive director to develop a strong board, the more confidence and respect the board will have for *your* work. This does not mean running the board; it means informing the board about issues that affect their governance role. It also means treating board members as individuals who have their own distinct talents and interests, which may not be evidenced in their group meetings. When a board is treated only as a group, it is difficult to have a meaningful relationship with them.

    There is a fine line in these relationships, of course, particularly when the board members are your boss. If you think about how you want to be treated by your employees, then the boundaries of the relationships with board members will be obvious.

2. **Employees.** At no other time has it been as challenging for nonprofit leaders as now, with the potential of four very different generational groups working under one roof at the same time. This calls for a more personal leadership style, not just a participative one.

    All generations value the ear of the boss, and having an open-door policy is as necessary as walking around. Years ago, the leader would *not* have had hallway conversations with employees about their personal lives (family, health, life goals, etc.), but today, NOT being interested in people's lives beyond work could be detrimental to your leadership effectiveness.

3. **Funders.** In recent years, nonprofit experts touted relationship building with donors as the driving force to fuel philanthropy; some call it friend raising, not fundraising. New staff titles like *donor relations* have replaced titles like *annual gifts* suggesting that the donor relationship is paramount

to the donors' gift size. This is all well and good, as long as this philosophical shift is honestly calibrated and not just a response to popular thinking.

Donors, in particular, want and deserve relationships that are respectfully appropriate within the context of their role with the organization. Having a personal as well as a professional relationship with a donor might be a good idea, so long as ethical boundaries are preserved. It is important to recognize that donors are not just the means, but also the ends, in themselves (Crutchfield and Grant 2008).

4. **Community Partners.** Call it community building, mobilizing, organizing, or networking—the more you extend yourself externally, the greater the visibility, the investment, and the collaboration that is generated for your organization.

   Crutchfield and Grant call it "nurturing nonprofit networks," which is number four on their list of success factors that make up high-impact organizations. Helping peers succeed and building networks of allies also advances your organization and generates respect as a positional leader. Promoting collaboration rather than competition has its advantages. "High impact organizations share their wealth, expertise, talent, and power with other nonprofits not because they are saints, but because it's in their self-interest to do so" (Crutchfield and Grant 2008).

5. **General Public.** Relationships with the general public will not be as personal as those with whom you work every day, but they are just as important because the public can be *the* constituency with the loudest voice.

   In the same way that a corporate sponsorship opens the door to high visibility, so do speaking engagements. When the public of nongivers hear and see the organization's leaders on a regular basis, they begin to consider the importance of that leader's organization: to associate with, to volunteer at, to make a gift to, and recommend to their friends.

   Nothing is as compelling as the stories that can be told when the platform invites them. Saying something in public has wider impact than one conversation with one person.

ENERGY OF FUNDRAISING LEADERSHIP

Differences Between Good and Bad

Leaders are the spark that ignites the fire in others when they act on positive emotions, speak to staff with a passionate voice, answer questions in an inspirational way or simply emit confidence and joy.

—James Boyle

The spark that leaders exhibit is really a reflection of their soul, their passion, and their joy. Acting as ENERGY, this spark manifests itself in their social consciousness, be it a desire to champion, advocate, or be a change agent. This internal energy awakens our motivations and our ability to motivate others to do extraordinary things.

When our energy is turned on, it's as if we are wearing a sticker on our foreheads that declares we are on fire. You can see it in our walk, in our talk, in the sparkle in our eyes, the tone of our voice, the intensity of our face muscles. When we walk into a room, we seem to light it up. When it's turned off, we are virtually invisible.

So important is positive energy as a leadership trait, it is the first thing trait-theorist headhunters look for. They call it *achievement drive*—a visibly high level of ambition, energy, and initiative.

With energy deeply ingrained in our psyche, we can tap it or turn it off. Energy seems to erupt like a volcano when we are onto something, and when we run out of steam, it subsides like a wet blanket over hot coals.

Besides being ingrained, energy is also contagious, in spite of it being high or low. High energy is replete with positive thoughts, creating enthusiasm and movement. Being content and happy about our life's path helps us tap into our good energy. Positive energy works like a magnet, attracting others who want to be with you, to be like you, to do what you do.

Likewise, stress and discontentment cause our good energy to wane or dissipate, and this, too, affects others. When we work too hard and too long, we become overwhelmed; numbness begins to set in. Low energy drains others, causing obstacles and even paralysis. This condition is not uncommon in high-stress jobs. Thus John Gardner, among others, suggests that leaders need to periodically take time and space to renew their energy, to clarify their future directions, to cleanse their minds of the here and now, and to renew their zest for life.

Not all people with energy seek leadership positions, but when they do, it's magical. Their intense zest for life, their *joie de vivre* and dynamism, naturally energize the entire organization.

I am reminded of the "CUBE," a poignant teaching tool that Hank Rosso designed for The Fundraising School located at The Center on Philanthropy.

His Cube is a visual reminder that sits prominently on the classroom tables throughout the weeklong Principles and Techniques course, which shows how all the elements of fundraising come together to construct an integrated development program.

He would point to each side of the cube and talk about the fundraising elements that are needed: Institutional Readiness on the top; Dynamic Functions on the bottom; Human Resources, Markets, Constituencies, and Case for Support.

He would go back to the side titled Human Resources, take his finger and slowly slide it down to the word *leadership* and say: This is the one element on this cube for which there is little if any substitution. Without leadership (he was referring to executive directors and board of directors), you (the development director) won't be successful at raising money, at least not for long.

His point: If you don't have leadership and positive energy at the top of your organization for fundraising, the fundraiser might as well look for another job.

Any executive director who wants to stimulate philanthropy must have intense energy for philanthropy and exuberance for fundraising.

No one else can be the *source* of the positive energy that drives fundraising—not the board, not the staff, not the professional fundraisers, not the donors. Only the executive director can provide the leadership impetus for fundraising to succeed.

Fundraising must be a strategic organizational initiative that values philanthropy as a partnership with others. In the absence of leadership from the top, fundraising is relegated to mere tasks at the bottom.

To recap from earlier in this chapter: The executive director must be the lead in shaping the vision, the core values, the guiding principles, the decision-making process, and in developing key relationships for fundraising to succeed.

This delegation of responsibility is affirmed in *The Nonprofit Chief Executive's Ten Basic Responsibilities*, the 2006 Board Source manual written by Richard Moyers. It says:

> The division of responsibilities around fundraising will vary widely based on an organization's size, the relative importance of contributed income, and the types of funding that the organization receives. One principle does hold true for most organization, from universities to homeless shelter: the Executive Director is one of the most important participants in building relationships with key individual and institutional donors and ensuring effective board involvement in fundraising (Moyers 2006).

To take the lead, energy is needed—but there are two kinds that deserve attention.

- POSITIVE ENERGY: Energy That Inspires and Stimulates
- NEGATIVE ENERGY: Energy That Deters and Contaminates

POSITIVE ENERGY

Energy That Inspires and Stimulates

> Leaders who can stay optimistic and upbeat, even under intense pressure, radiate the positive feelings that create resonance.
>
> —Daniel Goldman

Energy for fundraising comes from a place in your heart or your head that gives you the burning desire to carry a torch for something that is uniquely yours to champion, be it something personal, professional, or organizational—a belief that you and your community will benefit from your efforts.

The confidence that your donors will have in your institution will come as a result of their respect for your energy for fundraising. Why would others invest in ideas or issues with executive directors who are not leading the charge?

Beyond all the other leadership stuff, are executive directors expected to "ask"? Of course, they must. If they don't, why should anyone else?

The art and science of modern-day philanthropic fundraising is a process of asking not for yourself, but for others. When we ask potential donors, we are serving as conduits for those who are in need of the services that our organizations provide, be they students, artists, patients, or clients.

As executive director, you will want to acknowledge that people naturally want to give to something they deem important. It's not you they are giving to; it is you they are giving *through*. When you receive a gift, you have a responsibility to steward it; it's as if they lent it to you, to invest, with an expectation of a return.

For fundraising to be successful, it is essential that you, and all members of your leadership team, learn how to embrace fundraising, advocate for it, participate in it, and inspire it as a worthy endeavor.

The executive director's high-powered energy is the source of the organization's vision, credibility, and stewardship for fundraising.

- The executive director is the energy source of the institution's vision, when it is dependent on philanthropy.

- The executive director brings credibility to donors that the institution is well managed.

- The executive director ensures the stewardship of gifts that are made and wisely used.

The following checklist asks what you can do as well as what have you done?

POSITIVE ENERGY Checklist

- Have you established a charitable vision for the organization that is bold and palpable?

- Have you defined the precise role that philanthropy plays in your vision and goals (implying that without contributions your organization or program would not exist)?

- Are you the face and spokesperson for fundraising. Are you proud to ask people for a gift?
- Are you the go-to person for new ideas of what philanthropy might fund?
- Are you the champion for the act of philanthropy, not just for your organization, but for your larger community?
- Do you involve the board to do the same, by being spokespersons within the community and with their peers?
- Have you invited all employees to get involved in fundraising, not just the development staff?
- Do you know donors personally and well enough to receive unexpected generous gifts?
- Have you written a philanthropic values statement and asked people to embrace it?

Negative Energy

Energy That Deters and Contaminates

> Fundraising can bring out nervousness, embarrassment, or anxiety. These feelings arise when the conversation is all about money. We must deal directly with their fears . . . give them the opportunity to get over their mental blocks by having an honest, open discussion about their nervousness or anxiety about fundraising.
>
> —Gail Perry

Not all executive directors look at fundraising from a positive point of view; some still resist raising money because of the societal myths that money is power, good or bad. These views may hark back to a time when our parents taught us that the subject of money was taboo. We were warned not to discuss how much money we had or how much Dad made. We were told not to ask others for money out of embarrassment of being seen as poor. If we had to ask for help, it sent a message that we were not capable of taking care of ourselves.

When fundraising is measured only by how much money is raised (aka, the campaign thermometer) rather than the purpose it serves (what does the money do?), that's bad energy.

Fundraising is not really the functional task that it sometimes appears to be when people say, "Let's raise funds to do 'that'!" The *that* has to be defined and defended in terms of the benefits, which could be referred to as the mission product. I hesitate to use an analogy here that compares selling widgets to promoting ideas, because fundraising should not be relegated to terms like begging or selling. But when you are promoting ideas (as in fundraising), you still have to make those concepts as tangible and beneficial as any product, or people won't figuratively or literally "buy it."

When executive directors view fundraising as a degrading exercise of revenue generation, they naturally resist it. A negative attitude stems from a belief that fundraising is bad power; that is, taking or getting money. When asking for money is the equivalent of begging, who would want to participate?

Is asking for money a form of begging or selling? Is the asker the victim or the negotiator? The conduit or the steward?

After 40 years in the emerging profession of philanthropic development, I have come to see that gifting money for charitable purposes has far greater positive implications for the donor than it has negative implications for the asker.

Granted, some fundraising efforts are more asking focused, as opposed to receiving focused (for example, asking someone to be a sponsor for a charity walk). During my long career, fundraising has made a seismic shift from begging to selling, to receiving, investing, or borrowing.

Today's fundraising methods are more invitational and less implicational. When we invite someone to give a gift, we are not implying they should give. The choice is theirs. It's not a trade: "You give to my charity, and I will give to yours."

When fundraising has an underpinning of bad energy, resistance builds. If the executive director doesn't like it, no one else will either. If fundraising is not respected as an honorable way of inviting participation, it will be pure drudgery and unsuccessful.

The word *leadership* has a contextual meaning that is assumptively positive, not negative. Most say a person is a leader or is not a leader. But when someone is in a leadership position, people expect good leadership, not bad leadership. To me, saying someone is a bad leader is almost oxymoronic.

I think every executive director ought to take an oath to do no harm before he or she tries to do some good. For the balance of this chapter on leadership, we will assume that being a leader is being self-aware, trustworthy, open and honest, emotionally intelligent, authentic, valiant—good, not bad.

Never mind the favorable compliments or the cynical judgments directed at positional leadership. The plain truth is that leadership is coupled with followership, which provides the resources to fuel the leading of the organization's philanthropic agenda. As was said earlier in this chapter, in the nonprofit world, the concept of followership moves up a level to the concept of partnership, because relationships in the nonprofit sector tend to be more voluntary and much less subordinate.

With that in mind, everyone wins.

EFFECT OF ORGANIZATIONAL STAGES

Various Stages Will Alter Strategy

> We're all aware of the rise and fall of organizations and entire industries. . . .
> Since marketing experts acknowledge the existence of product-market life
> cycles . . . it seems reasonable to conclude that organizations also have life cycles.
> —James Gibson, John Ivancevich, and James Donnelly

Leading an organization requires a familiarity with the art and science of organizational development (OD) and an awareness of how leadership tactics change with each organization's life cycle (OLC).

Organizational leadership is akin to being at the helm of a great ship, maneuvering it deftly in the crosswinds. Armed with OD knowledge, leaders have the rudder to navigate both calm waters and stormy seas. Having an understanding of OLC, leaders use the appropriate sails to adjust to dissonance and align for synchronicity.

Today, most organization leaders use OD principles to improve an organization's problem-solving and renewal processes, through more sophisticated change and collaboration tactics, by applying behavioral science theory.

You may remember OD's arrival in the 1970s and 1980s if your degree is in business or if you were exposed in the workplace to the concepts of total quality management (TQM), team building, or learning circles. It is used (mostly by consultants) to evaluate and align how the organization's constituents function together. Experts in leadership studies, systems thinking, and organizational leadership, look at OD as a multidisciplinary ongoing approach that draws on sociology, psychology, and theories of motivation, learning, and personality.

OD emphasizes the human factors and the synergy between employees and the organization. As such, it assesses this relationship by gathering feedback from all constituents, via task forces, interviews, and surveys. Because the OD process looks for disconnect, it is neither a linear process nor a brief one. It is more holistic than static, given the need to make adjustments along the way.

Larger nonprofit organizations, such as educational and health care institutions, tend to be more aware of the theory and application of organizational development principles. Today, all graduate business programs include a course on how organizations emerge, develop, adjust, change, and grow over time. In the OD classroom, case studies on culture and change are used extensively. Most national conferences feature speakers and workshops on organizational leadership and management, and today, the majority reference life stage differences.

However, the theory of OLC organizational life stages or cycles is not as widely understood or applied concept as OD, particularly within midsize and smaller organizations or in newly formed organizations.

Organizational life cycles are the processes by which an organization moves through its various growth stages and cycles, influenced by both internal and external circumstances.

Organizational life cycles have their root in the work of psychologist B. W. Tuckman, who observed and interpreted how individuals work through phases (forming, storming, norming, performing, transforming), to become a group. He theorized that individuals who form a group apply *forming* behaviors by starting to clarify their goals. After time, a group enters the *storming* phase, when the individuals test their relationships by challenging each other. Next comes a phase know as *norming*, when group members can set group goals (as differentiated from individual goals) and establish a decision-making process that is inclusive. The group then moves to the *performing* phase, where the individuals within the group gain confidence and are able to have stronger and more productive interactions. Finally, the group enters the *transforming* phase (akin to Maslow's self-actualization), where the now-cohesive group of individuals is able to move beyond the present into the future.

But it was Richard Weber who borrowed Tuckman's group dynamic theory, turned it into a life cycle model, and applied it to nonprofit organizational behavior. He used human behavioral terms for his four growth stages: Infancy, Adolescence, Adulthood, and Maturity.

In a summary of OLC models, Quinn and Cameron wrote for *Management Science,* proposing that changes in organizations follow a predictable pattern that can be characterized by developmental stages. These stages are sequential in nature, occur as a hierarchical progression that is not easily reversed, and involve a broad range of organizational activities and structures.

The numbers of life cycle stages proposed in various works that have studied the phenomenon have varied considerably over the years. Some analysts have delineated as many as 10 different stages of an organizational life cycle; others have reduced them to three stages.

Organizational life cycle is an important model because of its premise and its prescription. The model's premise is that requirements, opportunities, and threats both inside and outside the organization will vary depending on the stage of the organization's development. The OLC model's prescription is that leaders must change their goals, strategies, and processes to fit the new set of issues. This implies that leadership culture must also change to adapt to new circumstances and situations.

Being unfamiliar with life stage concepts can create huge disadvantages. Earlier in my career, I was not aware of the predictability of organizational stages and cycles, and that lack of understanding caused missed opportunities and even erroneous assumptions. Today, as I consult, OD and OLC are the backdrop upon which I am able to diagnose internal challenges and strategic issues, which are profoundly different in each organizational stage and type. Once-popular boilerplate management assessment tools are now obsolete. No size fits all.

As part of my teaching on the subjects of leadership, philanthropy, and fundraising theory, I include a section on life stages and cycles because of the adaptation that is called for in the implementation of both ideas and systems. When students are first introduced to OD and OLC, their reaction is: "Wow, I just didn't get it. Now I know what's going on in my organization, and why."

In the United States, most nonprofit institutions are less than a century old, so the present-day diagnosis of life stages is relatively simple. An early life cycle is shorter than those that come later, with the average life stage between 10 and 25 years. Most nonprofits will be divided by only four stages: birth, adolescence, maturity, and seniority. A fifth stage is emerging, however, which will likely be accepted as a transformation period.

What those stages are called is really not very important. Different theorists, authors, and practitioners use different terms, depending on their personal interpretation and word choice. What is important is the idea of dividing organizations into life stages that are defined by different behaviors and needs.

In this chapter, we will use the simplified four-stage model to demonstrate the more obvious characteristics of organizational behavior.

Organization Life Stage Observations and Assumptions

1. Stages are not as distinct as they appear in graphic form; they are more dynamically motivated by internal and external influences (they don't manifest themselves in one fell swoop).

2. While most stages are sequential, it is possible for an organization to slide back into a previous stage rather than moving entirely into the next one with relative ease.

3. Some stages end up being longer than others because of limited resources, lack of leadership, or external market conditions. This means there could be plateaus where growth is less evident than in an earlier or later time.

4. Within each organization stage, parts of the organization could be experiencing different growth stages. For instance, a new program could be at the infancy stage, while other programs in the organization could be in adolescence or early maturity stages.

Analyzing an organization's growth stage or cycle appears elementary on the surface but it actually requires an in-depth evaluation by expert research analysts who can delineate the wide variety of intersecting factors that cause strengths to be strengths and weaknesses to be weaknesses, not just reflections of each other. The optimal way to ensure an organization's relevance in a changing marketplace is to apply external scans, market needs assessments, research mining, and in-depth strategic planning.

If you introduce a new project (at infancy) into an organization with a more advanced culture (at adolescence), the new one will have to play catch-up without compromising its own natural evolution toward stability.

So, what do organizational life and growth stages have to do with fundraising? Just like the larger organization, a development or fundraising program has its own life cycle of growth stages. The natural progression of building a fundraising program is exactly the same as growing an organizational, thoughtfully and deliberately.

Fundraising cannot be accelerated at a faster rate than other projects and programs. Like the organization itself, a fundraising program requires leadership, staffing, infrastructure, investment of resources, and time to grow relationships with clients and customers and eventually to create predictable patterns and outcomes.

The four stages covered here include:

- INFANCY: Vision and Values Create Impetus
- ADOLESCENCE: Infrastructure Demands Are Paramount
- EARLY MATURITY: Expertise and Expansion Are Evident
- SENIORITY: Transformation Needed for Sustainability

INFANCY

Vision and Values Create Impetus

> The primary question at this stage is "Can this dream be realized?" . . . the organization really is merely a dream of a better world that is inspirational and worth striving for.
>
> —Judith Sharken Simon

Vision and mission are the instigators for stage one, with dreams of what could be and should be. Although the original vision and mission may be altered throughout the course of the organization's existence, these two inextricable driving forces will continue to inspire people to step up as board members, investors, volunteers, employees, and more.

This stage is naturally entrepreneurial, with energy and enthusiasm at an all-time high. The source of energy at stage one is derived externally by new people gathering to create something that does not currently exist; their mutual energy turns into a dynamic force that results in the formation of a new organization.

At stage one, the organization will be attracting or appointing its first CEO, its first board of directors, and its first leadership team. This group (collective as well as individual leadership) will influence how the culture and the values are formed. Never again will there be as much freedom to shape organizational values and principles. Decisions will be intuitive but discerning; they will be optimistic but realistic; they will be experimental but unshakable.

The need to generate start-up funding is top of mind; asking people to invest is a birthright—no money, no mission. Raising funds for a new vision, in the opinion of some, is not only exciting, it is also relatively easy. All that's needed is a good case that resonates with people; this *shared desire* can accomplish something that has not been done (this way) before.

Others say it's difficult to start a new nonprofit venture, given the amount of capital that needs to be raised. As a measure of how easy it is, consider the growing number of new nonprofits that enter the marketplace each and every year. Regardless of your opinion about how many nonprofits are too many, we all know it's easier to raise money from foundations for new ideas than for something old.

A measure of how hard this stage is can be found in the number of organizations whose mission becomes obsolete and who get stuck in survival mode longer than they should. Currently, we are seeing more mergers, more acquisitions, more program cuts, and more closing of the doors. This proves that no stage of development guarantees that an organization is secure or impenetrable to outside forces, including threats never imagined like the recent economic recession.

The key to creating a stage one organization is to generate adequate funding and sufficient engagement to produce ample momentum to take it to stage two. Stage one is probably the shortest stage; the faster we move into stage two, the greater our chance of succeeding in the long run.

INFANCY Organizations

- Meeting agendas focus on market positioning and public awareness.
- Board members tend to be friends of the leader(s).
- Decisions are made spontaneously, not always tied to a written plan.
- Communications are intentional, upbeat, and frequent.
- People attracted to the mission are similar in personality and style.
- Attitude is "anything goes" and "we can do it."

INFANCY Fundraising

- Large start-up grants come from major funders or foundations.
- Grant proposals read like investment prospectuses.

- Fundraising is done by the top leadership, more informally than formally.
- The case for support is focused on a better tomorrow.
- Development program is not structured and often done by volunteers.
- Campaign activities call for a lot of celebrations and special events

ADOLESCENCE

Infrastructure Demands Are Paramount

> The key question at this stage is "How can we build this to be viable? . . . organizations at this stage are focused on establishing systems of accountability . . . but it also has numerous enticing intersections, choices, and challenges.
> —Judith Sharken Simon

The need to stabilize the organization's growth calls for more staff, space, systems, policies, procedures, and even politics.

Stage two organizations need a more centralized and unified direction. What was once external visionary leadership now shifts to internal managerial leadership.

The stage one's unfettered ingenuity and spontaneity requires stability and discipline. A new kind of leadership is called for, akin to the tough love given by our parents in our adolescent years. Tighter management practices are the answer.

Does this mean that the visionary leaders must leave? Sometimes yes, if they can't adapt to fit this more structured phase. Or no, if they are really flexible and wise enough to know it's time to surround themselves with experts in areas they are not.

Stage two requires a less individualized and more collective form of leadership to move the organization to the next level. Those fabulous founding ideas need to be solidly rooted in people power if they are to sustain the bumpy road ahead.

At this stage, the organization must grow its bench strength by expanding its organization chart vertically and horizontally: more positions of expertise on top and more support positions below. All hands on deck are needed from a multitude of functional disciplines: human resources, strategic planning, marketing, product development, customer/client relations, partner and collaboration work, technology, legal work, communications, resource development, fiscal management, physical plant oversight, and oversight and implementation of policies, procedures, and processes.

It's not just the leader who needs to change; it's the board of directors as well. The original visionary investors will not even like this next stage. It will be too process oriented for them, and they will want to move on to another venture philanthropy project. What's needed at stage two are management gurus or, as the children's nursery rhyme said, one butcher, one baker, and one candlestick maker.

In this stage, the board meeting agendas will look very different because the vision and mission have been accepted as fact and fate—no need to tweak them further; this is the true implementation phase.

The stage two organizational business model or chart, however, may need to be updated, as the revenue demands change. Funds are now needed for what is called *overhead* and *infrastructure*—both of which are questionable terms. Most people mistakenly think of overhead and infrastructure as a cost rather than an investment. This perception has been greatly influenced by the way our chief financial officers (CFOs) account the books and by the way watchdog agencies evaluate nonprofit costs. It goes without saying that overhead costs have become the executive director's nemesis. If they are perceived as too high, people think we are wasting money. If they are perceived as too low, people think we are not making good business decisions.

Exactly what is *overhead*? Organizational overhead is the ongoing administrative expenses that cannot be attributed to any specific business activity, but are still necessary for the business to function. Examples include rent, utilities, and insurance.

Exactly what is *infrastructure*? Organizational infrastructure includes accounting, fundraising, information technology, human resources, physical plant, and other common organizational elements that undergird a nonprofit's mission and programs.

Because funds are specifically needed for overhead and infrastructure in stage two, fundraising is more challenging because our case for *overhead* may appear ambiguous and even extraneous. We need to be very clear when asking for general operating support and to make a case that programs and services will not be effective or efficient without the necessary infrastructure.

When donors are close enough to an organization, they can see that general operating support is absolutely critical. Thus, at stage two, fundraising must emphasize the retaining of donors who have been supporters over time.

At this juncture, fundraising becomes a little more creative as we seek to attract greater numbers of donors who will adopt our organization as one of their favorites (meaning they will give regularly). Gone are the really large start-up grants, replaced by a multitude of smaller but loyal individual donors.

This stage of fundraising also has a focus on building infrastructure, that is, donor data-based management systems, policies for gift acceptance, and recognition programs. Methods of fundraising now include the annual fund drive, special events, a cadre of small foundation grants, and some corporate partnerships. While the fundraising methods are expanding in number, size, and style, all of them must generate as much revenue as possible to grow the administration and to cover the increased costs of fundraising.

ADOLESCENT Organizations

- The meeting agendas focus on management issues, infrastructure, and financial accounting.
- New board members are recruited for their management expertise in areas such as finance, audit, accounting, human resources, technology, and marketing.
- More staff members are hired for their knowledge, expertise, and skill set experience.
- The organizational policy book is growing in size and in content, but procedures are still determined at the department level.
- The organizational chart is much larger, requiring more than one page.
- There may be a waiting list for program and services.

ADOLESCENT Fundraising

- Professional development staff has been hired, and a development department has been established.
- The case for support is based on what the organization does and how much it costs to operate; the mission is prominent in the fundraising materials.
- Volunteers are recruited to serve on various committees, including fundraising projects.
- Special events, grant writing, and direct mail are the preferred fundraising methods.
- There is a fundraising goal, a budget, and benchmarks for the acquisition, retention, and upgrade of donor gifts.

EARLY MATURITY

Expertise and Expansion Are Evident

> The key question at this stage is "How can the momentum be sustained?" The organization is very stable, yet the same stability may make it stale as concerns for procedure slow creativity and growth.
>
> —Judith Sharken Simon

During stage two, the organization's growth tends to slow down while the internal support systems are fully developed, course-corrected, and augmented with tools to be more competitive in the marketplace.

By the time stage three comes about, the work done internally is ready to support a different kind of growth: program improvement, program replication, and program expansion. The organization should be relatively stable and ready to push the edges in professional delivery and market positioning. Strategies include community needs assessments, long-range planning, new business development, quality control systems, evidence-based practices, and diverse sources of revenue.

There are leadership changes, too, both in how the executive director leads and in how the board governs. Gone are the days of hands-on volunteer committees to draft the first HR policy manual. Gone is the original board member who headed up the first gala. It's not that volunteers are not needed—they are, but in different roles with different responsibilities.

The most obvious change is in the expertise of the board: management know-how is not needed as much as knowledge about the external environment. Board members who have insight and exposure to more global issues are preferred, as in the following examples:

- Knowledge of health care reform if on the hospital board
- Knowledge of cultural marketing if on the symphony board
- Knowledge of gaps in service delivery if on a homeless shelter board
- Knowledge of youth development metrics if on a social service board
- Knowledge of economic and employment trends if on a college board

Executive directors also need to have subject matter expertise and/or surround themselves with leadership team members who do, including marketing, finance, and fund development.

This is the optimal time for growing earned income; the services are at their highest quality; they are competitive; and they have an optimal ROI and the highest possible effectiveness and efficiency rates. Consideration will be given to new ventures: starting a for-profit arm to generate unrelated business income, instituting sliding-scale fees where none existed, partnering with a corporation on a cause-related marketing project, collaborating with another agency to increase service delivery reach and impact.

This is also the best time for fundraising because of the multitude of options. You could fundraise to start an endowment or grow a reserve fund, entertain the idea of a capital or special purpose campaign, or establish donor-designated accounts to raise more for high-priority programs or initiatives.

Each of the organization's individual programs could have its own fundraising project, targeting donors who might increase their gifts by designating to a program rather than to general operations. A big campaign could be undertaken to fund a specific initiative with the goal of attracting new donors at the major gifts level. Segmented constituent groups can expand their niche events by recruiting more volunteers with golf tournaments, walks and runs, and galas. And because foundations and corporations like to fund specific projects, this is the best time to double the revenue from them. Growth and progress correlate with the ability to secure additional resources: more income, more programs.

Working in a stage three organization is rewarding and secure. The salaries are equitable; there are enough human and financial resources to go around; there is room for innovation and some risk; new staff and board members stimulate new ideas and possibilities (Simon 2001).

EARLY MATURITY Organizations

- The board's composition and its agenda shifts to "achieving program excellence" and "increasing market share."
- The executive director hires subject-matter experts and advocates for evidence-based practices.
- The program directors are eager to infuse revenue streams for their own department's budget and willingly step into fundraising.
- Internal and external communications are sophisticated and targeted; no longer designed to inform, they direct people to act.
- Core programs are replicated, client reach is extended, sites are expanded, and new programs are added.

EARLY MATURITY Fundraising

- The number of designated gifts is rising, as is the average size of the gifts.
- The case for support is targeted to match the donors' interest with the organization's needs. Everything in fundraising is strategic.
- The number of development professionals has increased as the numbers of donors and dollars have grown.
- There is now a comprehensive written development plan that is approved by the board of directors and the director of development serves as a member of the CEO's administrative leadership team.
- Fundraising takes place 365 days a year; there is a separate campaign for each constituency group: the board, employees, top-level donors, special-interest donors, small family foundations, large national foundations, corporations, faith-based organizations, and the organization's neighbors.

SENIORITY

Transformation Needed for Sustainability

> The primary questions is "What do we need to redesign?" Mature nonprofits revisit one or more aspects of their organization . . . sometimes changing them drastically, sometimes only making slight innovations, as they rediscover who they are and how they fit in the changing world.
>
> —Judith Sharken Simon

At this stage, the organization mission has been optimized; mission impact is at its peak. In the best scenarios, everything is healthy, nimble, adaptive, evolutionary, and resilient.

The upside of stage four is that change processes are strategic and continuous, keeping the organization dynamic and resilient. The downside is that if anything is taken for granted, things will start to slide in the opposite direction. That's why some refer to this as the *re-state,* a point at which relevance is the common denominator.

A stage four organization is able to reflect on its strengths and reassess where it is going next. This process of reflection has lots of *re* words: renew, reassess, rebuild, restructure, reinvent, and reorganize. It's time to do a large-scale review of what has changed along the way and how relevant its existing identity, values, vision, and mission are to today's environment.

Most of our large-scale national nonprofit organizations are at this stage, and if we look carefully, we can see evidence of massive reinvention shifts: Red Cross, Girl Scouts, YMCA, The Conservancy, and the United Way. Each has issued edicts for local chapters to reinvent themselves, to merge with smaller units, and to rebrand their organization's image. The YMCA is now "The Y." The United Way is focused on "impact." The Girl Scouts have gone viral. The Red Cross is consolidating in a hub and spoke, and the Conservancy is all about grassroots collaboration.

A major downside of stage four is the likelihood that mature organizations are siloed—individual departments have micro-organizations inside the larger entity. Things feel less personal: HR requires everyone to use the same titles; Finance requires everyone to fill out the same expense forms; Technology insists that you can't use a newer version of Word because everyone needs the same program; the front desk no longer knows who you are when your spouse calls for you; the E.D. calls you by name only if you are wearing your nametag.

Things are so compressed that if you take a day off and don't log out, you are listed as "gone missing" or "on leave."

An upside of a stage four organization is that it is a predictable, reliable, and most probably one of the most secure and financially beneficial places to work. The chances of getting hired or fired are slim. You get 12 days vacation, 11 days sick leave, and although you now have to pay for your family members, a large portion of your medical insurance is still covered. Your best collegial relationships were forged here; your best professional innovations were created here.

It is no surprise that the board is no longer as hands-on as it once was, and while the employees know *about* them, few actually know them. In stage four, board members are recruited for their business acumen: They are top CEOs elsewhere, community leaders, high-powered donors, and mostly people who have paid their dues elsewhere. When they are in the boardroom, the discussions and the decisions are at a very high level.

But back at the employee level, sometimes you will feel the innovation energy moving forward, and at other times, you can feel the innovation drain. You acknowledge you work in a big place, and change at this juncture will require something big to jar it. This stage could be the longest one of all four. Some will spend their entire careers in this safe-and-sound stage four environment.

Fundraising in a stage four organization is equally as multifaceted and extremely sophisticated. By now, with decades of fund development in place, the donor pool is highly developed, replete with major gifts in the million-dollar range (or more). Every fundraising theory and practice is in place, working together to move donors from their first gift to their largest and most meaningful gift for whatever the organization's mission is. Annual campaigns, major gift campaigns, capital campaigns, and endowment campaigns are going on, often simultaneously.

For fundraisers who relish being in the midst of constant activity, a stage four organization is the place to be. There is room for the newcomer generalist, for the senior-level specialist, and for everyone in between.

A note about the recent economic downturn: For the first time in their history, stage four organizations are being adversely affected by external changes in the marketplace and in the economy. They are facing reductions in revenue from paying clients, patients, students, subscribers, members, and, in most cases, donors. Even the seemingly impervious endowment and reserve funds have been drastically reduced to a level never imagined. The recent economic recession has hit fast and hard.

Currently, I suspect that every stage four organization is more focused on the present than it is on the future, so we must wait to see if a stage five becomes a reality in the evolution of the modern-day nonprofit organization. If so, as noted earlier, it will probably be called transformation.

SENIORITY Organizations

- The board agenda is more often at 30,000 feet than at 3,000 feet.

- There was likely a national search to recruit the current executive director, who came with impressive credentials and a solid track record.

- Department heads act like mini executive directors; they have their own advisory boards, strategic plans, financial budgets, and organizational charts.

- There are departments that are more entrepreneurial than others, causing both healthy competition and unhealthy tension within the organization.

- The culture is now historically and symbolically rooted. Everyone knows what the expected behaviors and attitudes are, without reading the official values statement.

- The financial statement is now so complex that only accountants can understand it; the CFO is the second most important staff person next to the executive director.

SENIORITY Fundraising

- The development department has grown incrementally, utilizing every known technique and method to reach every prospect and every donor.

- In large organizations, it is possible to have at least 10,000 donors and as many as 70,000.

- Highly qualified and credentialed development staff will be assigned to the four gift areas: annual, major, capital, and planned giving.

- Only a small percentage of contributions are raised for general operating expenses, and these will come primarily from benefit events and unrestricted annual gifts; the majority of the gifts are generated and designated for specific programs, projects, or departments.

- The infrastructure in the development program includes the latest technology, including social media such as Facebook, text-giving, e-blasts, e-pledge, and other social networking activities.

EXHIBIT 1.1 FUND DEVELOPMENT GROWTH CHART

	Stage ONE: INFANCY	Stage TWO: ADOLESCENCE	Stage THREE: EARLY MATURITY	Stage FOUR: SENIORITY
LEADERSHIP FOCUS	Entrepreneurial Innovation	Resource Development	Program Expertise	Organizational Alignment
BOARD FOCUS	Vision, Mission, and Values	Structure and Financials	Expansion and Professionalism	Relevance and Vitality
MANAGEMENT FOCUS	Business Plan	Policies and Procedures	Quality Improvement	Resource Distribution
FUNDING FOCUS	Start-Up Gifts: Friends of the Founder	Annual Gifts: Individuals, Corporations, and Foundations	Annual, Major, Capital Gifts and Grants	Annual, Major, Capital, Legacy, Endowment: Gifts and Grants
CASE FOCUS	Future Opportunity	General Operating and Stabilization	Programs and Projects	Market Dominance and Impact

A fundraising program has four basic growth stages. Each stage requires a different leadership approach; each is designed to build a strong integrated fund development program. See Exhibit 1.1.

SUMMARY

This chapter has provided substantiation for and elaboration on the absolute need for the executive director to provide leadership to nonprofit organizations, as well as their fundraising program. It has pointed out the essential multifaceted ingredients of leadership that cause donors to resonate with your organization, versus resisting support for it. As complex as the topic of leadership is, there is one fundamental truth: Fundraising starts and ends with leadership. In the absence of executive director leadership, fundraising will fail.

The next chapter provides you with a background on philanthropy, including why people give, to whom they give, what share of market you might capture, and how much you need to invest in a fundraising program.

REFERENCES

AFP Research Council Think Tank. 2008. *Leadership, Governance and Giving.* www.afpnet.org/files/contentdocuments/2009_rctt_guide_1251517967859_7.pdf.

Bennis, W. G. 2003. *On Becoming a Leader: The Leadership Classic.* Cambridge, MA: Perseus Books.

Bolman, L. G., & T. E. Deal. 2003. *Reframing Organizations: Artistry, Choice and Leadership.* San Francisco, CA: John Wiley & Sons.

The Bridgespan Group Report. 2009. *Finding Leaders for America's Nonprofits.* Boston, MA.

Carlson, M., & Donohoe, M. 2003. *The Executive Director's Survival Guide: Thriving as a Non-profit Leader.* San Francisco, CA: John Wiley & Sons.

Cherry, K. "Leadership Theories—8 Major Leadership Theories." psychology.about.com/od/leadership/p/leadtheories.htm.

Collins, J. 2005, *Good to Great and the Social Sectors.* New York: HarperCollins.

CompassPoint Annual Reports. 2001, 2006. *Daring to Lead.* www.compasspoint.org.

CompassPoint Nonprofit Services, the Annie E. Casey Foundation, the Meyer Foundation, and Idealist.org National Study. 2008. *Ready to Lead? Next Generation Leaders Speak Out.* http://meyerfoundation.org/newsroom/meyer_publications/ready_to_lead.

Connolly, P. M. 2006. *Navigating the Organizational Lifecycle: A Capacity-Building Guide for Nonprofit Leaders.* Washington, DC: BoardSource.

Cornelius, Marla, Rick Moyers, and Jeanne Bell, *Daring to Lead 2011: A National Study of Nonprofit Executive Leadership.* San Francisco, CA: CompassPoint Nonprofit Services and the Meyer Foundation, 2011.

Cornelius, Moyers, and Bell 2011, Daringtolead.org.

Covey, S. R. 1992. *Principle-Centered Leadership.* Detroit, MI: Free Press.

Crutchfield, L. R., & H. Grant. 2008. *Forces for Good: The Six Practices of High-Impact Non-profits.* San Francisco, CA: John Wiley & Sons.

Deal, J. 2007. *Retiring the Generation Gap: How Employees Young and Old Can Find Common Ground.* San Francisco, CA: Jossey-Bass/The Center for Creative Leadership.

De Pree, M., 1989. *Leadership Is an Art.* New York, NY: Bantam Doubleday Dell Publishers Group, Inc.

De Pree, M. 1997. *Leading without Power: Finding Hope in Serving Community.* San Francisco, CA.

Gardner, J. W. 1990. *On Leadership.* New York: Free Press.

Gowdy, H., A. Hildebrand, D. La Piana, & M. Mendes Campos. 2009. *Convergence: How Five Trends Will Reshape the Social Sector.* San Francisco, CA: The James Irvine Foundation and La Piana Consulting.

Hall, H. 2006. "Growing Up: The Stages a Charity Can Expect to Go through as It Ages." *The Chronicle of Philanthropy* (April). www.qm2.org/CHRONICLE_OF_PHILANTHROPY__April_6_for_Website.pdf.

Heifitz, R., A. Grashow, & M. Linsky. 2009. "Leadership in a Permanent Crisis." *Harvard Business Review* (July-August): 62–69.

Hesselbein, F., M. Goldsmith, & R. Beckhard. 1996. *The Leader of the Future: New Visions, Strategies, and Practices for the Next Era.* San Francisco, CA: John Wiley & Sons.

Kouzes, J. M., & B. Z. Posner. 1995. *The Leadership Challenge: How to Keep Getting Extraordinary Things Done in Organizations.* San Francisco, CA: John Wiley & Sons.

Maxwell, J. C. 1991. *The 21 Indispensable Qualities of a Leader: Becoming the Person Others Will Want to Follow.* Nashville, TN: Maxwell Motivation.

McCall, M. W., Jr., & M. M. Lombardo. 1983. *Off the Track: Why and How Successful Executives Get Derailed.* Greensboro, NC: Centre for Creative Leadership.

McLean, G. N. 2006. *Organization Development: Principles, Processes, Performances.* San Francisco, CA: Berrett-Koehler.

Moyers, R. 2006. *The Nonprofit Chief Executive's Ten Basic Responsibilities.* Washington, DC: BoardSource.

Palmer, P. J. 2000. *Let Your Life Speak: Listening for the Voice of Vocation.* San Francisco, CA: John Wiley & Sons.

Quinn, R. E., & K. Cameron. "Organizational Life Cycles and Shifting Criteria of Effectiveness: Some Preliminary Evidence." *Management Science* 29, no. 1 (January 1983).

Reggio, R. E., & S. S. Orr. 2004. *Improving Leadership in Nonprofit Organizations.* San Francisco, CA: John Wiley & Sons.

Simon, J. S. 2001. *Five Life Stages of Nonprofit Organizations.* Saint Paul, MN: Fieldstone Alliance.

Stevens, K. 2001. *Nonprofit Lifecycles: Stage-Based Wisdom for Nonprofit Capacity.* Long Lake, MN: Stagewise Enterprises.

Straughan, B. 1999. *Four Stages and Four Challenges of Organizational Development.* Takoma Park, MD: Institute for Conservation Leadership.

Terry, R. W. 1993. *Authentic Leadership: Courage in Action.* San Francisco, CA: Jossey-Bass.

Tierney, T. J. 2006. *The Bridgespan Group Report: The Nonprofit Sector's Leadership Deficit.*

Wagner, L., & L. LeLaulu. 2005. "Fundraising, the CEO, and Servant Leadership."

W. K. Kellogg Foundation. 2008. *Intentional Innovation: How Getting More Systematic Could Improve Philanthropy and Increase Social Impact.* Authors Gabriel Kasper, Monitor Institute and Stephanie Clohesy, Clohesy Consulting.

www.hbs.edu/mba/studentlife/leadership_values.html.

Philanthropy Concepts

PRINCIPLES, MOTIVATIONS, IMPACT, AND CULTURE

It is important to note that philanthropy exists primarily because people wish to ameliorate problems or advance causes. "Organized philanthropy" exists because worthy organizations provide programs and services that require financial contributions. When the two come together—donors' interests and organizations' needs—philanthropy is a transformational exchange of values providing sustenance and substance to a democratic society.

INTRODUCTION

New world philanthropy is a natural human instinct to say how life could be and should be. Philanthropy is not mandated, not required, nor directed by someone else. It is the free and democratic choice of every individual, to give or not to give. Scholar Robert L. Payton gave it definition, as the title of his book: *Philanthropy: Voluntary Action for the Public Good.*

Individual philanthropy is a personal expression about what matters to each person; stemming from their personal values, spiritual beliefs, and often, an interest in making their community a better place to live. When individuals decide to give to a nonprofit organization, it's because they trust the leadership and value the mission.

Collective philanthropy is the pooling of many contributions by nonprofit organizations to fund their *public good* mission and achieve greater impact. Since philanthropy is the litmus test of trust and value, we say it affirms a nonprofit's relevance and its popularity.

Individual philanthropy and collective philanthropy (like voting), becomes a consensus builder for not only one organization, but an entire community and country.

History demonstrates that there is no limit to what and where people will give of their time, talent, and treasure. New World philanthropy is broad and all-encompassing: from the arts and science, to education and the environment, from museums and monuments, to poverty and hunger, from illness and health care, to religious causes and moral agendas.

Some would say that political advocacy qualifies as philanthropy, but that conversation will be reserved for social scientists and political pundits.

For you the executive director, philanthropy is not just a method of generating much-needed revenue; it is one of the principal ways to position your organization as a valuable community asset.

With an entire sector devoted to the philanthropic pursuit of partnerships, philanthropic fundraising is not something to shy away from. It is something to be zealous about.

If your organization does *not* attract philanthropy, an inadvertent but contrary message may be implied, that you do not need your community's input or financial support. If you don't fundraise, the public does not have an opportunity to validate their trust in what you do—which could lead to mistrust around your organization's relevance and value.

As a nonprofit leader, when you embrace philanthropy as "community building" you automatically make a compelling *rationale* for fundraising, which inspires everyone around you to help raise money: The board of directors, the development department staff, your program staff, and volunteers.

When you lead the fundraising charge, you affirm that the purpose of philanthropy is to raise the mission, and one way to do that is to raise money (not vice versa).

Chapter 2 covers:

- PRINCIPLES of Organized Philanthropy: Spiritual and Democratic Ideology
- MOTIVATIONS of Personal Philanthropy: Discovery of Complexity and Complications
- IMPACT of Community Philanthropy: Measurable Economic and Social Benefits
- CULTURE of Organizational Philanthropy: Foundation for Successful Fundraising

PRINCIPLES of Organized Philanthropy

Spiritual and Democratic Ideology

> The philanthropic tradition is older than democracy, older than Christianity. . . .
> It gives form and purpose to personal and social life that cannot be provided by
> the self-interest of economic enterprise or required by the mandate of political
> institutions.
>
> —Robert L. Payton

A contemporary book on fundraising must acknowledge that philanthropy has historical, sociological, philosophical, ethical, theoretical, and practical roots that have produced many iterations and ideologies.

Most early forms of philanthropy were motivated by religious beliefs and customs that spurred acts of giving to those less fortunate. Charitable behaviors were first chronicled some 3,700 years ago, beginning with the Egyptian Book of the Dead, proceeding through the Old Testament, into ancient Greece and Rome. Christian tithing was present in the Middle Ages, as evidenced in the hierarchical alms-giving collections, leading to the creation of the famous Elizabethan Poor Laws.

These treasured traditions and habits of generosity were firmly embedded in the human psyche when Europeans set out to brave the New World. Without restraints, the New World freedom seekers added a new dimension to Old World philanthropy: The right to express oneself, with and without religion.

In just the past century, the once simple Greek interpretation, *love of human-kind,* has been expanded in dimension and dynamics, shaped by our cultural heritage and values. New World philanthropy is the accumulation and culmination of our human evolution; it is the convergence of traditional religious beliefs *and* newfound democratic principles.

Once a single act of expressed goodness, just one word (*philanthropy*) is now an ideology and way of life. In the United States, it is a conscious effort to build a civil and diverse society.

New World philanthropy is best described as a four-part dynamic: a *tradition,* a *spirit,* a *sector,* and an engagement *process,* all designed to improve life. These four parts *organize* the giving and the receiving of contributions.

Many ask, is philanthropy a noun, a verb, or an adjective? Or all of them? John D. Rockefeller, an early leader in the philanthropic movement, contemplated its meaning as a *noun:* The support mechanism for the nonprofit sector—what they do, rather than what they hoped to accomplish. Others suggest that philanthropy is a *verb*—more than the act of giving or the act of raising money, it is the *outcome* that philanthropy stimulates, the building of community.

Fundraisers, in particular, use the words *philanthropy* and *fundraising* interchangeably. Of late, development professionals refer to their work as *philanthropic fundraising* to emphasize that it is mission focused, in contrast to an exclusively money-raising endeavor (and in part to distinguish themselves from political fundraisers and paid telemarketing solicitors).

For me, the definition of New World philanthropy is multifaceted:

- Philanthropy is our fundamental impulse to say how life should be or could be. It is both conscience and catalyst.

- Philanthropy is an initiative that occurs when we want to advance a cause or ameliorate a problem.

- Philanthropy is the litmus test of caring and trusting communities. It is essential to a civil society.

- Philanthropy is more than altruistic (benevolence, if you will) and more than egotistic (self-love, so to speak). It is a combination of both, finding its place on a continuum of giving and receiving (implying a relationship and reciprocity).

- Philanthropy is intentional, expressive, and action oriented.
  As an *intention,* philanthropy separates moral and ethical actions from simply doing.
  As an *expression,* philanthropy is the democratic spirit that keeps a county strong and free.
  As an *action,* philanthropy is the freewill contribution of time, talent, and treasure.

As an executive director, it is advantageous for you to know how philanthropy became organized *and* understand how fundraising evolved from its earliest form of begging to a sophisticated form of values exchange. In the absence of this knowledge, you will not be as well equipped to champion the practice of philanthropy, nor to promote best-practice fundraising techniques.

When you understand why certain practices emerged, you will be better able to course-correct your current strategies and to advance philanthropic fundraising with more clarity, creativity, and commitment.

In this New World, we expect our nonprofit leaders to be the chief advocates of an organizational culture that exists to serve others and to be of social benefit. We don't want our leaders to be self-serving; we expect them to go beyond their own organization and inspire a stronger philanthropic culture within their larger community.

If you want a great fundraising program, you will want to construct your own unique ways of generating gifts on four levels:

- TRADITION: Way of Life that Advances Communities
- SPIRIT: Can-Do Approach of Generosity and Gratitude
- SECTOR: Designated for Inspiration, Ideas, and Ideals
- PROCESS: Connecting Donors and Recipients

TRADITION

Way of Life that Advances Communities

Philanthropy permeates American life, touches each one of us countless times in countless ways; philanthropy provides the resources for some of the most important activities that give shape and substance to our efforts to be a free and open and democratic society.

—Robert L. Payton

Since the founding of the United States, foreign visitors have commented on the uncommon persistence of Americans to voluntarily form new nonprofits to address social problems.

But make no mistake: The philanthropic *tradition* of the New World is not merely an extension of the Old World traditions of charitable almsgiving or poor relief. This American tradition is different.

It is based on the freedom to *pioneer*—to develop experimental programs, enrich new forms of cultural life, and improve self-help for neighbors, at any and every income level. It is the expression of collective freedom, to do what individuals cannot do alone and what governments will not do. Some have referred to this kind of philanthropy as *improvement theory.*

This free philanthropic tradition has flourished since our nation's founding because it has been nurtured, cultivated, enhanced, and advanced. It is uniquely democratic as a result of its individual parts:

1. The volunteer gathering of like-minded people,
2. Who create a formal or informal voluntary association,
3. To develop solutions and strategies to address a shared issue,
4. By garnering gifts of time, talent, and treasure,
5. To accomplish the established mission.

It is our rich tradition to respond to acute social needs, our impulse to nurture social justice, and our desire to advance an equitable quality of life. But it is the action that follows that makes U.S. philanthropy a unique cultural dimension.

Acts of philanthropy have forged a permanent kind of Tocquevillean behavior, *institutionalizing a democratic process* to build and maintain a civil society. Advocacy for change is deeply rooted in our nonprofits' DNA and our public policy making is firmly grounded in our constitution. When declaring independence in 1776, our country's founders observed that governments get "their just powers from the consent of the governed." As early as 1793, associations were springing up out of the churches to develop strong agendas that would ultimately influence public policy and create laws.

Social reform (aka social improvement theory) was an impulse that forged our philanthropic tradition, creating social policy agendas like child welfare, women's rights, prison reform, treatment of the emotionally and physically disabled, foreign aid, social work, public safety, protection for refugees and immigrants, and medical research.

An endless number of U.S. institutions emerged to serve and strengthen community institutions: libraries, museums, civic organizations, universities, hospitals, arts and cultural institutions, and charitable coalitions like the

United Way, which have strived to connect concerned citizens around critical community issues.

Civic engagement was also an underlying theme of organized philanthropy. The *tradition* of voluntary action through voluntary associations provides the nonprofit sector with its infrastructure: its socialization, problem solving, and leadership; its quality of life; and its public power and community self (Gurin and Van Til 1990).

The collective, action-oriented response that is indicative of our philanthropic fabric is the combination of many constituency-led coalitions.

Our philanthropic *traditions* include:

- FAMILY traditions of volunteering time with local associations
- CHURCH traditions of supporting mission work here and abroad
- SCHOOL traditions of taking up collections or sending cookies to troops overseas
- INDIVIDUAL traditions of writing checks each and every year to our local charities
- CORPORATE traditions of social responsibility and sponsorships
- GOVERNMENT traditions of responding to international catastrophes

As a tradition, philanthropy is a way of life on two levels; the micro level that advances individual communities and the macro level that elevates an entire nation. It is the American way of expressing both sentiment (for something) and skepticism (against something).

Our philanthropic traditions (beliefs acted on) are formed naturally when people act them out naturally and automatically pass them on to future generations. By their nature, values are socially ingrained, forming cultural trust. Momentum alone will not ensure their vitality or endurance; they must be nurtured and reaffirmed as they travel through time.

As a Nation, we must continue to encourage participation, debate, and criticism around our public policies to ensure that our founding documents remain intact and that the "government of the people, by the people, for the people, shall not perish from the earth."

Organizational TRADITION   Just as communities are more or less philanthropic, organizations are, too. When nonprofit organizations have a long established tradition of philanthropy, donors are greater in numbers and more generous in dollars.

As executive director, you will want to establish or nurture a tradition of philanthropy in your organization, not just for today but because it is essential for sustainability. The following questions will help you discern what is needed.

TRADITION of Philanthropy Checklist

- How does your organization talk about its own tradition of philanthropy? Do you celebrate those who founded our organization? Do you tell stories to build a sense of history and purpose?

- Do your donors feel a sense of ownership for your organization? Is it one of their favorite charities? Do they have a role to play that makes them feel they are part of the organizational family?

- Do you have engagement and recognition activities to encourage donors to establish lifelong patterns of giving? Will these traditions, such as belonging to a heritage society, be passed on to their family members and their friends?

- How do you publicly celebrate your organization's philanthropic traditions? Do you host an annual philanthropy recognition event?

- Do you give awards for continuous giving at 5 years, 10 years, or more?

- Do you reach out to the next generations to help adult donors teach their children about philanthropy in ways that perpetuate the expressed values of that family? Do you seek and welcome family gifts, where multiple members of a family pool their contributions to leverage what they hope to accomplish?

SPIRIT

Can-Do Approach of Generosity and Gratitude

> The history of American generosity is rich and complex, and it extends over three and one half centuries. But the core elements of the story do not change. Our economic and social progress is powered by a virtuous engine . . . with four parts that work in a continuous, reinforcing cycle: generosity, opportunity, prosperity, and gratitude.
>
> —Claire Gaudiani

If the American philanthropic *tradition* is based on repetitive acts of community building, then the philanthropic *spirit* is a can-do attitude based on deeply held expressions of generosity and gratitude, or what some call *relief theory*.

When we say that philanthropy has a spirit, words like *values* and *virtues* come first to mind. Others follow: *benevolence, stewardship, conscience, catalyst advocate, innovator,* and, more commonly, *doing good.*

The spirit of philanthropy was a prevalent theme in the Native Americans' way of life. Meeting Columbus at his first landfall in the New World, Indians were reported to be "ingenuous and free, willing to give anything asked of them, with as much love as if their hearts went with it" (Bremner 1988).

American immigrants were of the same mind and spirit, albeit more theologically rooted. The foundation of their philanthropic spirit was decidedly Christian, a code of conduct for those who came to create communities that would be better than those they left. Religious freedom was the driving force; the doctrine of stewardship was the literal belief in the brotherhood of man as children of God.

Strong ties between spirituality and giving still exist; time has not altered that. A report titled *Faith and Philanthropy: The Connection between Charitable Behavior and Giving to Religion* reveals that households that give to religion are at the heart of giving to the nation's nonprofit organizations. Spiritual and religious values influence donations and volunteerism to all types of nonprofit organizations, not just houses of faith.

- More than 85 percent of religious-giving households also support secular organizations.
- Fifty-two percent of all households give to both religious congregations and secular organizations, but those households account for 81 percent of all donations.
- Households that give to both types of institutions give more to religion ($1,391) than households that give only to religion ($1,154).

Philanthropy as a *spirit*, derived from spiritual beliefs, spiritual values, and spiritual desires, is our country's moral compass and our democratic catalyst.

The notion of doing good has no socioeconomic basis; its spirit protects the environment, prevents disease, improves education, enhances the arts, preserves historical landmarks, and sustains the needs of charity. Philanthropy is an expression of generosity, opportunity, prosperity, and gratitude

Organizational SPIRIT   As executive director, you not only want a *tradition* of philanthropy, you want to instill a spirit of philanthropy; the first is doing (improving), the second is caring (relieving). That spirit is probably the same one that created your organization; the same one that drove tough decisions; the same one that lingers in the hearts of your oldest and most loyal donors.

If you ask yourself the following questions, they will help inspire you to rekindle the "fire" that fuels a spirit of philanthropy.

SPIRIT of Philanthropy Checklist

- How do your organization's employees and recipients (students, patients, clients, customers) view the role that philanthropy plays in your organization? Are they aware that philanthropy pays for something that would not exist without contributions? What is that something?

- Does your organization honor or celebrate the different forms of philanthropy: time, talent, and treasure? Do you show the dollar value of volunteer time in your annual report? Do you list your honor roll of volunteers in the same way you list donor names?

- How would you describe your organization's philanthropic spirit? Is it based on advocacy for social justice? Is it the pursuit of a scientific breakthrough? Is it an expressed passion for art?

- Do you encourage your donors to designate their gifts to programs or projects of their choice? Or do you prefer undesignated gifts so you can use them as you want? Whose choice is best, yours or theirs?

- What do the words *generosity* and *gratitude* mean to your organization? Is generosity only associated with gifts of high dollar amounts? Is gratitude less when the gift is insignificant? Is there equity in your behaviors with all levels of giving?

SECTOR

Designated for Inspiration, Ideas, and Ideals

> No country in the history of the world has so creatively and effectively combined philanthropy and government service . . . when we as individuals, volunteer our hard-earned dollars to advance society by freely giving from our own pockets, government taxes us less.
>
> —Michael Marsicano

In the United States, three well-founded sector systems are in place; they assure that injustice and inequity is mitigated to the extent that it is constructive.

First, the government, or public sector, regulates a process by which every person, through taxation, shares in the responsibility of supporting the public good.

Second, the business or private sector, based on free enterprise, offers endless opportunities for self-initiative.

Third, the independent or philanthropic sector offers citizens, individually and collectively, the freedom to advocate, ameliorate, or advance causes of their choosing. It is the designated place for inspiration, ideas, and ideals.

The very essence of the nonprofit sector is derived from the public's belief that the people can address social issues more effectively than government by delivering services that are independently determined and voluntarily subscribed. And as the smallest sector, at times it has been one of the loudest, most diverse, and influential voice in our nation's acculturation.

The central benefit of the philanthropy *sector* lies in the value-added dimension it brings to the government and marketplace sectors. The philanthropic sector does things *differently* than the other two sectors, making society complete in the following ways.

The nonprofit sector is organized to:

- Fill gaps
- Experiment with new ideas
- Serve controversial constituencies
- Provide a forum for public policy
- Remain free from economic influences
- Speak for and against issues

Not only does the public promote the creation and existence of non-profit ventures with pride, but they also fully expect nonprofits to operate in a less costly and more productive fashion than the private or public sectors.

Thus, the credibility of nonprofit organizations depends to a large extent on the public's perception of its effectiveness and efficiency. Our public trust rates are challenged whenever a nonprofit fails to meet our expectations; scrutiny is fueled in government and consumer watchdog groups.

Held to higher standards, the nonprofit sector also faces stronger criticism when it falls short. The nonprofit sector is where citizens cast their vote for what matters to them by giving to charitable organizations they trust. When a cause or a charity is not the recipient of broad-based philanthropy, one has to ask if their mission or need is real and relevant. If more is given than needed, one must ask if the solution is sufficient and realistic.

Donors, in particular, want a return on their investment that is equivalent to or in excess of what they receive from the government sector; our public trust standards are very high because we use a moral or social calculus to measure the value of our gifts (Gaudiani 2004).

Public trust doesn't come automatically; it has to be earned. Bottom line, people want their money's worth.

Organizational SECTOR   As executive director, beyond building a *tradition* and a *spirit* of philanthropy within your organization, you need to ensure that philanthropy becomes an independent program (i.e., a sector). As a separate program, philanthropy must have a designated place to fill gaps, stimulate ideas, serve as the catalyst for change, and demonstrate measurable results.

To develop your organizational version of the *sector*, you might ask the following questions.

SECTOR Program of Philanthropy Checklist

- What is the size of your organization? How big should it get? How many more people could you serve? Should you add more programs?

- How many other organizations exist that are just like yours? Are you duplicating services, or are there gaps? Should you consider merging or creating a nonprofit sector coalition to expand reach and reduce costs?

- Have you compared the budget, the business model, and the market position of other similar organizations, locally and nationally? What can you learn from them? Could you teach them about your successes and failures?

- Is your organization overly reliant on one or two sources of funding? What are your plans if one of those funders were to go away? Do you need to search for other sources of philanthropy revenue or explore fee-based services that would reduce your risks?

- Do you encourage entrepreneurship in your employees? Do you reward good ideas? Do you encourage people to take risks that they won't be punished if they don't work out?

PROCESS

Connecting Donors and Recipients

> We are living in a time of profound social, cultural, and economic change. It is important that philanthropy, long held as the means for alternative solutions to pressing problems, grows through each of us to better support the crucial issues of our time.
>
> —Tracy Gary

Philanthropy also operates as an interactive, dynamic *process,* an assembly of parts that together comprise the whole subject—the noun, the verb, and the adjective must be connected. This process is referred to as *civic engagement* theory.

As a *process,* philanthropy has two layers: *individual* and *organizational.*

Individual PROCESS Throughout their lives, individual donors go through their own process to define and refine their chartable views and philanthropic objectives.

Individuals generally start giving because they are expected to (or feel they have to) and eventually reach a point where they want to (freeing themselves from expectations, to decide for themselves). This progression is a personal journey, which produces both internal self-actualization and external rewards.

Tracy Gary, author of *Inspired Philanthropy,* describes this individual process as a life path that aligns a donor's values with their giving practices. She theorizes that obligatory giving is the first step of giving, followed by social giving, next by passionate giving, ending with strategic or transformative giving (Maslow like).

The first stage of philanthropy tends to be *traditional* since it is directed toward basic needs, such as blankets and food for flood victims and temporary housing for homeless families. Traditional philanthropy is also about social maintenance giving to established educational, social, religious, and cultural institutions. Gary says traditional philanthropy "is based on responding to, treating, and managing the consequences of life in the existing social order as it is."

The last stage of philanthropy tends to be more *transformational* since it is more about analyzing and responding to the cause than to the effect, seeking out answers to questions that deep dig into societal change or triggers that will alleviate poverty or make education and health care more accessible. According to Gary, transformational philanthropy "strives to fund solutions that are proactive rather than reactive."

This adaptation from giving for charity (traditional) to giving for change (transformational) has no schedule, no deadline, and no barometer. It's a process of individual discovery about what each of us can do during our lifetime to achieve our own self-actualization.

A caution for those who are new to the subject of philanthropy: Too often, the act of philanthropy and the word *philanthropist* are associated with iconic wealth and/or grandiose giving. Public interest in society's powerful elite during the late-nineteenth and early-twentieth centuries has created an impression and a myth that money is the driver of charitable and philanthropic giving. Even today, it seems that powerful and wealthy individuals get more press with their giving than the average person next door.

But let's be clear: In the United States, philanthropy is the privilege of every citizen, regardless of income, age, education, or social status, and the nonwealthy are often more generous with what they have to give. Research also tells us that all ages, regardless of wealth, are equally as generous with what they give.

The key to a successful fundraising program is the ability to *spark* an interest in someone, and encourage them to go through a *process* that eventually moves them from traditional giving to transformational giving.

Organizational PROCESS   The organizational philanthropic *process* focuses on the ultimate connection of the donors' values and the organizations' values—with as many as four or five touch points/people in between.

In organized philanthropy, many people are involved in the organized *process of philanthropy*, as follows:

- The philanthropist who is motivated to give
- The facilitator through whom the gift is made
- The leader(s) within the institution who will accept the gift
- The providers who deliver or perform the funded service
- The recipients who have needs and issues

This process is best articulated in Exhibit 2.1. It is not a static form, but a continuous flow of connections that dynamically reconnect over and over again.

When the philanthropic process is organized around the values of reciprocity, cooperation, mutual respect, accountability, and commitment, all of the participants are beneficiaries.

Having a *tradition, a spirit and a sector* of philanthropy in your organization is not enough, you also need a formal *process* to fully implement all the philanthropic transactions and transformations.

A philanthropic culture within your organization requires all four elements, the same way the nonprofit sector depends on all of them.

As the executive director, you might ask the following questions to see how you can create effective and efficient *processes* that build donor trust and loyalty.

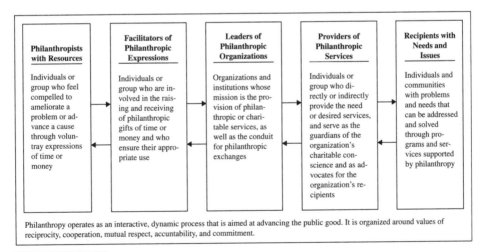

Philanthropists with Resources	Facilitators of Philanthropic Expressions	Leaders of Philanthropic Organizations	Providers of Philanthropic Services	Recipients with Needs and Issues
Individuals or group who feel compelled to ameliorate a problem or advance a cause through voluntray expressions of time or money	Individuals or group who are involved in the raising and receiving of philanthropic gifts of time or money and who ensure their appropriate use	Organizations and institutions whose mission is the provision of philanthropic or charitable services, as well as the conduit for philanthropic exchanges	Individuals or group who directly or indirectly provide the need or desired services, and serve as the guardians of the organization's charitable conscience and as advocates for the organization's recipients	Individuals and communities with problems and needs that can be addressed and solved through programs and services supported by philanthropy

Philanthropy operates as an interactive, dynamic process that is aimed at advancing the public good. It is organized around values of reciprocity, cooperation, mutual respect, accountability, and commitment.

EXHIBIT 2.1   THE PROCESS OF ORGANIZED PHILANTHROPY

PROCESS of Philanthropy Checklist

- Does your organization have a process in place that is seen as a human or social exchange, starting with the donor and ending with the recipient?

- Do the people in the middle stand in the way of connecting donors to recipients, or do they facilitate linkages between them?

- Are your process steps donor centered, or are they driven by process policies and procedures? Does the person who opens the gift envelope look at who signed the check, note whether it is a joint or single account, and inquire what it is for?

- What kind of processes do you have in place to thank a donor within 24 hours? How often do you report to each donor how the gift was used and what it accomplished?

- Do you have a process in place that alerts you to a second gift or third gift in the same year?

- Do you have a once-a-year campaign, or do you solicit gifts year-round, so that the donor's desire to give at a particular time can be honored, rather than making them wait for your next campaign?

- Do you have someone on your staff who can advise a donor how to establish an individual process of inspired philanthropy? Do you have the tools necessary to encourage donors to write their own philanthropy mission?

MOTIVATIONS OF PERSONAL PHILANTHROPY

Discovery of Complexity and Complications

> Philanthropy is a creative expression of that part of yourself that cares about and believes in the potential for change. The most effective philanthropy joins your interests and experiences with current needs and seeks desired outcomes for the public good, not self gain.
>
> —Tracy Gary

The study of who gives and why has been an ongoing pursuit by both scholars and practitioners for decades.

We have an intuitive picture of the primary motives behind the act of giving, from fundraising practitioners who have interpreted donor behaviors along the way. But recent motivational and behavior studies by scholars have given us a more comprehensive picture. They illuminate how complicated motivations really are when we add in demographic and psychographic variables.

Sources of research include:

- Economists and public administrators have conducted research on the tax implications of charitable giving, focused on factors such as education, employment, marital status, household income, wealth, and tax policy.
- Psychologists have focused on predictors of individual motivation to give, such as altruism, sense of community, and/or having been helped by a charitable organization.
- Sociologists have examined the motivations for giving, as well as the context and culture of the giver and the giver's affiliation with an organization.
- Market researchers have looked at the effectiveness of certain solicitation techniques and market segmentation approaches in connecting donors with causes.
- Fundraising practitioners have used internal analysis of giving indicators, supported by the national research on giving and volunteers that is collected and published by Giving USA.

Explaining in more detail what all the motivational elicitors or exhibitors are would take much more than a chapter section; it would take an entire book. This section will cover:

- DEMOGRAPHICS: Conditions that Predict Probability
- PSYCHOGRAPHICS: Values and Attitudes that Predict Inclination

In the following chapters, we will explore further what you need to know about donor motivations of high-potential constituent groups and how to apply market segmentation, targeting, and communications to these groups.

DEMOGRAPHICS

Conditions that Predict Probability

> Generosity is a value shared by the well-to-do and the not-so well-to-do. It is shared across races and ethnic origins. . . . More Americans give than vote, eat fast food, or watch the Super Bowl.
>
> —Claire Gaudiani

Giving is a statement about what matters to each of us. It is an accepted fact that roughly 70 to 80 percent of all Americans make gifts to charity. Trying to determine who gives more or less in proportion to their income is much more complicated and difficult.

Here are a few facts:

- Americans give more per capita than any other nationality, followed by Canadians.

- Tax deductibility is not the sole reason people give, but it may be a benefit of giving.

- People who give tend to also volunteer, and vice versa.

- People who attend a house of worship tend to give more than those who do not.

A study by the Center on Philanthropy, *Generational Difference in Charitable Giving and Motivations,* found that all generations are equally generous. Even so, we do see significant differences in the way generational groups (Great Generation, Baby Boomers, Gen Xers, and Gen Yers) go about their giving.

There are also differences by gender, ethnicity, religion, and affiliation; differences between married and unmarried persons; differences between Americans, Canadians, and the rest of the world . . . and the list goes on.

The CCS study showed that higher income and higher education levels are associated with a greater likelihood of giving to charity and with higher average gift amounts. Study findings categorized three different motivations tied to three different income groups:

- Among lower-income donors (income less than $50,000), the phrases that resonated for giving were "helping to meet basic needs or helping the poor help themselves."

- Donors with income between $50,000 and $100,000 were more likely than donors in either higher or lower groups to say that they gave to "make the world a better place."

- Among donors with income of $100,000 or more, the phrases selected as motivations for giving included "those with more should help those with less" or "making my community better."

Research tells us that gender plays a role in giving and that women are a high-potential constituency. A 2010 study by Deborah Mesch at the Women's Philanthropy Institute points out that women are more generous than men.

- In every income group, female-headed households are more likely to give to charity than male-headed households.

- In all but one income group, women give more than men.

- Female-headed households give more than men in comparable households except in the widow-widower category.

The more we know about our donors' demographics and psychographics, the better we are able to develop personalized fundraising strategies that cause them to consider gifts to our individual organizations. Field research about donor behaviors points out the need to understand internal motivations alongside external elicitors as we craft our messages, stories, videos, and communications.

Today's donors want to make a difference, see real impact, and understand the return on investment of their gifts. It goes without saying that the messaging and case for support needs to appeal to particular constituencies' motivations.

The theory of marketing is a welcome tool when applied to donor and prospect research; it requires us to segregate high-potential prospects from unlikely prospects, which increases the number of *yes* responses and reduces the number of *no*'s.

Giving USA divides gift sources into the following four categories:

1. **Individuals.** Seventy-three percent or $217.79 billion came from individuals in 2011.

   Individual donors are the predominant givers in the United States, by number and by dollars. This fact must be taken into consideration when creating a fund development program, because individuals have always been and will always be the core of philanthropy for your organization. Individuals have proven to be predictable and loyal and have a greater lifetime value than any other gift source.

   They should represent at least 70 percent of your donor base and have at least a 70 percent retention rate. Within this category will be individuals who give $25 a year and those who give $25,000 a year, those who give only once and those who give every year for decades.

2. **Bequests.** Eight percent or $24.41 billion came from individual bequests in 2011.

   Individuals who leave end-of-life bequests are significant in dollars (not in numbers). Every nonprofit needs a formal fundraising program to solicit and steward bequests from individuals.

   This source of giving is not acquired or developed easily; it takes an environment of relationship building and trust to earn the confidence of individuals who will award a portion of their life earnings to your organization.

3. **Foundations.** Fourteen percent or $41 billion came from private, corporate, and community foundations in 2011.

   As a category of givers, foundations give proportionately a small amount of dollars through a formal grant-making process, but their grants tend to be significant in size for a nonprofit.

   They are organized by tax statute and by association with each other, influencing public policy and social responses. Within the category of foundations are four subtypes: independent, private, and family foundations; corporate foundations; community foundations; and institutional foundations.

4. **Corporations.** Five percent or $14.55 billion came from corporate businesses in 2011.

   The smallest source of giving comes from the business sector, independent of corporate foundations. This fact must be taken into context, because formal giving is just one dimension; businesses give also of their time (their employees as volunteers) and their talent (giving you loaned executives, marketing support, and even printing your annual reports). Additionally, a partnership with a well-respected local business is likely to influence others to give, so there are unreported contributions triggered by cooperation.

PSYCHOGRAPHICS

Values and Attitudes that Predict Inclination

> Available literature shows that charitable giving arises from a complexity of motives, attitudes, and demographic attributes. Some may give out of altruism, while others give out of egoism. Others find mercy, humility, obligation, tax deductions, and access to elite business and social networks as motives for giving.
>
> —Andrew Ting-Yuan Ho, thesis student

Why do people give? Once again, the answer to this question cannot be found in a sole research document or explained in a single sentence. There are many dimensions of motivation, with numerous themes, including self-interest and self-esteem, sympathy and empathy, social justice and social norms, as well as gratitude and reciprocity.

First, there is the debate whether donors give for altruistic reasons or for narcissistic reasons. Some speculate that giving decisions are rational (as in financial); others believe they are emotional (as in empathy). The head versus heart discussion is interesting, but the *why* people give is not black and white; it is more apt to be a shade of gray. *Fundraising approaches use cases that range from charitable to change-oriented to stimulate a wide range of motivations.*

Second, psychologists generally agree that people have internal motivational beliefs and values that cause them to act in certain ways (some are more philanthropic than others). These motivations are theirs alone, to be acted on by them, implying that people cannot really be motivated. However, their preexisting motivations can be externally elicited, much the way many behaviors are triggered. A natural desire to help requires stimulation. *Fundraising techniques (personal solicitation, phone calls letters, and special events) were designed to elicit them.*

Third, behavioral scientists have determined that internal motivations are more likely to be multiple in nature, rather than singular (suggesting that each decision to be philanthropic may be different in each case and exclusive to each person). *Donor research is designed to uncover what exists and where.*

Fourth, market researchers have discovered external elicitors that are more effective than others, achieving greater impact when sequenced (numerous messages, circumstances, or activities), as opposed to just one. *Fundraising utilizes sophisticated communications to do this.*

Fifth, professional fundraisers have concluded that a donor's motivations (and elicitors) can change over time; we see that people go through stages of giving, from checkbook charity to transformational philanthropy. They also have different interests at different life stages. *There are four types of fundraising campaigns to address these stages and situations.*

From our observations, intuition, experience, and research, we can assume that some people have inherited a tradition of philanthropy, others have learned how to give through their experiences, and a small number will never see the benefit of giving.

We can also assume that a caring society has a responsibility to expose people to the joys of giving and encourage them to integrate generosity and gratitude into their lives.

It is also fair to say that no one should think less of those who do not give, since philanthropy is a personal choice.

There are six predominant motivational elicitors seen in donor behavior:

Have Linkage, Interest, and Ability   People need to be and feel *linked* to an organization's leadership and purpose, they need to have a natural *interest* or affinity for the type of mission, and they need to have some financial *ability* to make a gift that would make a difference. In the fundraising lingo, this is called the LIA.

- *Linkage* refers to a connection, an affiliation, or an access point between a donor and a cause, or someone representing that cause.
- *Interest* refers to a particular interest in an issue or an affinity for an organization's mission, which is in sync with the donor's values.
- *Ability* refers to a donor's capacity and inclination to make a financial gift that makes a difference.

The individual and combined weight (say on a scale of 1 to 5) of these three indicators can help predict who will be more or less likely to give. If people are not connected and not affected, they are probably not going to think about making a gift, regardless of whether they have the ability. If they are strongly linked and greatly interested, they will make more than a token gift.

They are Asked   Another time-honored elicitor of philanthropy is the familiar claim that people give, if they are asked. If people aren't asked, they may not give, but there are observations of generosity from people who gave without being asked. Perhaps it's all in the definition of *ask*. To most people, that word *ask* conjectures a formal request for money.

The ask, of course, can be subtle or it can be overt, as you can see from the following:

- Would you be willing to support this cause?
- Would you consider a gift to this organization?
- Would you join us in funding this project?
- Can we count on you to make a gift?
- What size gift would you like to make?
- Can we put you down for a gift of $___?

Where the *ask* gets complicated is with different generations. The Great Generation is accustomed to asking friends to support their favorite charities. But Baby Boomers are more comfortable with an invitational or an indirect ask from the executive director. Gen Xers are actually more comfortable with a direct ask than a roundabout approach from someone representing the organization (board member or staff member).

Another time-honored principle is that people give to people. Research based on a national sample of more than 8,300 donors confirmed that people actually give more when they are asked personally by someone they know.

The following findings are impressive:

- Donors gave 19 percent more to secular charities when someone they knew asked for a gift in person (or $987 average).
- Religious donors who were asked to contribute gave 42 percent more when asked in person by someone they knew ($2,904).

Asking in person does not guarantee an automatic *yes*. Even when asked, today's younger inexperienced donors will want to take time to think things through, so asking someone who is not yet fully informed is likely to generate an early "no" or "I'll think about it." They may need to be more involved and engaged before being asked, as well as more familiar with the art of giving.

Are Informed and Influenced   There is yet another donor group that doesn't want to be asked; they want to be involved or invited in first. These are often the technology-savvy corporate executives who make it a practice of researching everything before they invest. When they decide to give, it's on their terms.

Seemingly unsolicited gifts still have an element of prior influence. Somewhere along the way, a self-motivated donor who carefully selects a charity of choice may have been influenced by comments from trusted friends or marketing messages from the charity. In reality, asking for a gift has many forms, from oblique to overt.

We also know that women are more likely to give only after they have checked out a charity by volunteering there. Once involved and satisfied that an organization meets their criteria, they start giving.

Younger donors are more likely to research charities before deciding to give to them, and they are heavily influenced by their peers through social media. This means that donors can be more involved than anyone at the charity realizes; their friends are in the know.

Recent research also tells us that having a connection is critical to donor retention:

- Nearly 38 percent of donors stopped supporting an organization that they had previously supported because they no longer felt connected.

- Twenty-six percent stopped supporting at least two organizations that they had previously supported because they no longer felt connected.

See the Benefits   Someone will ultimately benefit from a charitable gift; the best-case scenario is when both the donor and the recipient have mutual reciprocity. It's easier to see how the recipient benefits, but it gets more complicated with "how" donors satisfy their motivations.

For instance, a gift to Haiti Relief might be stimulated by an altruistic or theological belief (benefiting someone else). Still, the donor will benefit from feeling a sense of satisfaction that he or she has done a good thing.

A gift to the Opera Company might be stimulated by a more narcissistic need (to get the best seat in the house). Still, the organization and artists benefit because they have an appreciative audience.

A gift motivated by one end of the continuum (altruism to egoism) is not better than the other, unless, of course, it conflicts with your organization's views or challenges your integrity.

For some donors, there are tangible benefits such as getting a building named after them or receiving recognition items. There are endless examples of incentives and benefits in the public media world of fundraising, ranging from T-shirts, to mugs, to coupons and CDs.

While some donors gravitate to tangible premiums or are incentivized by them, others abhor them or decline them because they seem like a waste of donated money.

Research tells us that a benefit, whether intangible or tangible, is key to long-term giving. An interesting research study discovered that for donors, in spite of their desire to make a difference for others, how they benefited or achieved personal fulfillment mattered.

- Fifty-five percent said they gave because of the impact on their quality of life.

- Forty-six percent said they gave because they got personal fulfillment.

But what might be even more important to fundraising professionals is the high level of need they have for results. Sixty-nine percent have a preference for giving to charities that provide donors with measurable results.

Need to Affirm Identity When a person decides to make a gift, they consider what they *have* to give. One principle driver of philanthropy involves the person's identity: who they are and how they see themselves. Their identity includes not only their treasure, but also time and talent to give.

If they see themselves as reasonably well off or *blessed*, they don't have any problem giving money. When someone is young and climbing a career ladder, they may give their time or talent—because they don't have the money. Both types of gifts are equally as valuable to the donor. In fact, at certain times of our lives, time may be more valuable than money.

Our identify is reflected in how we give as well as the amount we give, and what we give for.

If a donor needs a psychosocial experience to affirm their identify, they may choose to give through a special event. If a donor has more identity than he/she psychologically needs, they may choose to give an anonymous gift. If a donor needs a lot of affirmation from others, he/she may choose to make a public gift for something tangible and visible. Point is: We give what we have to give at each phase of our life.

Schervish and Havens' research uses "the identification model" to study how and why individuals come to identify with the needs and aspirations of others. They say "It is not the absence of self that generates generosity but the presence of a caring self." In some ways, this is similar to de Tocqueville's civic concept of enlightened self-interest or "self-interest properly understood."

The most important element of their model is *Communities of Participation* which includes both formal organizations as well as informal connections. "Being connected to an array of such life-settings is the basis for people becoming aware of needs and choosing to respond."

The identification model of charitable giving is essentially about relationships, stems from self identification, connections with others, involvement in activities, and inspiration to give.

Many Reasons for Giving, Not Just One The list of reasons for giving is long, complex, and not entirely understood, because of the personal aspects behind philanthropy. The Minnesota Council of Foundations suggests that giving comes from one or more of the following motivations:

- To help fulfill one's life goals and passions
- To feel a sense of value and satisfaction
- To leave a lasting imprint on society while making a significant difference
- To perpetuate a certain viewpoint or philosophy
- To unite family members around a purposeful mission
- To honor or memorialize a friend or loved one
- To give something back to a community
- To fulfill a responsibility or desire to be a leader in a community
- To connect with others who share one's interests and passions
- To benefit from tax advantages
- To express gratitude or to say thank you

As was mentioned earlier, motivations are more likely to be multiple than singular. Eugene Temple, former executive director of the Center on Philanthropy at Indiana University, states that his organization's studies also find varied and multiple motivations: "Typically, people give because they identify with a cause . . . there are people who feel a responsibility to give back . . . and often people will say if they are asked by the right person, they will give." A recent study pointed out that one in five donors give to charity to "help meet people's basic needs."

It's Easy Fundraising experts say there are only three basic ways to solicit a gift: in person, by mail, by phone. There are, obviously, multiple variations of each form.

To *make* a gift, the same principle follows: people give in person, by mail, and by phone. They use a variety of giving vehicles to do this: cash, check, electronic transfer, credit card, stock gifts, and, of course, various forms of planned gifts (art, property, possessions).

Experience tells us that the smaller the gift, the greater the possibility it will be in change or cash (using the Salvation Army Red Kettle as an example). The larger the gift, the greater the likelihood it will be an electronic transfer of stock.

In recent years, there has been a decline in the effectiveness of direct mail, which has reduced the number of personal checks needing to be processed. Increasingly, donors are using electronic banking systems and charge cards for their gifts; it is much easier for them, resulting in gift processing efficiencies.

Another significant trend is an increase in monthly giving via payroll deduction or automatic bank transfer. Not only does incremental gift pledging make it palatable for the giver ($20 a month is barely noticed), but it is more lucrative for the charity. It also appears that people who give monthly keep giving from year to year, without having to make a new decision every year. So retention rates are higher, in addition to larger cumulative giving.

IMPACT OF COMMUNITY PHILANTHROPY

Measurable Economic and Social Benefits

> Creating social benefit is both a personal and professional goal for an increasingly diverse set of players who bring evolving needs and expectations, are informed and enabled by emerging tools and technologies, and are increasingly emboldened to create new organizational structures to achieve common goals.
>
> —The James Irvine Foundation/La Piana Consulting

The central benefit of the nonprofit sector is the value-add it brings to the other two sectors, government and business.

The nonprofit sector has a unique role that operates very differently: Although the smallest of the three sectors, the nonprofit sector has at times been the loudest and the most influential voice in the acculturation of diverse peoples.

The nonprofit sector fulfills a host of important functions; many of them operate independently, and others act as virtual extensions of government programs. Nonprofit organizations have fulfilled a variety of functions that enable citizens to contribute to the overall well-being of their communities. As such, they are building and maintaining a civil society.

Perhaps the most important sign of recognition that the nonprofit sector is beneficial to American society is its general exemption from federal income tax. Add that to the fact that donations are tax deductable. This might be proof alone, but defense must be offered beyond historic decisions—the nonprofit sector must continue to defend its purpose if it wants to maintain its position.

There are two ways to measure impact.

- SOCIAL: Engagement of People Community Building
- FINANCIAL: Monetary Impact to the Global Economy

SOCIAL

Engagement of People in Community Building

> Nonprofit organizations provide the basis and the infrastructure for forming
> social networks that support strong communities. They are frequently the vehi-
> cle for mobilizing and empowering residents—serving as counterpoints and
> conduits for community preferences.
>
> —Elizabeth T. Boris

According to political scientist Robert Putnam, nonprofit organizations are the
foundation of community-level social capital, not just in the United States but
in other advanced industrial countries as well. He suggests that social capital is
important for a variety of reasons:

1. It allows citizens to resolve collective problems more easily.
2. It greases the wheels that allow communities to advance smoothly.
3. It widens our awareness of the many ways in which our fates are linked.
4. The networks serve as conduits for the flow of helpful information.

The concept of social capital, or civic engagement, is that certain people
have access to valuable resources. *Social capital* is defined as "access to resources gained by virtue of the frequency of connections with others."
Expand this concept to many people, and you have entire communities
who, because of their expanded value exchanges, have multiplied their social benefits.

There are distinct benefits to living in a community with high levels of social
capital, including the protection of democratic governance, self-sufficiency
through gainful employment, a safe and secure environment in which to live,
and the assurance of a good quality of life.

- Child development is powerfully shaped by social capital of trust, networks,
  and norms of reciprocity within a child's family, school, peer group, and
  community.
- In high-social-capital areas, public spaces are cleaner, people are friendlier,
  and the streets are safer. Mutual trust, frequent interactions, and reciprocal
  activities among neighbors are known to reduce crime rates.

- There appears to be a strong relationship between possession of social capital and better health and happiness via networks, membership, and interaction. High-social-capital communities have markedly better health outcomes and lower age-adjusted mortality.

- Social capital can help to mitigate the insidious effects of socioeconomic disadvantage with the growing presence of nonprofit organizations, including those that help people train for and find jobs. Since employment is often tied to networking, it requires a wider network with access to more introductions, more information, and better opportunities.

The 2000 Social Capital Community Benchmark Survey revealed that social capital has a significant effect on the quality of life in communities and people's general satisfaction with their lives. Those living in communities high in social capital are much more likely to report greater personal happiness than their counterparts in low-social-capital communities.

As such, the extent to which people volunteer to help others is the most commonly used measure of the nonprofit sector's capacity of people's connection to each other: "For the 1.23 million charities, social welfare organizations, and religious congregations in the United States, giving and volunteering is at the heart of citizen action."

- Citizen action (including philanthropy) can even "profile" a community as more or less philanthropic. Ironically, high-income is only one indicator of philanthropic behavior. Civic engagement, community need, advocacy by leaders, spiritual traditions and corporate participation all influence both citizens and entire communities to be philanthropic.

- Some cities, like Seattle and the Washington, DC area, have higher rates of philanthropic participation in part because of higher-than-average income. But taxpayers who live in low-income states like Alabama and Georgia give more than wealthier states. Taxpayers who live in high-income states like New Hampshire and Alaska give less on average than poorer states.

- Kansas is among the 10 most generous states, despite having one of the highest poverty rates and a low ranking of high income. Wyoming, on the other hand, has one of the lowest number of taxpayers who report giving to charity, but they donate enough to rank among the 10 most generous states in the United States.

Bottom line: Whenever and wherever the public *values and trusts* their nonprofit organizations, a community-wide culture of philanthropy is formed, is nurtured, and flourishes.

FINANCIAL

Monetary Impact to the Global Economy

> During the past decade, the rate of growth of nonprofit jobs outdistanced the rate of growth of for-profit jobs in every year except one, and in that year they were nearly tied.
>
> —The Johns Hopkins Nonprofit Economic Data Project

According to Independent Sector, the U.S. economy greatly benefits from the nonprofit sector in many ways, but four measures stand out: revenues, employment, contributions, volunteer value.

First, in 2009 the nonprofit sector employed 13.5 million people (10 percent of the nation's workforce) and paid $668 billion in wages (9 percent of all wages), representing 5.5 percent of the nation's gross national product. (The Johns Hopkins Nonprofit Economic Data Project) More specifically, the U.S. nonprofit sector employs:

- Nearly 18 times more workers than the nation's utilities industry.
- Fifteen times more workers than the nation's mining industry.
- Nearly 10 times more workers than the nation's agriculture industry.
- About five and a half times more workers than the nation's real estate industry.
- Nearly three times more workers than the nation's transportation industry.
- About twice as many workers as the nation's wholesale trade, finance and insurance, and construction industries.

Second, the nonprofit sector (charities that file 990s) reported revenues of $1.4 trillion and assets of nearly $2.6 trillion. That revenue figure is comprised of earned fees, government grants, and an impressive $290 billion in philanthropic gifts and grants, made voluntarily and without benefit except for a tax deduction, by people across the nation. That $290 billion in donations is truly an indicator of public opinion.

Third, contributions to charitable organizations in 2011 are estimated at $298.42 billion (a 4% increase over the revised estimate of $286.91 billion in 2010).

Fourth, about 63.4 million Americans (or 26.3 percent of the adult population), gave 8.1 billion hours of volunteer service worth $173 billion in 2010.

What is most impressive about the U.S. charitable sector is the diversity of programs it offers. The 501(c)(3) organizations in this network fall into eight major categories:

1. **Religion.** Religion garners 35 percent of the philanthropic pie, and is 100 percent dependent on philanthropy for its operating budget.

For the record, religion has always received the highest percentage and captured the largest share of the philanthropic pie. The *why* is obvious, given our constitution of religious freedom and our deeply ingrained spiritual values.

Religious giving is stimulated by a sense of belonging to a group that shares and honors its spiritual mandates. The majority of religious institutions are houses of worship. As a member, there is a cultural expectation that you will share in the expenses to operate the programs, services, and missions. After all, this is *your* spiritual home.

In many religious institutions, giving is required as a tithe. In some, there is another form of pressure coming from peers: Leaving the collection plate empty as it passes by could be viewed as symbolically sacrilegious. Giving is so prevalent in religious organizations that guilt may be self-assumed if one is not able to do one's part.

In spite of being the largest subsector, very few religious organizations have professional development officers on staff; the fundraising is done by the organization's religious and lay leaders. From the pulpit, they ask their members to pledge an amount for the year, broken down into weekly or monthly collections (via envelope for the plate or an electronic bank transfer). This method of fundraising is extremely successful, since it brings two financial goals together: the entity's annual operating budget and the amount each member can and will give annually from his or her income. The case for support in religious organizations is very simple: to advance their religious beliefs.

Beyond religious giving to houses of worship, there are hundreds of thousands of religious organizations that go beyond worship; churches were some of the first in the United States to start social service programs to help people with basic needs. And they transfer a significant portion of their contributions to other charitable organizations.

2. **Education and Research.** Education receives 14 percent of the philanthropic pie, which underwrites a small percentage of the general operating budget, a large percentage of which is raised for capital improvements.

   The education subsector is comprised of educational institutions that are accredited and credentialed, including private and public colleges and universities, elementary and secondary schools, and noncommercial research institutions. Typically, an education program (such as a literacy project) that is not housed in an accredited institution would fall in another category, possibly social services.

   Private and public higher education institutions were the first nonprofits to hire fundraising consultants and fundraising professionals; they were also among the first to practice all four of the fundraising approaches: annual, capital, major gift, and planned. It goes without saying that fundraising is usually very organized and professionally staffed.

The need for philanthropy is in the financial gap between student fees and the real cost of hiring faculty and maintaining school buildings. Philanthropy is sought for unrestricted gifts to balance the budget, to underwrite individual student scholarships, to fund academic chairs, to support research projects, and to grow endowment accounts. Capital campaigns and endowment campaigns are big business in the education subsector, accounting for the majority of money raised each year in the United States and Canada.

Next to religious organizations, educational institutions have the second most natural constituency to reach out to for philanthropic support: alumni. Having benefited from an education (which directly influences their ability to do well in life financially), most alumni are inclined to give back, in part because of their pride of association with their classmates and the institution, but also because they believe they can help others be successful. So giving to your school is a little like standing up for mother and apple pie.

3. **Human Services.** Human services receives only 9 percent of the philanthropic pie, but contributions range from 10 percent to 90 percent of an organizations' operating budget.

The human or social services subsector appears *old* when you trace the roots of philanthropy back to the earliest days of the Hull House and Boy Scouts. But the social service sector continues to be more prone to change than other subsectors, making a vast majority of the agencies appear *new*. After all, the essence of this sector comes from its desire to ameliorate social problems, not perpetuate them. Capital and endowment are not large priorities for this sector; service is.

Next to religious causes, the human service sector is highly dependent on philanthropy from individuals, in addition to being dependent on grants from all sources (government, foundations, and corporations). Over half of the revenue in human service organizations usually comes from fees. Government provides just under half of their revenue. The balance or shortfall comes from private contributions.

Fundraising came late for most of the present-day social service agencies, not necessarily because they could not use philanthropy, but because they resisted having to beg for money to provide services that every person should be entitled to. When, as a subsector, they entered the marketplace, they did so with great clarity of case, creativity of approach, and zealousness to attract people to their cause.

What kinds of people give to human services organizations, if not the service recipients? Others who can relate to the problem that is being addressed because they know someone who has addictions, family issues, mental health conditions, or special needs. We can see a strong sense of empathy in social service donors and a genuine desire to provide immediate care, as well as funding systemic solutions. Social service donors tend to give annually and occasionally very generously; they do not see social service issues as going away, but they do want them to diminish, so they will give as long as they can see improvement.

4. **Health Services.** Health Care receives only 8 percent of the philanthropic pie, but it attracts some of the largest major gifts.

The health care subsector includes all health-related institutions, organizations, agencies, and associations from hospitals to public clinics, nursing facilities, and national health causes. Each raises money differently, using different cases and attracting different donors.

For instance, hospitals have very sophisticated development programs geared to attract gifts from former patients. Nursing facilities and hospice agencies generally attract end-of-life and memorial gifts (all one-time gifts). National health causes tend to raise money directly from those who are affected by a disease and from families and friends who hope for a cure.

Why do people give so generously to hospitals that seem to skirt the line between being a nonprofit and acting like a for-profit? Donor behavior has very little to do with tax-exempt status, save for a small percentage of high-wealth donors whose giving is designed to improve their tax status. Most donors give to make a statement, and no one feels more compelled to say thank you than a satisfied patient. Giving to health care institutions is generally an emotional expression of appreciation as well as an investment in an organization that the donor may need the future, or a contribution toward a cure.

If we or a loved one is diagnosed with a disease, it is hard to resist making a gift to an organization whose research mission is to cure that disease. These are the gifts we give, without being asked.

5. **Public and Societal Benefit.** Public Society Benefit organizations receive 8 percent of the philanthropic pie, but that slice is growing every year.

This subsector is kind of an enigma, a catchall and sometimes a passthrough. It is comprised of a large and growing number of private and community foundations, along with civic, social, and fraternal organizations like the United Ways and Jewish federations. This subsector also includes organizations focused on civil rights, voter education and registration, public policy research, social science research, and community and neighborhood economic and civic development. It also includes leadership development programs.

Legally, they are nonprofit organizations, but technically they do not deliver frontline services: They primarily receive, raise, and give away money or advocate for a position or cause. Since they do not act like other subsectors, their inclusion in Giving USA tends to skew the other sectors' relative positions in the marketplace.

In 2010, the public society benefit subsector received approximately 7 percent of all gifts greater than $1 million that were publicly announced in the media and tracked on the Center on Philanthropy's 2010 Million Dollar List.

6. **Arts, Culture, and Humanities.** Arts, Culture, and the Humanities receives 5 percent of the philanthropic pie and do the best job at generating fee-based income from the same constituency.

The arts and culture subsector encompasses all types of museums (from arts to science to history), most performing arts (dance companies, opera, symphony, choral) and various types of cultural and science organizations.

Arts and cultural organizations function on the narrowest margins of profit within the nonprofit sector because of their dependence on a physical space designed to suit their distinct form of art. This dominance of space and art form mandates a more commercial culture than other nonprofits.

Most people who contribute to arts and cultural organizations do so as part of their enjoyment of the institution's experience, be it front-row seats, access to the green room, or invitations to opening night. The words *patronage* and *aficionado* come to mind when we look at donor behavior in this subsector, both historically and in the modern world. No longer the sole purview of the wealthy, the arts and culture subsector now attracts all socioeconomic levels.

Fundraising in this subsector is more dependent on parties, galas, and special events—all providing the important psychosocial benefits that donors are looking for.

Donors to the arts tend to be lifelong givers and have often been influenced by previous generations to support a particular art form, be it a ballet company or a museum with masterpieces.

7. **International and Foreign Affairs.** International Affairs receives 5 percent of the philanthropic pie, but this subsector is exploding.

   Overseas relief and human development organizations have grown in number and in fundraising status during the past 20-plus years. With the advent of technology, people can see what is happening across the planet in real time; they also can view the effects of world events that compromise human existence.

   Most international organizations work from two platforms: immediate relief and longer-term sustainability. Adverse human conditions require the basics of food, water, medicine, and clothing in the form of aid. Once stabilized, people need to rebuild their houses, install wells, grow crops, and become self-reliant. Institutional efforts require both government resources and philanthropic responses.

   International organizations use fundraising strategies that are directed to the grassroots attracting hundreds of thousands of small gifts from across the globe. Donors are motivated to give to international causes for the same reasons they give to disaster relief; their gifts are emotional, spontaneous, and often one-time, rather than repeatable.

   The challenge in fundraising for this growing and important subsector rests with assuring people that their gifts are more than a Band-Aid.

8. **Environmental and Animals.** The Environment and Animals subsector attracts 2 percent of the philanthropic pie and is dominated by a few large organizations who garner most of the gifts.

   Giving to environment and animals includes zoos and aquariums, botanical gardens and horticultural programs, humane societies and other animal rescue organizations, wildlife and habitat preservation groups, and organizations working for pollution abatement and control. The subsector also includes programs for environmental education, outdoor survival, and beautification of open spaces.

   While only 2 percent of the philanthropic pie, these organizations cannot exist without support from the public in the form of memberships, donations, gifts of property, and bequests.

   Membership is, for many of these organizations, their largest source of revenue beyond grants. Are memberships considered fees or gifts? The answer could be one or the other or both. Most memberships entitle the purchaser to a discounted ticket rate to use the facility and/or receive publications; some include a tax-deductible gift portion.

   What motivates people to buy or give to organizations in this subsector? Primarily, a love for the natural world and its inhabitants. For many people, the environment is their church, a place where the greater powers that be exist.

- ATTITUDE: Perception Influences Opinions
- ADVOCACY: Communications Shape Cultures
- ACTION: Aligning Cultural Ideas and Ideals

CULTURE OF ORGANIZATIONAL PHILANTHROPY

Foundation for Successful Fundraising

Building a strong values-based culture—or building a strong performance culture—is a strategic, intellectual, and often difficult process. It requires a substantial commitment from the organization in terms of time and resources, but the payoff can be substantial.

—McKinsey & Company

Although all nonprofit organizations depend to some extent on philanthropic support, not all are successful at raising funds. The primary difference is the presence or absence of what is termed *philanthropic culture*.

As I have worked with organizations across the country, I have seen firsthand how many struggle with the very same issues: boards that don't raise money, program staff who refuse to share names of potential supporters, donors whose gift of money is valued more than their input, development programs with imposed and impossible goals, and CEOs who say they'll help with the fundraising but show up only for the recognition dinners.

When the job of fundraising belongs to only a few people, philanthropy cannot thrive. To raise the kind of resources that are needed in today's competitive marketplace and into the future requires a carefully crafted organizational culture that views philanthropy as artful and joyful, not drudgery and pain.

The term *philanthropic culture* was popularized in the past decade to describe how the best nonprofit organizations embrace philanthropy: It promulgates the ideal environment for fundraising.

In the broadest context, the term *philanthropic culture* describes how a group of people embrace the principle of voluntarily sharing and stewarding their resources for the benefit of others. In democratic societies, the term is often used to differentiate a caring philanthropic sector from a financially driven commercial sector or a politically mandated government sector.

When nonprofit organizations are said to have a philanthropic culture, it is implicit that philanthropy is essential to achieving their mission. There is widespread acceptance of philanthropy as a core value, and everyone has a role in promoting it. As such, fundraising has a rationalized and respected existence.

The espousal of a philanthropic culture requires an institutionalized investment of resources in the education, engagement, and renewal of cultural values, hence the references in this chapter to organizational dynamics of "attitude, advocacy, and action."

This section focuses on how nonprofit organizations can introduce and integrate philanthropic beliefs and principles into their vision, mission, values, and behaviors. Successfully doing so will result in an integrated and inclusive approach to fundraising that emanates from the center (the figurative soul) of an organization and is embraced by all (the figurative body).

CULTURE Principles

ATTITUDE: Philanthropy is critical to the mission.
- Philanthropy is understood, respected, and needed.
- An investment is made to embrace and inspire it.
- The goal is to build vital and viable communities.

ADVOCACY: Fundraising is everyone's job.
- Philanthropy is taught and reciprocated.
- Fundraising is a source of pride.
- Everybody can articulate a compelling case.

ACTION: Donors are valued for more than money.
- Donors are seen as voluntary partners in mission.
- Community input is sought, and ideas are welcomed.
- Gifts are wisely stewarded, and intentions are honored.

For some, the concept of a philanthropic culture can be a little elusive.

You can list the characteristics of a culture when it values philanthropy by its give-and-receive exchange relationships, but it generally cannot be reduced to black-and-white simplicity. It is based on integrity, transparency, and ethical principles. It is a form of mutuality. A philanthropic culture is built with three ingredients.

ATTITUDE

Perception Influences Opinions

A philanthropic culture is an organizationally pervasive mindset, shared at all levels in the organization, that the organization is both interested in and worthy of charity investment, so much so that every internal constituent understands how their role impacts the net desired outcome, which is that benefactors act on their desire to further the organization's plan.

—Gary Hubbell

In my opinion, a philanthropic culture is decidedly Toucquevillean, in that it constitutes a gathering of people with shared missions and goals.

When this hypothesis is applied to organizational behavior, internal constituents are viewed as *partners* in mission work (board, volunteers, administration, employees). As such, their attitude stimulates an expanded collective synergy that results in *partnerships* with external constituents (clients, donors, grantors) to fund the delivery of mission services (via contributions of time, talent, and treasure).

This deliberate interconnecting of people around core values to achieve charitable missions is the most basic form of community building. Herein lies the essence and enigma of the term *philanthropic culture.*

As I have used the term in classrooms and practice, I am advocating for fundraising attitudes that create caring community behaviors, not solely because more money would be raised but because more people would appreciate the power of working together for the benefit of others. Not a new idea, at all. It was one that Ward and Pierce, the YMCA's first fundraisers, espoused at least 100 years ago.

Admittedly, we cannot dismiss how gifts of money are critical to our mission, but to focus primarily on the money is missing the point of civic engagement and the relative influence that volunteer time and talent bring to social change. A few psychological studies suggest that the latter (volunteerism) is the underlying stimulus for financial philanthropy.

In recent years, volunteerism has unfortunately taken a back seat as professionalism has emerged. This situation does not bode well for the development of authentic philanthropic cultures.

As Hank Rosso (1991) promulgated in the formative years of fund development, volunteerism is the tenet of fundraising. Professional fundraising expertise does not mitigate the need for volunteers. That would be tantamount to removing the word *voluntary* from Payton's description of philanthropy.

Philanthropy, in all forms, is the litmus test of a community's concern for an organization's mission. If internal constituents give of their time, talent, and/or treasure to support their own charity, they send an endorsement to the greater community that theirs is an organization worthy of support from others. If, on the other hand, internal or external constituents say, "No thanks," there is probable cause that the current mission is no longer relevant.

As implied, fundraising serves as the mirror of an organization's understanding and regard for philanthropy.

As Claire Gaudiani asserted in her book *The Greater Good:* "The United States is not generous because it is rich, it is rich because it is generous." She argues that generosity is a long-standing tradition of a people who, while rugged individualists, also seek to build and share community.

Generosity, we all know, is not the purview of the rich. Nor is community building the purview of the common man. Both are natural human instincts of democratic nations.

ATTITUDE Checklist

- How does *leadership* really feel about philanthropy as a core value?

- Does the organization authentically embrace this type of culture, instill it, and inspire it? Or does it resent and resist dependence on it (albeit subtly)?

- What is your rationale for *fundraising?*

- Does the organization promote a culture of giving because it raises the community's philanthropic involvement, or is fundraising done merely as a competitive pursuit of the community's donors?

- What you hear in the hallways: "We are entitled to charity because we do good works." "We need the money to balance our books." "We want to involve people because they bring resources, including ideas." What you hear can give you the clues.

- To what extent are *donors* valued? Are donors seen as partners in the delivery of services and fulfillment of the mission, or are they simply another source of revenue?

- Is there a donor orientation to fundraising (welcoming designated giving) or an organizational predominance (we know best how to spend it)?

ADVOCACY

Communications Shape Cultures

Organizations that operate with a culture of philanthropy understand three things: the value of organizational culture, the importance of philanthropy, and the inextricable link between philanthropy and fund development.

—Simone Joyaux

Building a philanthropic culture, particularly when it doesn't exist, is hard work. The resolution comes when leadership *advocates* it. When leadership is firmly committed to the concepts and familiar with processes that influence cultural change, the outcomes can be amazing.

There are multiple ingredients of a philanthropic culture and at least two dimensions. The first is a perspective from the inside, looking out (the organizational view), and the second, a perspective from the outside, looking in (the donor community view). Intertwining the two are the attitudes, advocacy, and actions that form the glue of a cultural bond.

1. **From an organizational or professional point of view,** culture is the substance that causes people to connect to an organization. It dictates how people think and behave and is so influential that it defies contradictions.

    Culture is the force and the spirit that brings internal values, attitudes, and beliefs into sync, giving an organization the power to connect with external constituents and secure financial resources. Culture can be an asset, when healthy, and a hindrance, if dysfunctional.

    To assess the presence or the absence of a philanthropic culture, one need only look at the attitudes around fundraising and donors and assess if anyone is advocating for it (rather than being passive about it).

    If you were to objectively evaluate the status of your organization's philanthropic culture, you would assess at least three conditions:

2. **From a donor and community point of view,** all organizations have personalities that can be felt, if not described. The culture of an organization comes through loud and clear, from the moment you walk in the front door or hear the voice of someone answering your phone call. Several axioms come to mind: "First impressions are lasting impressions" for donors as they construct their views, reinforced by whether the organization "walks the talk."

    The concept of a philanthropic culture may be elusive to donors, in the sense that it is hard to define in concrete terms. It is more about feelings and intangibles. However, if philanthropy is valued, it is very obvious in the way the organization treats you as a donor, a grantor, and a volunteer.

    Donor satisfaction is probably the highest measure of a philanthropic culture.

    When donors are ultimately satisfied with their decision to give through us, they tend to give without our asking. I am not talking about automatically supporting the annual fund each year; I am taking about discerning, rational, and meaningful behavior, the kind that causes donors to advocate for an organization in an unsolicited manner.

Once again, if you were to evaluate the status of your culture, you would consider several donor-oriented conditions.

If all of these *satisfaction* conditions are met, your donors cannot resist advocating to others, because doing so affirms a belief that your organization also merits support.

Organizations with institutionalized philanthropic cultures tend to be inclusive in their actions. Their face of philanthropy is diverse and democratic, not the exclusive purview of those with wealth or influence. It belongs to people who want to be a part of something that improves the community.

Elizabeth Lynn and Susan Wisely (2006) provide us with an indicator for assessing the motivations of our donors. They have identified four interrelated yet distinct traditions of philanthropy:

1. Relief

2. Improvement

3. Social reform

4. Civic engagement

The last and most mature organizational tradition is civic engagement, which seems symbiotic with the stated rationale for building philanthropic cultures within organizations. Civic engagement is motivated by donors' desire to increase their own civic participation, which subsequently builds and nurtures larger communities by increasing connections (which incidentally fueled the formation of community foundations across the United States).

Concurrently, "communities of participation" is Paul Schervish's first of eight factors that he deemed sufficient to induce at least a minimal level of philanthropic response. His research findings indicate that "communities of participation" have the strongest and most consistent relationship to giving behavior.

Charitable giving is largely a consequence of forging a connection between the existing inclinations and involvement of individuals and the needs of recipients. As implied by Schervish, philanthropic fundraising is a dynamic that integrates the giver with the receiver (literally and figuratively); it is not intentionally a one-way transfer.

In cultures that are philanthropically configured, donors are more likely to be recognized for what they bring to the table (beyond financial resources), clients are respected for what they need (not just what we think they need), employees are seen as specialists in service delivery (serving naturally as advocates), and board members are tapped for their expertise (not blamed for the institution's shortcomings).

A philanthropic culture may, ironically, be more dependent on the stewarding of relationships and contributions already garnered, rather than being contrived to get more.

To quote On Course Consulting, which specializes in organizational development: "Organizations that have adopted a culture of philanthropy have matured in their development efforts: they have evolved from a focus on money to a focus on building lasting relationships.

ADVOCACY Checklist

- What are your donors' understandings of your *mission/case*?

- Are donors able to articulate what contributions are needed for, in a way that is compelling, urgent, and critical? Can they point to several programmatic initiatives, explain how services are delivered, and describe the benefits of a $1,000 gift versus a $10,000 gift?

- What is the level of donor consciousness for gift *stewardship*?

- Do donors know exactly where their gifts were used, how they were used, and what happened as a result?

- Do they express themselves with words like "I made a difference"? Can your donors tell someone else that your organization is effective and efficient in what it does?

- Do they have any idea what percentage of the budget is dependent on philanthropy? Would they select your organization if they had $1 million to give away?

- What kind of donor and volunteer *participation* does your organization have? The measure of involvement is not limited to numbers, figures, or percentages. It has more to do with the quality of the experience. Some may prefer to volunteer on a board or a committee; others may be inclined to work behind the scenes.

- Did your donors learn something? Was the donor's time and talent used wisely? Were the donors successful? Would your donors like to participate again?

ACTION

Aligning Cultural Ideas and Ideals

A philanthropic organizational culture is an understanding of and respect for the way philanthropy helps an organization achieve its mission. A culture in which every member of the organization understands the role they can play in achieving fundraising goal.

—Philanthropic Trends, KCI Spring 2004

One might dispute that a philanthropic culture could exist without fundraising, but it is doubtful that anyone would contest that fundraising could thrive without it.

An organization's *attitude* about the integral role of philanthropy, I grant you, is hard to measure in concrete terms. What is being said one day could change a perspective tomorrow if a major government grant came through. Or when an organization *advocates* for philanthropy, it could do it rhetorically because of an impending campaign. There is plenty of evidence of that in strategies for higher education capital campaigns. But *action* is another matter, and it is ever so easy to measure.

In a philanthropic culture, the most significant indicator is that everyone shares the responsibility for creating it, sustaining it, and celebrating it. The work of philanthropy is an organization-wide value and responsibility; fundraising is not relegated to the development office.

Action starts at the top of an organization, with the CEO and the board, affirming that community involvement is essential to their charitable mission. A philanthropic culture (internal) plays out in the following actions:

ACTION Checklist

- The CEO is the primary advocate for philanthropy.
- The community's insight and input are sought after.
- The board members seek all forms of gifts, without apology.
- The leadership team integrates philanthropy into operations.
- Everyone is held accountable for caring relationships.
- The CFO promotes donor-directed fund-accounting and reporting.
- The program staff create and promote strong cases.
- Clients or recipients serve as spokespersons.
- Other staff steward donors and dollars linked to their programs.
- Everyone in the organization has some contact with donors.
- Volunteers are sought after for their insight, input, and impact.
- Every major decision asks: "What would our donors and volunteers think?"

Actions by the organization's leaders and employees, of course, are not enough. Their actions have to work in concert with fundraising activities.

A philanthropic culture and development and fundraising practices are inextricably linked. Stacy M. Vanden Heuval confirmed this in her 2006 master's paper, *Philanthropic Cultures in Healthcare Organizations*:

> Developing the organizational elements, behaviors, attitudes, and opinions necessary for creating a culture of philanthropy in healthcare organizations should be addressed simultaneously with developing best practices in fundraising in order that success can breed success. The efforts for building a stronger organizational culture and for improving fundraising practices are mutually beneficial. (Vanden Heuval 2006)

What is the Role of Development Staff? Why is it Important to Clarify Terms? They are the facilitators, catalysts, advocates, stewards, and the conscience of a philanthropic culture.

Fundraising is not the primary responsibility of development professionals; building a philanthropic culture is. The most successful development professionals—those who consistently facilitate the most extraordinary gifts—take their job very seriously and their role very broadly. Their fund development programs are more than narrow fundraising efforts that focus on a campaign goal thermometer. They strive to build relationships that result in the formation of philanthropists (of all financial means), as opposed to getting donors. Their programs perpetuate the philanthropic tradition and nurture the spirit of giving and receiving.

In philanthropic cultures, development professionals influence the environment by encouraging everyone to be involved in the philanthropic process in some way. In a 1994 article, Deal and Baluss address the role that development professionals play in strengthening an organizational culture:

> The further nonprofit organizations allow the cultural values to shift away from the responsibility to contribute ideas, services, and human capital to improve society, the more difficult fundraising becomes. Fundraising professionals should help nonprofit institutions renew their symbolic cores and strengthen their links to donors and beneficiaries. (Deal and Baluss 1994).

The first step in building a successful development program is clarifying differences between *philanthropy, development*, and *fundraising*. Understanding the relationships among these activities forces fundraisers to reflect on why and how they do their work, rather than on what they do or how they do it.

Philanthropy is the giving-and-receiving exchange that fundraisers facilitate; *development* is the management of all the required relationships; *fundraising* encompasses the methodologies and functions themselves.

In a philanthropic culture, fundraising professionals view the entirety of development as a means of enabling donors to fulfill their philanthropic dreams and create a society that reflects their most deeply held values. Development becomes the process of helping people move from prospects to philanthropists. It is the sum of all fundraising efforts to acquire, renew, cultivate, educate, and serve donors. It is a long-term approach that helps people discover how donors can be an agent for good, along with others.

There is sufficient evidence in the field to suggest that a philanthropic culture produces a form of philanthropic fundraising, which is more successful than charitable or commercial fundraising.

The difference between a professional development program and a narrow commercial fundraising program is much like the difference between charity and philanthropy.

Charitable Fundraising.   Charity focuses more on the problem than on the solution. It is expressed in what the organization needs, rather than what the community wants or needs. Charity is a limited concept that tends to be crisis oriented, indicating a weakness of some sort, for which there is almost always a sense of apology. This crisis orientation leads to a form of begging for support that results in almsgiving; it is impulsive, based on emotion, and often limited in its gift amount. Charity is short-term by nature, requiring minimal commitment and eliciting limited satisfaction on the part of the giver. The benefit is directed toward one person for one time, rather than to many people for all time.

Some examples of charity or commercial fundraising activities are:

- Cause-related marketing activities, which are purchases, not gifts.
- Special events, such as golf tournaments, with no mission connection.
- Raffles, gambling, and auctions, where focus is on the item, not the recipient. Some religious giving, causing guilt to give every Sunday.
- Those annual funds where you give but cannot designate.
- Most a-thons, where you do it once, for a friend

Philanthropic Fundraising.   Philanthropy, a much broader concept than charity, is aimed at systematically solving the problem—as is philanthropic fundraising. It is based on carefully devised plans, built on previous successes that together garner a sense of pride.

Philanthropic fundraising focuses more on the community than on the organization and, as such, benefits many people. It requires a deliberate investment on the part of the giver and produces a satisfying outcome for both giver and receiver—resulting in a transaction, rather than a transfer.

Philanthropic fundraising is donor focused but always in balance with the interests and the concerns of the recipient.

Some examples of philanthropic or donor-focused fundraising (external) activities are:

- A donor development plan with everyone's name, next to the donors.
- Constituency segmentation with targeted communications.
- Giving choices for donors (cases) and giving methods (timing).
- Recognition tailored to donor intent, not just donor size.
- Personalized asks and thanks—no boilerplate.
- Existing donors receive more attention than prospects do.

If and when a philanthropic culture is fully institutionalized (implying there are stages associated with its evolution), fundraising is actually more creative, flexible, and spontaneously strategic.

Why is Fundraising a Program?   At its most mature stage of integration into all aspects of an organization's culture, the development department is respected as a program, equal to all other service delivery programs. Its customers are community donors, and its service is the delivery of education, engagement, and stewardship via philanthropic transactions.

An organization with a philanthropic culture has the ability to do more than influence its own donors, board members, volunteers, employees, and customers; it actually has influence to raise the level of philanthropic behavior in the entire community!

A philanthropic culture is hard work, you can be sure. It means:

- Falling on the side of the donor, by meeting their needs, sometimes before we meet ours, but never doing harm in the process (which means not taking money for something we don't need but not allowing worthy programs to be eliminated because not enough can be raised, today).
- Working harder to tailor, to segment, to personalize, to be clear, to communicate effectively, to operate efficiently, and to continue to question: Can we do this better?
- Taking risks to cut programs when they are no longer relevant and going out on limbs to add critical new programs before they are fully funded.

To list all the indicators or rudiments of a philanthropic culture would create a list so long that we would lose clarity in the minutiae. In this chapter, I list the critical few absolutes, from which longer lists are elaborated in other chapters.

An environment that is *not* philanthropic has the following behavioral indicators derived from myths about money, about voluntary giving, and about the difference between philanthropic and charitable fundraising:

A Culture that Is Not Philanthropy

- Leaders believe their charitable services *should* be supported by the philanthropy of others, not themselves.

- Staff think that board members, wealthy donors, and others in the community *should* make contributions because of the good work the staff deliver.

- Board members think they *should not* be asked to fund raise because that is not the reason they were recruited.

- Volunteers feel they *should not* make a financial contribution when they are giving of their time.

- Professional and program staff think fundraising *should* be the responsibility of the person who was hired as a fundraiser.

- Clients feel the organization *should* give them services, no matter how they are funded.

- Clients, customers, recipients, and beneficiaries believe they *should not* have to reciprocate, even if they have the ability.

In the absence of a philanthropic culture, fundraising can go on—it just won't go as far.

SUMMARY

This chapter has provided insight into the nonprofit sector and why philanthropy is the expression of people's unabated opinions and intrinsic values—you just can't keep people from supporting what they really care about. Understanding how philanthropic motives drive people's actions to give time, talent, and treasure is paramount if you want to be successful at fundraising. More important, this chapter explains how a philanthropic culture enables that success and the lack of a philanthropic culture deters it.

The next chapter focuses on the structure of a fund development program, covering the historic evolution of organized fundraising, in addition to the *how-to* of developing a program, staffing it, and preparing a development plan.

REFERENCES

Backer, T. E. 2004. "Philanthropy and Community Change: How Consulting Psychology Can Contribute." Conference Paper. APA Society for Consulting Psychology Midwinter Conference.

Backs, G. W. 2002. *Talking the Walk & Walking the Talk: Philanthropic Culture in Alberta's Nonprofit Sector.* Master's thesis, Saint Mary's University of Minnesota.

Boguch, J. 1994. "Organizational Readiness for Successful Fund Development: A Systematic and Holistic Approach." *New Directions for Philanthropic Fundraising* (Fall).

Bremner, R. H. 1988. *American Philanthropy,* 2nd ed. Chicago: University of Chicago Press.

Clotfelter, C. T. (ed.). 1992. *Who Benefits from the Nonprofit Sector?* Chicago: University of Chicago Press.

Crowley, G. J. 2005. *Nonprofits and Civic Engagement: Benefits and Challenges in Building Social Capital.* Pittsburgh: Coro Center for Civic Engagement.

Deal, T. C., & C. S. Baluss. 1994. "The Power of Who We Are: Organizational Culture in the Nonprofit Setting." *New Directions for Philanthropic Fundraising* (Fall): 5–16.

Gary, T. 2008. *Inspired Philanthropy: Creating a Giving Plan and Leaving Legacy.* San Francisco, CA: John Wiley & Sons.

Gaudiani, C. 2004. *The Greater Good: How Philanthropy Drives the American Economy and Can Save Capitalism* New York: Henry Holt.

Gaudiani, C. 2007. *Generosity Rules: A Guidebook to Giving.* New York: iUniverse.

Gowdy, Heather, Alex Hildebrand, David La Piana, & Melissa Mendes Campos. 2009. *Convergence: How Five Trends Will Reshape the Social Sector.* San Francisco, CA: The James Irvine Foundation and La Piana Consulting.

Gurin, M. G., & J. Van Til. 1990. "Philanthropy in Its Historical Context." In *Critical Issues in American Philanthropy: Strengthening Theory and Practice,* ed. J. Van Til. San Francisco, CA: Jossey-Bass.

http://store.givingusareports.org/.

Hubbell, G. J. 2004. *Forces for Change: The Coming Challenges in Hospital Philanthropy.* Falls Church, VA: Association for Health Care Philanthropy.

Huebler, J. Philanthropy Described in Democracy in America by de Tocqueville (Learning to Give), a graduate studies paper.

Isaak, J. K. 2004. *Capital Campaigns and the Development of a Culture of Philanthropy in Higher Education.* Master's thesis, Saint Mary's University of Minnesota.

John Hopkins Nonprofit Economic Data Project. http://ccss.jhu.edu/wp-content/uploads/downloads/2012/01/NED_National_2012.pdf

Joyaux, S. P. 2001. *Strategic Fund Development: Building Profitable Relationships That Last.* Burlington, MA: Jones & Bartlett.

Joyaux, S. P., & T. Ahern. 2008. *Keep Your Donors: The Guide to Better Communications and Stronger Relationships.* Hoboken, NJ: John Wiley & Sons.

KCI. 2006. *Building a Philanthropic Organizational Culture: Philanthropic Trends.* Toronto, ON: Ketchum Canada.

Lynn, E., & S. Wisely. 2006. *Four Traditions of Philanthropy: The Civically Engaged Reader.* Chicago: Great Books Foundation.

McGinly, W. C., & K. Renzetti. 2005. "Expanding the Role of Philanthropy in Health Care." *New Directions for Fundraising* (December).

McKinsey & Company, prepared for Venture Philanthropy Partners. 2001. "Effective Capacity Building in Nonprofit Organizations." http://www.vppartners.org/sites/default/files/reports/toc.pdf0.

Minnesota Council of Foundations. http://www.mcf.org/donors/why.

Payton, R. L. 1988. *Philanthropy: Voluntary Action for the Public Good*. New York: Macmillan.

Putnam, R. 2000. *Bowling Alone: The Collapse and Revival of American Community*, New York: Simon & Schuster.

Rosso, H. A. 1991. *Achieving Excellence in Fundraising*. San Francisco, CA: Jossey-Bass.

Sargeant, A., & E. Jay. 2004. *Building Donor Loyalty: The Fundraiser's Guide to Increasing Lifetime Value*. San Francisco, CA: John Wiley & Sons.

Schervish, P. G. 1997. "Inclination, Obligation and Association: What We Know and What We Need to Learn about Donor Motivation." In *Critical Issues in Fundraising*. New York: John Wiley & Sons.

Significant Gifts, a study commissioned by Campbell & Company and conducted by the Center on Philanthropy at Indiana University (2009). philanthropy.iupui.edu/Research/giving_fundraising_research.aspx.

Statistics are from the 2007 Bank of America/IUPUI study of high-net-worth donors.

Statistics from the 2000 Social Capital Community Benchmark Survey. www.ropercenter.uconn.edu/data_access/data/datasets/social_capital_community_survey.html#.T758R7BYuf4.

Urban Institute. 2010. *The Nonprofit Sector in Brief: Public Charities, Giving and Volunteering*. Washington, DC: Urban Institute.

Vanden Heuval, S. M. 2006. *Organizational Culture as It Relates to Creation of a Culture of Philanthropy in Healthcare Organizations*. Master's thesis, Saint Mary's University of Minnesota.

Williams, K. A. 1998. "Donor-Focused Strategies for Annual Giving." In *Creating an Environment for Philanthropy to Flourish*. Burlington, MA: Jones & Bartlett.

Wuthnow, R., & V. A. Hodgkinson. 1990. *Faith and Philanthropy in America: Exploring the Role of Religion in America's Voluntary Sector*, Jossey Bass Nonprofit & Public Management Series.

www.bc.edu/research/cwp/publications/by-topic/motivation.html.

www.campbellcompany.com/Portals/22807/docs/Generational%20Giving%20Study%20Executive%20Summary.pdf.

www.kciphilanthropy.com/lang/en/.

www.oncourseforsuccess.com/.

www.philanthropy.iupui.edu/Research/docs/2009CCS_FinalReport.pdf.

www.time.com/time/business/article/0,8599,2048696,00.html.

Development Concepts

PROFESSION, PROFESSIONALS, PROGRAM, AND PLAN

This chapter examines how fundraising became the organized discipline and profession that it is today. Concepts of leadership and philanthropy help define the theory of fund development, but the strategies and methods still have to be executed. Fundraising wasn't always the professional, credentialed business proposition and career path . . . it had/has tangents and tribulations; various forms of begging and selling; elements of purism and commercialism; criticism and celebration.

INTRODUCTION

Call *fundraising* by what it is or by a fancy name; the following terms are used interchangeably by nonprofit professionals: *institutional advancement, resource development, philanthropy relations, fund development,* or just plain *fundraising.*

The Association of Fundraising Professionals embraces all the terms, pointing out that some are more expansive and others more restrictive. *Fundraising* is an honorable term, not to be shied away from—but you can use whichever one you like, they all mean: The development of relationships that produce contributed financial resources, including but not limited to individual gifts, memberships, foundations, grants, corporate partnerships, planned gifts, and legacy requests.

Your first step in building a successful fund development program is to understand and utilize the proper terminology of commonly used words: *philanthropy, development, fundraising.* These three little words are used alone and in phrases, often interchangeably.

A *philanthropy exchange* is the giving and receiving relationship that links donors, a cause, and the organization's respective fundraisers.

A *development program* is the strategic management of relationships, systems, processes, and procedures.

A *fundraising activity* encompasses the methodologies, vehicles, and the tactical functions for each relationship approach.

Inversely and structurally, *fundraising* is the way we raise money, *development* is the way we operationalize a department or program to raise money, and *philanthropy* is the causation of people's desire to give.

Fundraising leadership is not something to relegate to others; it is honorable work, and it starts with you, the executive director. If your view of fundraising is positive and you are proud to be a fundraiser, everyone else will be, too.

This chapter is about the fund development profession, the professionals, the department, and the development plan. Because of the relative newness of the fundraising profession, you will benefit from knowing its history, its professional stance, its strategies, its need for "organization" theories, and its results.

Most important to you, the executive director, this chapter offers a section on how to identify characteristics and skill sets of development professionals who will best fit your organization and work in tandem with you to achieve great results.

Chapter 3 covers:

- PROFESSION of Fund Development: From Begging, to Selling, to Marketing
- PROFESSIONALS in Fund Development: Characteristics, Credentials, and Compensation
- PROGRAM for Fund Development: A Comprehensive, Multifaceted Approach
- PLAN for Fund Development: Articulation of Metrics and Methods

PROFESSION OF FUND DEVELOPMENT

From Begging, to Selling, to Marketing

> Fundraising is a noble calling because responsible philanthropy will help to change institutional injustice.
>
> —Archbishop Desmond Tutu

First, it is extremely useful for executive directors to know a little about how fundraising came to be a recognized profession, starting in the United States. Second, it will help you understand why U.S. ideals of organized philanthropy are now being replicated across the globe.

It may be no surprise to you, but after years of fundraising history and universality, experts have acknowledged there is not just one best way to do it.

Oh, sure, there are the fundamental underpinnings of the way we raise money, but donors are so very different, as are cultures of communicating. What works in Great Britain does not work in India. What works in a large university does not work in a small environmental group. What works with a donor who is making a first gift does not work with a donor who is making a last gift.

When we understand the genesis of core fund development principles, we are better equipped to adjust a particular fundraising approach, when needed, to better position our organization in the marketplace.

Knowing the nuances and the variations, along with the time-honored principles, will help you inspire the innovation needed for today's complex fundraising environment. Eventually, fundraising principles and techniques boil down to how to *build relationships* with people who want to make a difference during their lifetimes.

The profession of fundraising (or development) is a true *form of leadership:* a dynamic function and interaction that ebbs and flows with each need, each type of donor, and each situation. It has long been said that fund development is a combination of art and science, and history proves it.

There is a common myth that anyone can learn how to do fundraising. I do not share that opinion. I think it takes someone unique to be a great fundraiser, and history also supports that. The list of the greats is not very long, but the list of aspirants is.

A review of many sources leads to several pivotal points in history where philanthropy shifted from gathering to giving, from begging to asking, and from commercialism directed at the masses, to a sophisticated marketing exchange process. Some of the greats led those changes.

A historical perspective validates that certain principles have remained intact throughout the centuries, including the campaign method, peer solicitation, psychosocial events, and donor recognition. But they need to be adjusted for each and every donor and organization.

The following historical eras are arbitrary, since they are my own interpretation of the various stages of fundraising. History is still being written, and someday there will be a single comprehensive source beyond the incomplete sources cited here:

- PIONEERS (1641 to 1904): Moral imperative to collect contributions
- CAMPAIGNERS (1905 to 1960): Consultants codified campaign theory
- TECHNOCRATS and INNOVATORS (1960 to 1990): Merged a calling into a career
- REFLECTORS and CORRECTORS (1990 to 2005): Shifted to a donor-focused culture
- RESPONDERS (2005 and beyond): Faced Expansion, Retraction, and Globalization

PIONEERS (1641 TO 1904)

Moral Imperative to Collect Contributions

Fundraising began as a moral imperative, which justified a dignified form of begging and collections (beyond almsgiving). When fundraising began, it was largely to save souls, assist the unfortunate, and underwrite efforts for a better society. Giving was the obligation of those with more, to help those with less.

Some historians and writers theorize that fundraising had its start at Harvard University in 1641, when the Massachusetts Bay Colony sent three clergy to England to raise funds to "educate the heathen Indian." It is reputed that one of the three returned with 500 pounds, one became a rector in England, and one wound up on the scaffold!

Not to be outdone, the College of William and Mary and Yale University followed suit. By securing grants from their provincial governments, they spurred contributions from individual wealthy donors upon their return to America.

Think about how lead grants still influence gifts from individuals today. Can you use this technique in other ways than capital campaigns? Is giving influenced by what others do?

By 1739, fundraising was both spontaneous and sporadic, becoming more widespread than anyone realized. For example, a young English evangelist by the name of George Whitefield was credited with traveling the country to take up collections for poor debtors, disaster victims, and orphanages and to underwrite books and financial assistance for hard-pressed colleges. I doubt he was the only one.

Slowly, fundraising moved beyond collecting alms to serious asking. Imagine being there when Benjamin Franklin provided these instructive directions:

> *In the first place, I advise you to apply to all those whom you know will give something; next, to those whom you are uncertain whether they will give anything or not, and show them the list of those who have given; and lastly, do not neglect those whom you are sure will give nothing, for in some of them you may be mistaken. (Van Til and Associates 1990, 14)*

By the early 1800s, fundraising *campaigns* were more frequent and more sophisticated (by early standards); they used personalized face-to-face solicitations and even personalized letters. Prospects of the time were predominantly the wealthy, and recipients were more often those without means.

Some historians arbitrarily date the emergence of fundraising to 1889, when Andrew Carnegie advanced his Gospel of Wealth and when Jane Addams and benefactors established Hull House in Chicago. Those two events affirmed the notion that the wealthy themselves believed they had a duty to give.

Think about how this notion persists, with Bill Gates leading the charge to persuade other American billionaires to donate 50 percent of their wealth to charity.

CAMPAIGNERS (1905 TO 1960)

Consultants Who Codified Campaign Theory

Fundraising became organized, combining both a moral and a logical approach, resulting in the formalization of the campaign method augmented by communications and engagement tactics, directed at the general public. The campaign method gave birth to the annual fund campaign, the endowment campaign, and many other enhancements.

Some fundraising scholars cite the YMCA's 1905 capital campaign in Washington, DC, as a watershed in fundraising history because this event coalesced all the known ingredients of the campaign method into a single intensive, highly organized, widely publicized, volunteer-led effort to raise a lot of money, fast.

YMCA leaders Charles Sumner Ward and Lyman Pierce said behind the decision for this highly organized approach was something more than a mere improvement in fundraising; it was an attempt to establish an ideological perspective that fundraising was a form of ministry, a call to make the world a better place. For Ward and Pierce, it wasn't the asking for a gift they criticized, it was the approach to fundraising, justified by saying they wanted to do more than raise money, they wanted to raise men. Fundraising as an expression of moral stewardship became embedded as an ideological perspective (Cutlip 1965).

In 1911, a well-known consultant, John Price Jones, introduced a second major ideological perspective by declaring that fundraising was also a *business.* For Harvard's $10 million endowment campaign, Jones drew on his background in journalism and advertising to recruit a professional staff of fundraisers who applied businesslike, commercial, and secular principles to campaigning (Cutlip 1965).

The onset of World War I influenced a series of life-altering events that would exceed government's capacity and know-how to deliver human services. The nonprofit sector was pressed into action. Fundraising broadened its scope from wealthy individuals to private foundations and people of other income levels. With this expansion came larger and broader organized campaigns, supported by highly skilled consultants and fundraising staff.

By the mid-1920s, the ideologies of the YMCA (idealists) and Jones (realists) schools of thought seemed to merge: Campaign fundraising was a philanthropic enterprise, a moral endeavor (a calling) that made excellent business sense (a career).

The number of capital campaign consulting firms swelled to more than 20 in New York City alone. Their clients included leading colleges, churches, and community chest organizations; they ran campaigns for college buildings, memorial football stadiums, and the first endowment funds (Bremner 1988; Broce 1986).

Think about how we utilize the expertise of consulting firms today. We still hire consultants to do our campaign feasibility studies and to provide counsel and advice for our major campaigns. Campaign consultants have the expertise in campaigning; most development directors do not.

With the onset of a nationwide recession, President Herbert Hoover conceptualized an effort that would involve the entire country. He created the Organization for Unemployment Relief and recruited 100 business leaders to oversee what is reputed to have been a $175 million campaign, utilizing *communication* strategies to an extent never before imagined. (Bremner 1988).

The campaign method was further augmented during World War II with another element, *paid advertising.* National war fundraising campaign messages on screen and in print were prominent, plentiful, and powerful.

During the 1940s, yet another element was added, *public education.* The American Cancer Society was the first to incorporate public education *and* donor solicitation into their fundraising materials, a strategy that would have long-lasting implications for the fundraising profession.

The late 1950s set the stage for the successful multimillion-dollar capital campaigns: Harvard, Duke, Stanford, and Chicago universities confirmed that bigger, better, faster campaigns were in and here to stay.

The concept of the matching challenge grant originated in this period, through the Ford Foundation's Special Program in Education, a fundraising tactic that remains successful today.

The first annual fund campaigns were designed as extensions and replications of the original capital campaign methodology. Mechanically structured and bottom-line oriented, the annual fund raised money for operating costs rather than capital improvements, and asked for gifts that were smaller and repeatable, rather than a large one-time gift.

The legacy or endowment campaign method was designed to generate planned gifts from donors who wanted something tangible beyond capital projects to fund, such as academic chairs and named scholarship funds.

History tells us that the first successful fundraisers were true campaigners (consultants, paid staff, and volunteers) with a combination of people-centered characteristics and business-minded skill sets. Time has not altered this effective duality; in fact, it has proven to be essential.

Think about whether your next major campaign should raise awareness for your institution, educate prospects and donors about the issues you face, or just raise money. Much can be said about how campaigning can achieve multiple goals.

TECHNOCRATS AND INNOVATORS (1960 TO 1990)

Merged a Calling Into a Career

This period of fundraising was the most eclectic, the most ambitious, and the most sales oriented. The organized world of fundraising was a social enterprise for both nonprofits and for-profits. This emerging profession now had its cynics and critics; it would have to regulate itself or be regulated.

The next 30 years of fundraising moved exponentially faster than the previous 200 years. The ministry-business of fundraising became a financially profitable venture and a popular social enterprise, embedded in every type of nonprofit organization across America.

Staff fundraisers now outnumbered fundraising consultants. They were employed within higher education, hospitals, arts and culture organizations, animal welfare, environmental causes, human and health services, and combined fund appeal organizations like the United Way.

By the 1970s, the once self-taught and experiential field of fundraising had become a business strategy in its own right, looking a lot like its sister professions (public relations, advertising, and marketing). Fundraising reached across every socioeconomic level, pushing philanthropy to 2 percent of the GNP.

Think about the fact that this number has not changed measurably since it was first calculated. What does that mean? Does it mean that philanthropy is an economic decision or a philosophical decision or both, which goes across all socioeconomic levels?

Meanwhile, this *everybody's* philanthropy was fueling a host of ancillary for-profit businesses that also fueled the economy. New companies popped up all around the nonprofit sector to do the business side of charity. Among them were fundraising software businesses, direct mail printing and mailing companies, cross-country telephone calling firms, and PR and communication firms that specialized in nonprofits or added nonprofit product lines.

The need to recognize more donors and more gifts gave birth to premium-award businesses who could manufacture anything you might imagine: brass nameplates, engraved brick pavers, weatherproof building-size lettering, wall plaques with inserts for repeated gifts, and tree-of-life sculptures recognizing legacy gifts. You could have your logo imprinted on virtually anything: paperweights, personalized mugs and key chains, car window stickers, etched-glass awards, refrigerator magnets, and stylized pens.

Think about what you do to recognize donors. Do you do something different for a donor who makes a large gift versus a donor who makes medium-size gifts every year? What kind of recognition do your donors want . . . a plaque, a paperweight, a T-shirt?

Social fundraising events and cause-related marketing became a cultural norm. Everywhere you looked there were mega benefit galas, nationally televised telethons, walkathons, raffles and auction events, pass-the-envelope neighborhood campaigns, celebrity benefits, national cause campaigns (aka Statue of Liberty), and numerous marketing ventures (American Express, Hershey).

The 1980s saw the emergence of the fundraising specialist, whose acumen in a specific area of fundraising was highly desirable—given the size and scope of larger, year-round campaigning. Job advertisements called for expertise in special events, prospect research, direct mail, grant writing, and major gift solicitation. Specialists were beginning to replace the generalists who gained their experience by doing it all. Fundraising was no longer a one-time position; it had become a career.

By the 1980s, this male-dominated profession attracted a significant number of women (albeit still small in number proportionately to men), whose presence brought a new and different perspective to relationship building. Socialized to be community change agents and family protectors, women saw fundraising as a way to raise women and raise money, in much the same way that Pierce and Ward did for men at the turn of the century. Women, to a large extent, influenced what would be called the donor-focused approach to fundraising.

Advanced technology made it possible to increase fundraising effectiveness and efficiency: to reach more prospects and solicit more donors, to connect with them more expediently and frequently, and to manage and process every step with electronic acuity.

Everything appeared to be moving forward in an orderly fashion when the highly visible business fundraising approach began to feel a little too commercial, a little too sales focused, and on the verge of a slippery slope.

Both the public and the fundraising professionals began to ask: What was this business of fundraising: a calling, a career, or profit-motivated impersonal reach into the pocketbook for self-gain?

There were symptoms that the pendulum from the early years of raising men had slid over to the other side; everything seemed to be about raising money. There were life insurance gimmicks, excessive cause-related marketing, Sunday afternoon telemarketing, charitable gambling, and the scramble for corporate endorsements via public sponsorships.

These seemingly commercial tactics were soon the target of public criticism—some warranted, some not. Critics (inside and outside the profession) claimed the nonprofit sector was becoming too profit minded. They alleged that increased knowledge (via technology and other business-minded advances) conflicted with professional development. Worse, they cautioned that profit-minded approaches produced quick-fix fundraising techniques that had no sustainability.

Think about what you may be doing in your fundraising program that ends up on one side or the other of authenticity versus commercialism. And what you are going to do about it?

Threats were coming for more regulation, more certification, and more transparency. The technocrats and innovators had ventured a little beyond that cutting edge to pseudo-commercialism. In spite of their enormous success, the time had come to question whether fundraisers live for or on philanthropy.

REFLECTORS and CORRECTORS (1990 to 2005)

Shifted to a Donor-Focused Culture

The 1990s was a turning point; the next 15 years were spent course-correcting the delicate balance between fundraising as a calling and as a career, challenging a view that the organization's needs were no more important than a donor's interests (and needs) . . . the two were equally important.

During the 1990s, professional fundraisers reflected more on their roles and intended impact. Professionals were entering the field with marketing know-how and formal fundraising education. They were students of a new philanthropy, determined to create a more balanced approach to fundraising. They called it *donor-focused* fundraising.

Nonprofit organizations were eager to challenge the business-as-usual attitude. The fundraising environment was changing all around by major social, economic, political, and competitive pressures.

New approaches were designed to meet the new donors in a more responsible way. It was time to:

- Better understand donors, their motivations, and their interests through research.
- Segment donors into similar, discrete constituency groups.
- Select and communicate specific needs to different donor segments by way of an exchange.
- Ensure a form of case management for each donor, allowing him or her to move more naturally into a relationship of giving and receiving.
- Provide a higher level of donor stewardship, recognition, and self-actualization.

The 1990s fundraisers looked very different from their white male predecessors of the 70s and the 80s. Their faces were more diverse, their titles were more reflective of their expertise, their experiences were augmented by the study of philanthropy, their fundraising techniques were creative iterations of the original campaign method, and their approach was marketing oriented.

Not only were women well represented in this group of fundraisers, but there were people of every ethnicity and religion, of every age and every background.

Think about who's on your development team. Is there enough diversity to challenge assumptions? Is there enough expertise to find the answers? Are your fundraising techniques old and tired or ahead of the game? To what extent does research guide your decisions?

For this generation of fundraising professionals, continuing education classes were not only readily available but essential to one's resume. Continuing education courses were now classified as cradle to grave: for entry-level, mid-level, senior-level, and even advanced executive-level fundraisers.

By the mid-1990s, the profession of fundraising was strengthened with the emergence of academic philanthropic studies, field research projects, and the establishment of best practices with metrics.

Along with the innovation and fast-paced expansion of fundraising activities, there came a concurrent demand for ethical principles, advanced practice standards, cost/benefit analysis, and benchmarks.

On the horizon was also a new donor type that Baby Boomer fundraisers would have to reckon with . . . Baby Boomer donors! Unlike their predecessors, they wanted information, transparency, accountability, and a say in the organization's decision making.

RESPONDERS (2005 AND BEYOND)

Faced Expansion, Retraction, and Globalization

Fundraising became firmly rooted in the belief that donor motivations are complex and personal, which demand a donor-centered approach solidly rooted in marketing theory. More and more, fundraising programs used sophisticated, comprehensive, and strategic approaches to build sustainable philanthropy. Gone were one-time emotive charitable fixes. Today's fundraisers have opportunities to change their corner of the world and live to see it.

Between 2005 and today, fundraising experienced two extremes: rapid expansion and economic retraction. We entered this "what else is new?" phase with innovations fueled by technology moving so fast that it appeared every aspect of fundraising was open to reinvention.

Nothing had challenged the face of fundraising more than the emergence and dominance of new generation groups who were not at all like their grandparents when it came to philanthropy. Fundraisers now had to create fundraising techniques for each of them.

As a reminder, fundraising was created and established by white men, and therefore the original approaches needed to be adjusted for other genders, generations, and cultural and ethnic groups. Today's responders are doing just that.

Generational complexity (a major challenge to fundraising) demands different strategies for each constituency segment. Fortunately, market research has given us a much better perspective of how very different the four generations are in values, attitudes, and lifestyles. Knowing more about the Great Generation, Baby Boomers, Gen Xers, and Gen Yers is essential to good communication, but even more important when talking to them about philanthropy. (More information is provided in Chapter 4 about how to segment with targeted communications.)

Gender differences, too, have become more distinct, and we have discovered that women have a higher potential than originally thought. Until now, women played a relatively minor role in giving and in asking. Men dominated both aspects: They had the money to give and the influence to ask others. Women were participants but seldom initiators.

Oh, my, how times have changed. A recent research study by the Women's Philanthropy Institute (WPI) at the Center on Philanthropy declared that women's likelihood of giving exceeds men's in 8 of 11 charitable causes: religious institutions, organizations that help the needy, health care and medical research, education, youth and family services, community, international, and combined purposes like the United Way.

Think about how you approach women differently than men for donations. Do you have a separate program to solicit and recognize just women, like a giving circle? What about couples?

Technology has globalized fundraising. News about national disasters can now be transmitted in a nanosecond, creating a new level of prime-time crisis-giving donors.

Inherent motivations to give to people in crisis has always existed, but with immediate-response vehicles such as online clicks or social media texting, more people tend to give first-time or extra gifts to human plights.

Response to 9/11, Katrina, the tsunami, and Haiti are dramatic examples of human generosity to those close to home as well as on the other side of planet Earth. People tend to give to crisis causes because of spontaneous empathy and with the thought it is a one-time gift, not a long-term commitment; as such the gifts are great in number but small in size.

Academic and practitioner research has provided twentieth-century fundraisers with greater information about donor motivations. Although still in its infancy, academic research (related to fundraising) is beginning to influence fundraising practice by affirming what works and what doesn't.

At this point, research on donor opinions and behaviors is still narrow and limited; most studies rely on single surveys from relatively small numbers of participants. Only one known longitudinal study is being tracked by the Center on Philanthropy (COPPS). But the time will come when both academic research and practical research are as fundamental to fundraising as they are to fields like psychology, social work, and medicine.

Think about what kind of research you collect and whether that knowledge could be shared with others? Do you invite graduate students to use your organization or your fundraising program to do class projects or work as interns?

The innovative responses to changing times resulted in highly skilled and sophisticated fundraising professionals who were rewarded with higher salary levels and passage onto their respective organization's leadership teams. Fundraising is no longer an office in the basement; it is next to the right hand of the executive director and the board of directors.

Where is fundraising going? Given the current post-recession environment, it is difficult to be sure, but Holly Hall is as good a futurist as one might find. Not only has she been a writer for many years for the *Chronicle of Philanthropy*, but also she was one of my favorite students in the St. Mary's University of Minnesota Philanthropy and Development Master's program. Holly is not a fundraiser per se; she is an observer of fundraising and philanthropy. Who better to predict the likelihood of near-future trends? She predicts:

1. Expansion of money-making ventures: Fundraisers will be required to help find and manage new efforts to seek revenue.

2. A growing pool of older donors: Fundraisers need to better understand the aging process, since the number of Americans 65 and older will nearly double in the next two decades. They need to hone in on the subtle differences between people in their 60s and early 70s and those who are much older.

3. Demand for technology savvy: The growing number of donors who use social media has intensified donors' interest in interacting with charities. Fundraisers will have to understand the techniques of community organizing, not simply sending direct mail appeals.

4. Globalization: As wealth grows outside the United States, more charities will see fundraisers who understand how to raise money across borders. Fundraisers will need to understand the giving styles of a multitude of very different ethnic groups and minorities.

5. Meaningful interactions with donors: Fundraisers need to meet donors' increasing expectation for interactions on their own terms with charities.

A Note to Executive Directors

I would not seriously consider hiring a development professional who did not know something about the history of fundraising. How else will they know what has worked, not worked, and might work? After reading this brief history section, be sure to pass it on to your development staff, so everyone can be on the same page.

PROFESSIONALS IN FUND DEVELOPMENT

Characteristics, Credentials, and Compensation

> The fund development professional needs to have the vision of YOUR organization, as well as understand the communities you operate in . . . they need to believe in the magic of the possible, yet have a firm grasp on what is relevant and important; follow a bold and arduous course and reach beyond their grasp for the golden ring.
>
> —Gail L. Warden

Make no mistake, it is a palpable challenge to hire a fundraising professional who shares your vision and is totally capable of running with it. There are thousands of qualified professionals out there looking for a job, but there are only a few who are right for you.

As executive director, you need someone who relates to you on many levels, someone who pursues your aspirations and at the same time has your back.

You need a fundraising professional who has a high level of expertise to lead and manage your development department, just as you need a financial expert to run your accounting department with industry-approved regulations and a human resource specialist to ensure that your workforce is equitably recruited, trained, and evaluated.

If you hire the right person, the benefits are enormous: Dollars flow in, donors recommend your charity to others, goals are met, and fundraising is easy and pleasurable.

If you hire the wrong person, the risks are enormous: lost time, wasted resources, missed contributions, and even damaged relationships. With the wrong staff, fundraising feels hard.

In my opinion, the best fundraisers are those who embrace the dual concept of fundraising: both a calling (ministry) and a career (business). Great fundraisers who are drawn to the field have a strong desire to make the world better and a keen interest in working with people.

Great fundraisers seem to have inherent abilities to communicate on many levels; they think strategically as well as tactically. A great fundraiser is drawn to certain types of nonprofits (e.g., health care versus the arts, grassroots versus global) because of a value orientation and will not take just any job!

The following questions, answers, and examples will give you most of what you need to know to hire the best person, with the optimal fit for both of you.

You will find information on:

- CHARACTERISTICS: Expertise, Competencies, and Conscience
- CREDENTIALS: Education, Experience, and Certification
- COMPENSATION: Equitable and Competitive Salaries
- JOB DESCRIPTION: Roles, Responsibilities, and Expectations

CHARACTERISTICS

Expertise, Competencies, and Conscience

> Wanted: Fundraiser whose entrepreneurial spirit, cross-cultural knowledge, and analytical abilities match their skills in building strong personal ties to donors. A good understanding of the aging process or experience in grass-roots organizing is a plus.
>
> —Holly Hall

No doubt you have heard the horror stories associated with hiring a fundraiser, only to have them raise nothing or jump ship when they get another offer that pays more! Or you have heard the oft-referenced complaint that development officers move every 18 months (not true for senior fundraisers). But what about the development directors who have stayed too long; because the board has an attachment to them, you can't get rid of them.

Yes, lots of nightmares are out there, but there are also plentiful tales of the best fundraisers who have generated millions of dollars in gifts and helped donors achieve their highest levels of aspiration.

According to Holly Hall, people skills are no longer sufficient for fundraisers; they must possess multiple talents to compete for donations in a changing marketplace.

Today's fundraisers need analytical skills *and* people skills, suited to the particular job they are being hired for. They need to understand what people respond to and be aware of how donors make choices.

Who are the best fundraisers? Are there certain characteristics that sort of guarantee success, a near-perfect list of behavior traits that will help you hire someone who won't let you down?

Several of my colleagues have pursued this knowledge quest, and I would be remiss not to give them credit. Hank Rosso (now deceased), Lilya Wagner, Gene Temple, and Bob Fogle are all authors of books and articles about the characteristics and skills of the best fundraisers. Although each has a particular opinion about what kind of individual is most likely to succeed, they are in consensus on two determinants of success:

1. Fundraising professionals need *leadership* skills.
2. They need to serve on the organization's *leadership management team.*

The best fundraisers are leaders in the truest sense. Their leadership doesn't come from position or power; it is inherent in their honorable character, their reputable knowledge, and their honed skills.

According to Lilya Wagner, author of *Leading Up,* professional fundraisers learn the art of leading up by listening, analyzing, and influencing. They serve by example, motivate others to action, exercise influence, and develop and share the executive director's visions. They help others catch the vision, plan and lead the action, consider the desires and feelings of others, achieve consensus in a group, and obtain practical results.

The leadership skills that fundraisers must have range from the concrete, such as bringing a group together for planning, to the ephemeral, such as developing and sharing a vision of what can be. They are required to engage on two levels; they must think strategically and act practically. They must accomplish extraordinary goals, meet high expectations, be on the cutting edge, and inspire a dynamic culture of connectivity.

At the highest level, fundraising professionals think about what they do, implement principles instead of following technical blueprints, and have an ethical basis for every decision (Wagner 2005).

Many years ago, when pondering what the requirements for best fundraisers were, I examined my own job description and discovered it barely touched on what needed to be done. It said raise money (but it didn't say how), it said to develop relationships with many constituencies (but it didn't say how or who), and it required me to build a stable base of support by being a good communicator (but it didn't say how or what). That day, I wrote down the leadership characteristics and traits that I wanted in a development director. Perhaps the following description will help you find the right person.

The best fundraisers are first and foremost technical experts; after that, they are your organization's facilitators, advocates, catalysts, stewards, and the conscience of your charitable mission.

Expertise   The first requirement of effective fundraisers is knowing their craft and being able to apply the techniques skillfully.

The best fundraisers know everything about how to raise money, including the theory and practice of annual giving, major gift giving, capital campaigns, and legacy giving. They understand and can apply all the solicitation tactics: personal, mail, telephone, and special events.

They have a highly developed knowledge of donor behavior, prospect research, cultivation steps, and acknowledgment processes. They are versed in how and when to use acquisition, renewal, and upgrade techniques that result in a larger, stable donor base.

They also know what doesn't work, and they constantly evaluate fundraising performance using the latest technology and metrics. They are ready to turn on a dime to increase performance or to respond to the newest approaches.

Their competencies are in line with Association of Fundraising published standards, and they continue to be educated about the latest fundraising trends and practices.

Facilitators   As facilitators of the philanthropic process, fundraisers must be able to hear everyone in the process and make sure they all have a chance to express themselves.

The best fundraisers recognize that philanthropy begins with the donors, who may need to be educated about how to give in order to realize their own aspirations, not be forced into contributing to something less meaningful. They are sensitive to donors' motivations, desire recognition, giving priorities, and need for involvement.

They understand that fund development is an indirect profession, ultimately practiced through others. They recognize the importance of teaching about the role that philanthropy plays in the institutions; they teach up (to executive directors and board members), down (to volunteers and staff), and across (to program directors and leadership team members).

Teamwork, they know, is the basic tenet of a strong fundraising program. They coach and lead others to bring out the best in them.

The best fundraisers help organizations adopt philanthropic values and philosophies, build donor-responsive systems, and incorporate strategies necessary to attract and retain philanthropic support, now and in the future.

Advocates   Philanthropic fundraisers are the voice for their cause in the community, all rhetoric aside.

They know the issues intimately so they can speak about them without resorting to annual reports, brochures, or telephone scripts. Whatever the issue (children, disease, shelter, education, culture, the environment), they live and breathe it.

The best fundraisers stand ready to help program staff articulate their dreams in ways that bring the case to life. They help develop the rationale for investing in programs and projects that benefit others. And they continuously demonstrate that philanthropy is more about receiving money than raising it.

They advocate for service excellence because that is what recipients deserve and donors expect. When services are insufficient or lacking, they use their voices to trigger the institution's conscience.

They are deliberate in their decision to affiliate with an organization whose mission mirrors their own values. Sometimes they are fortunate to have an opportunity to make their affinity for a particular cause a lifetime commitment.

The best fundraisers are the voice of the profession, too. They strive to be the very best by understanding the craft and its subtleties. They not only possess a technical knowledge of fundraising but also understand the philosophy and the theory, and they defend them. They research, write, and teach. They give away everything they have learned, and they continue to grow.

They know that their profession is one without competition; it is a vocation of collaboration. They serve as role models and mentors. Through their enthusiasm and commitment, they encourage talented colleagues to enter the profession and provide them support and guidance.

Catalysts   Philanthropic fundraisers articulate the vision of the institution and serve as change agents for social good; they are both courageous and tenacious.

The best fundraisers are the voices of both their donors and their organization's recipients. This means they carry messages of concern and praise. They transmit critical questions and give well-informed answers. They understand the complexity of meeting human needs and accept the resultant successes, as well as the disappointments.

When they speak, they do so with informed opinions, the concerns and desires of their donors, balanced by the cry for help and hope of the recipients. They speak out with patience and understanding, with gentleness and advocacy, with emotion and intelligence.

The best fundraisers seek out the organization's intrepreneurs (the term for entrepreneurs who work within organizational systems), helping them define their dreams and working diligently to fund them.

Their energy is endless in pursuing those dreams, inspiring others to action, and knowing when to lead and when to follow. They build mutuality while pushing for the highest possible attainment, yet understand and resist the obvious risk of becoming self-serving.

Stewards   As frontline recipients of philanthropic gifts, the best fundraisers recognize the responsibility for stewardship.

It is their responsibility not only to accept a gift in a meaningful way, but also to regard these funds as their own (figuratively): managing them prudently, investing them wisely, and expending them judiciously. They must know precisely where funds go and what good they do.

They accept that their stewardship role is one of moral action. Accountability begins when they make a case for support that spells out realistic goals and objectives that make later accountability possible. Their practice must be open, candid, and ethical.

They love raising money. They love to educate and challenge others to raise money. They love to represent the mission of the organization or the institution they work for. They get excited about the very concept of sharing an opportunity with a donor to invest in the quality of their community.

Conscience Fundraisers stand at the critical intersection between their organization and the community they serve.

This linkage requires balancing the competing, sometimes conflicting demands and expectations of staff, colleagues, volunteers, trustees, and donors. They must serve as the organization's charitable conscience.

The best fundraisers assume responsibility for acting as the social conscience and saying things others won't when the charitable mission is at risk of being swallowed up by corporate strategies. They are the ones to ask the tough questions that sometimes make people uncomfortable. They tug at people's elbows and ask, "What's going on here?"

They are passionate and compassionate. They are socially conscious—demanding that the client, the student, or the patient come first, no matter what. They do everything in their power to ensure that their organization is effective in its reach and to its recipients.

In all they do, the best fundraisers are ethical above reproach. They follow the strictest interpretation of the profession's code of ethics and take no action that would undermine the credibility of the organization or of philanthropy itself.

The best fundraisers practice philanthropy in their personal affairs and encourage others to give and to volunteer their time to deserving causes, not just their own.

Please note that one of the best resources for determining what professional fundraisers need to know rests with the Association for Fundraising Professions. They have chronicled and catalogued the skills, knowledge, and competencies required of professional fundraisers to perform their job responsibilities at various levels (entry level, mid-level, and advanced) and areas of practice.

CREDENTIALS

Education, Experience, and Certification

> It may be that, as stewards of the tradition, we ourselves do not have a full understanding of why "voluntary action for the public good" is so important. One of our first tasks, then, is to educate ourselves.
>
> —Robert L. Payton

Most other professions have utilized education and certification as principal measures of professional status. This practice began with physicians, lawyers, educators, and even social workers; during the 19th century, education and certification were extended to professionals working with money, including financial analysts and fund development officers.

What levels of education, certification, and experience should you look for when hiring?

Education Educational degrees offer evidence of the person's discipline to acquire development knowledge where certification shows evidence of the ability to apply it.

It doesn't matter so much what their undergraduate major is, or even their graduate degree. For instance, a background in anthropology will bring a curiosity of evolution that translates to being interested in people and their linkages; a background in marketing will bring a perspective about what makes people respond to one thing but not another.

Fundraising candidates who do not have a formal education augmented by an interest in lifelong learning (aka continuing education) suggest to me that they are not interested in achieving professional stature.

At this juncture, there are a limited but growing number of professional fundraisers with graduate degrees in philanthropy or development. The number correlates with the number of universities offering graduate programs.

We see even more taking advantage of the increased number of university-based CEU certificate programs in fundraising. For example, the University of St. Thomas in Minnesota offers a spring and fall fund development series of classes for aspiring and experienced fundraisers, who, upon completion of nine sessions, receive a fundraising certificate. Every year, this sell-out CEU program graduates approximately 25 participants. Since its inception in 1999, nearly 6,000 participants have taken classes in fundraising.

Another popular continuing education program is located at Indiana University–Purdue University, Indianapolis (IUPUI) in the Center on Philanthropy. The Fundraising School offers a year-round series of classes on campus in Indianapolis as well as in San Francisco, Chicago, and New York. All their classes are CEU based, taught by experienced fundraising professionals, and supported by research.

Formal and continuing education are critical components of the fundraising profession; this is a changing field that requires exposure to new ideas.

Certification Certification in fundraising is a measure of tested bench strength. CFRE and ACFRE certifications are well known and growing as hiring prerequisites. The CFRE (Certified Fundraising Executive) connotes that a professional fundraiser has experience, expertise, and ethical standing in the professional community. CFRE International, the provider of this certification, reports there are currently 5,404 certificants, with the vast majority in the United States.

Does certification mean that holders are the *best* fundraisers? Not necessarily: There are many fundraisers who do not hold the credential by choice. For those who do, however, you can be assured that they take fundraising very seriously and have made a commitment to it as a profession.

The ACFRE (Advanced Certified Fundraising Executive) connotes the highest level of professional certification. It boasts only 98 certificants, who have achieved the rigorous process of a multilevel peer review process that focuses exclusively on advanced management, leadership, and ethics within fundraising.

As an aside, getting a certificate as part of an educational program does not offer any evidence that the attendee has been tested, nor does it imply success. Only CFRE and ACFRE credentials hold certification status in the professional fundraising industry.

Experience Experience is an essential consideration when hiring a development director, because it takes time to learn the work.

Fundraisers tend to go through a growth cycle that is sequential and logical, which is divided into three main stages. You want to hire one that fits the particular stage of your organization and your development program.

1. **The Beginners.** When fundraisers first enter the profession, they are called beginners because of where they are in the experiential learning process, even if they bring senior-level skills from another field such as marketing, law, or estate planning. This stage is the time for learning the *how-tos*, the everyday functions and tasks ranging from putting solicitation letters *out* to receipting gifts *in*. It does not take long for beginning fundraisers to learn the mechanical techniques of direct mail, telephone solicitations, volunteer recruitment, and special event or campaign management.

2. **The Advancers.** When fundraisers move beyond the how-tos to the *what-tos*, they learn and apply the theoretical aspects of fundraising. At mid-level, they begin to place more emphasis on the relationships created because of the interest people have in working together to achieve a common mission. At the advancing stage, fundraisers do background research on prospects and donors, recruit and manage volunteers, and develop relationships with key donors and program staff. They have naturally moved from task-oriented functions to a higher level of interactive functions.

3. **The Integrators.** At the last stage, fundraising professionals move to the *whys* and the *ways* of the philanthropic process. Their focus is now macro *and* micro, on the whole organization as well as on developing

and maintaining interpersonal relationships with executive leadership, boards, volunteers, and donors. At this juncture, they can integrate the strategic and tactical facets of fundraising by *facilitating partnerships* between donors and the organization. At this stage, fundraisers are actively involved in the organization's strategic planning and they spend the majority time managing people, not things.

Until just a few years ago, it was unthinkable to hire someone without at least five years of professional fundraising experience. Times have changed. As a result of the most recent recession, the nonprofit sector has been challenged by the influx of very talented for-profit professionals who, in mid-career, have decided to abandon their ideas for ideals.

If the type of fundraiser you are looking for is not looking for you, you may want to consider hiring someone outside the profession with transferable skills.

The hiring debate between the old-timer fundraisers and the newcomer entrepreneurs will go on for years, since it takes at least 3 to 5 years to establish a pattern that can be judged successful or not. But I say, "Why not?" Transferable experience shortens the learning curve.

SPECIAL SITUATION Checklist

- If you are starting a *new development program,* you will want someone with experience in building infrastructure and relationships (the management-leader type).

- If you are initiating a *major gift program,* you will want someone who loves to ask people for money and is good at training volunteers to open doors (the directive leadership type).

- If you are heading toward a *capital campaign,* you need someone who has campaign experience because everything for the next few years will be driven by solicitation deadlines (the analytical leadership type).

- If you want to *augment and reinvent your development program* and take it to the next level, you should look for someone who is a true change agent, someone who gravitates to big turnarounds and, by nature, thinks outside the box (the transformative leadership type).

- If you are a *national or international organization* with donors all over the map or an advocacy group, you want someone with flexibility and a desire to travel, as well as with expertise in volunteer management and special events (the servant leadership type).

COMPENSATION

Equitable and Competitive Salaries

> *U.S. News & World Report* listed fundraising as one of its "Best Careers" for 2009 and beyond . . . and not only does the hiring of fundraising professionals continue to grow in the slow economy, but so do the salaries offered.
>
> —*The Chronicle of Philanthropy*

In a recent interview, Tim Seiler, director of the Fundraising School at the Center on Philanthropy, IUPUI, said: "When you are trying to find a person with a high level of experience, the ethical approach to fundraising, and all that, it's a very short list that comes to mind."

The demand for great fundraisers has exceeded the market availability, especially for senior fundraisers.

Today's truth is that really great fundraising professionals are scarce and hard to come by . . . and tend to stay much longer than believed. Times have changed and the number one reason to move on is for greater responsibility and increased pay. How is this different from any other career track? It isn't.

Clearly, the longer a fundraiser stays, the larger the payoff for everyone: the donors, the organization, and the fundraiser personally—as long as the position has growth potential (responsibility and pay). The cost of losing a great fundraiser is high: It costs charities 65 to 83 percent of a fundraiser's annual salary to replace that person, according to research by Penelope Burk/Cygnus Applied Research.

But it's a two-way street, isn't it? Fundraisers also perform when they have a great boss. Burk's research reveals that fundraisers want to work for leaders who allow them to work independently (55 percent), who ask for and value their input (53 percent), who encourage them to ask questions (49 percent), and who give them credit for their ideas (48 percent).

Still, 37 percent of the fundraisers Burk researched said they left their last job for a higher salary, and 48 percent said they would leave their current job for higher pay. This points out the importance of being competitive with your salaries and other job enhancements, like expanded management responsibilities, job flexibility, and other low-cost benefits, as well as having succession plans.

In 2009, *U.S. News and World Report* said that fundraisers with eight or more years of experience could expect a salary range of $54,900 to $92,700. The report also gave fundraising careers a grade of A in all categories, including job market outlook, prestige, and job satisfaction. As the market demand exceeds the market availability of highly successful, experienced fundraisers, salaries will continue to go up.

Salaries tend to be in the highest range in health care and higher education and in the lowest range in social services and the arts. It goes without saying that the top of the range is reserved for the development directors, the major gifts officers, and the planned giving officers. The larger the goal and the larger the department, the higher the salaries for all levels, based on the fundraiser's scope of responsibility and experience level.

Don't skimp on salary if you want to get someone who is the perfect fit for your organization. A $10,000 differential in what you offer is small change and an insignificant investment that will be returned 100-fold in a few years.

You might be thinking that fundraisers should simply be paid on a percentage of what they raise, and while that sounds reasonable on the surface, it presents a very high risk for undue influence and self gain. To base salaries on a percentage of gifts generated is deemed unethical by the Association of Fundraising Professionals' Code of Ethical Standards. Why? Very simply, fundraising is not a sales function that influences people to buy something they need. I guess you could say that people (donors) *need* to give, but realistically, this must be the donor's choice, not influenced by the fundraisers for their personal gain.

Note: The Association of Fundraising Professionals releases a report regularly on the salary ranges and the compensation of fundraisers, which you can view on their website.

JOB DESCRIPTION

Roles, Responsibilities, and Expectations

A CEO said to me recently when I asked what qualities he was looking for in a VP for Development/Advancement, "Give me candidates who can command a room." It's all about leadership!

—Colette Murray

As executive director, your job is to organizationally lead fundraising; your development director's job is to departmentally lead fundraising. But you are a team, moving back and forth together between strategy and tactics, organization and department, external and intermal. How your development director views your role is as important as how you view theirs.

Their role is to lead and manage the day-to-day activities and through times of change, to aid in determining direction, and to move an organization from where it is to where it needs to be. Their role is to shape the philanthropic culture, use the best management tools, ensure resources are used wisely, mobilize support from others, and build a solid base that is sustainable in years to come.

Here's a list of responsibilities that can be used in a position description in hiring your director of development.

DEVELOPMENT DIRECTOR POSITION DESCRIPTION

Position Purpose

- The director of development serves as a valued member of the administrative team, with accountability to the chief executive officer.

- The director of development is responsible for providing dynamic and creative leadership of development and communications.

- This position is responsible for planning, designing, and managing all efforts to broaden public awareness of the agency's mission and to generate financial and volunteer support to help underwrite its programs and services.

- This position requires leadership attributes, strong interpersonal skills, management competencies, communication abilities, and ethical principles.

- This director of development's performance is based on the achievement of financial/philanthropic goals that are established in concert with the organization's development team.

Roles and Responsibilities

- Participate as a member of the administrative leadership team to help set overall agency priorities and objectives that will be achieved through philanthropy.

- Provide ongoing analysis and assessment of the philanthropic environment, within and outside the organization, to ensure that development strategies and functions are relevant and thriving.

- Work with the board development committee to establish short- and long-range development plans and programs that will maximize philanthropic potential. Strategies include annual giving, major gifts, foundation and corporate grant seeking, endowment funding, planned gifts, capital campaigns, and special projects as needed.

- In concert with agency administration and committee members, identify, validate, and prioritize programs that depend on philanthropic support. Prepare case statements, case messages, and care materials to convey effectively a sense of relevance, urgency, and realistic attainment.

- Provide the research necessary to identify and qualify constituent markets. Determine how each market will be solicited and by whom.

- Work with the board committee to establish opportunistic and realistic giving goals for each constituent group and for each program and project, as well as for each fundraising methodology.

- Develop and implement fundraising approaches and methodologies that will successfully communicate the organization's needs while matching donors' interests. Oversee prospect identification, donor acquisition, donor renewal, and donor upgrade programs that generate increased financial support.

- Ensure an environment of collaboration between volunteers and staff. Provide information, education, and training so volunteers can be involved actively and successfully in fundraising efforts.

- Initiate and maintain positive exchange relationships with donors, funders, board members, volunteers, program staff, and clientele. Provide opportunities for involvement and engagement.

- Oversee efforts to acknowledge, recognize, and cultivate donors. Ensure that all philanthropic funds receive the highest level of stewardship.

- Work with the board Communications Committee and agency administration to develop a communications plan that will achieve an increasingly high level of community awareness for the agency's mission.

- Oversee donor education and awareness activities, including promotion, brochures, newsletters, media, audiovisuals, tours, presentations, and cause-related marketing.

- Design a department infrastructure that ensures all resources are used wisely and all strategies are implemented successfully.

- Develop policies and procedures to govern development and communication activities according to rules, regulations, and approved practices.

- Hire, train, manage, and evaluate development staff who are responsible for daily operations, general communications, public education projects, donor events and activities, database management, donor research and relations, report generation, and acknowledgments.

- Maintain a work environment that supports teamwork, diversity, and respect for individuals.

The bottom line is that the role of your development director is to reach the financial goals established for the organization. They should not be expected to reach goals that they haven't had a part in creating. Remember, they are the experts in philanthropy. The fundraiser needs to determine how many donors will give, how much, and when. They are the only ones who can accurately predict what can be raised. This is not your CFO's expertise; it is, however, actually making the budget balance.

If your fundraising goals are realistic and based on solid evidence of constituency potential as well as tested case relevance, the development director and development team (including board members, leadership and program staff, fundraising staff, and volunteers) should not have trouble reaching them. They do need to be held accountable for these goals. If the goals are not reached, then you, the executive director, must ask if this is the right development director for you and your organization.

For me, reaching a financial goal is the ultimate measure of a development director's performance. There are secondary goals and many important benchmarks (which will be discussed later in this chapter under performance measurement), but the big one is the dollars raised against established budget.

In addition to meeting goals my best hires have the following experiences, expertise, and ability. You might ask yourself the following questions:

Best Hire Checklist

- Are they committed to and have an affinity for a particular aspect of the nonprofit sector (not just any charitable organization)?

- Have they been influenced by events in their life that cause them to want to solve a social problem or advance a cause (are passionate and compassionate)?

- Do they have a natural desire to build relationships (really like people)?

- Can they influence donors to want to join their cause (are great communicators)?

- Are they generous and humble (write their own check first) and do not need to take credit for what they do?

- Do they seem to be natural-born leaders (are posed to lead from the bottom, the middle, or the top)?

- Do they approach fundraising as a marketplace business proposition (are smart and savvy)?

- Are they able to measure their own success based on donor satisfaction, not just how much money they raise (they measure outcomes, not outputs)?

- Do they use metrics and benchmarks to achieve the highest possible goals (do their homework and strive for excellence)?

- Have they exhibited stewardship with human and financial resources (are zealous about ethical practices)?

PROGRAM FOR FUND DEVELOPMENT

An Integrated Seemless System

> Raising funds is both a joy and a curse for Executive Directors. The joy comes when you are successful in sharing your passion and vision . . . the curse comes when you feel that your entire job is about fundraising, and things aren't going well.
>
> —Mim Carlson and Margaret Donahoe

Joy or curse, it's all what you make of it.

Fundraising is not only a noble profession, but also an organizational program of strategic importance to the client group it serves, your *donors*.

Helping donors make wise decisions that fulfill their needs and interests is something that deserves program status within your organization. A development department should not be in a subservient role to just raise money for your other programs; it needs to be a free-standing program on its own merits. Donors are the development department's constituents, and they desire expert services to meet their needs.

This section elaborates three aspects that can make or break a successful fundraising program:

- STRATEGIES: An Integrated Development Program
- RESOURCES: Adequate Infrastructure and Systems
- TEAMWORK: Key to Unleashing Energy and Talent

STRATEGIES

An Integrated Development Program

> The overall fundraising program when it is fully integrated and carefully managed, positions the organization to conduct and manage fundraising at the most effective level.
>
> Timothy L. Seiler

Today, fundraising is substantiated by a considerable body of knowledge of proven fundraising theory, codified principles and research-substantiated practices. More importantly, there is an enormous opportunity to influence and advance the professional practice as new types of donors emerge.

Going forward, you will see a stronger integration of fundraising practices, into a more cohesive but segmented fund development program. You will see:

- More *seamless* fundraising (a blending of annual, major, capital, and legacy giving)

- More *personalized* fundraising (utilizing CRM, constituency relationship management)
- More *transformational* fundraising (addressing the new donor's need to make a higher impact)

The *integrated development program* is the ideal best-practice approach to fundraising in the modern world. It incorporates every aspect of fundraising by linking and integrating the following: theory to practice, strategies to tactics, procedures to performance metrics, policies to stewardship, approach to methods, and outputs to outcomes.

An integrated development program does not exist as a freestanding strategy; it is an extension of *your* organization's long-range plan. As such, it articulates how fundraising strategies and objectives will be executed to produce a revenue stream that underwrites your organizational priorities established by the larger strategic plan (not someone else's).

For instance, if your strategic plan is to build a new campus, the fundraising strategies would include implementation of a multiyear capital campaign, possibly with an endowment component. If your strategic plan is to expand current operating programs into other geographic regions, the fundraising strategies will include targeted methods to acquire new donors from those cities, counties, or states.

From an *internal* or organizational perspective, an integrated development program is the plan of action for how the toolbox of fundraising elements, techniques, and tactics come together to generate the largest number of gifts from the greatest number of high-potential donors.

From an *external* or donor perspective, an integrated development program is a point of entry by which donors make a gift that is timed for them: It could be a one-time gift to honor a friend; it could be an initial test gift to see if a charity is good for them; it might be a gift to show appreciation for services received; it might be a repeat gift stimulated by a front page newspaper article.

Because there are so many variables, you want and need a sophisticated integrated development program that:

- Seeks four types of gifts:
  Annual gifts, major gifts, capital campaign gifts, and planned/legacy gifts.
- Achieves four stages of giving:
  Acquisition, renewal and upgrade, and over-and-above gifts.
- Uses four different fundraising approaches:
  Personal solicitation, telephone calls, electronic/direct mail, and special events.

It sounds mathematically formulaic, but an integrated development program is anything but. It depends on an artful mastery of psychological and social skills that tie organizational readiness and donor responsiveness together.

The integrated development program is a collection of best-practice components assembled to produce a dynamic human and organizational process that connects people to values, values to mission, mission to outcomes, and so on. The absence of any component could cause fundraising to fail.

The process of building an integrated development program is presented here as a series of components, in a logical order, but a modification of the order (or sequence) can accomplish similar results. However, the absence of any best-practice component will diminish the intended impact; all components are needed for fundraising readiness.

Organizational culture has an enormous influence on the readiness of each component; some are naturally stronger and intact, and other components are weaker and require more attention. The talented fundraising professional will know how to synchronize all of them.

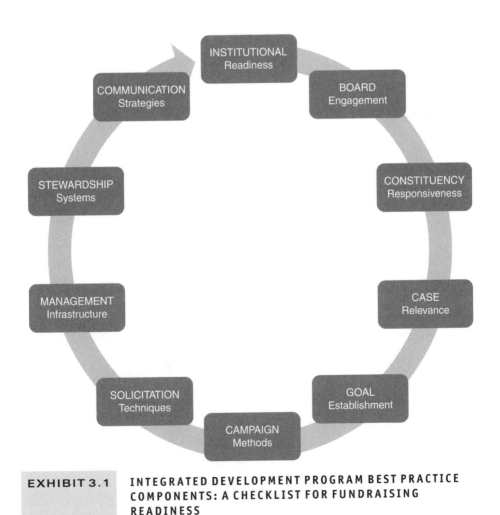

EXHIBIT 3.1   **INTEGRATED DEVELOPMENT PROGRAM BEST PRACTICE COMPONENTS: A CHECKLIST FOR FUNDRAISING READINESS**

Your goal as executive director is to insist that all of the 10 components are operating at their peak. To stay at peak, you want to regularly assess and fine-tune individual components (akin to adjusting a high-quality timepiece with intricate gear parts that need an occasional cleaning or oiling).

If your organization is putting together its first fundraising program, it could take as long as three to five years to assemble all these components and have them in good working order. If your fundraising program only needs an update, the fine-tuning might take only one year. This time projection and allocation points out how important ongoing evaluations are.

Regular assessments (audits) inspire proactive change; they help you stay tuned to the outside environment; they minimize ineffective and inefficient practices. For instance, a special event has a life of its own (as little as 3 years, as long as 10 years), necessitating reinvention along the way or elimination altogether. If you are starting a new planned giving program, you might not see results for five to seven years, so you must give annual and major giving your full attention to ensure steady cash flow. If your annual renewals are slipping, you might consider dropping acquisition efforts until you stabilize retention.

Regardless of your situation, to effectively raise money, you need all components in good working order, and to do that you need an audit every few years.

When all 10 components are intact and in sync, an organization will have the greatest likelihood of generating philanthropic support. The executive director's job is to insist that each component be assessed on a regular basis to ensure that every opportunity for fundraising is capitalized. See Exhibit 3.1.

RESOURCES

Adequate Infrastructure and Systems

> The very best fundraising managers are both problem solvers and solution enablers . . . successful fundraising management is the convergence of good people relationships and good business practices.
>
> —Elizabeth A. Elkas

Having a comprehensive development office is as important to fundraising as having a development professional to run it. The first key word here is *office,* meaning that a comprehensive development program cannot be run out of a briefcase, any more than any of your other programs that deliver services to key constituents.

Realistically, the development office, department, or program is a micro version of your larger organization, and as you build it, the development program will need to go through the same series of growth stages: *infancy, adolescence, early maturity,* and *seniority.* Its ability to raise money will correlate with its stage, meaning at infancy it will cost more to raise a dollar than at adolescence, where efficiencies will come with repeat gifts. This cost/benefit ratio goes back to the axiom "it costs money to raise money."

The second key word is *comprehensive,* meaning that a large multifocused development program will raise more than a small single-focused one (i.e., one with only special-event fundraising). With a comprehensive integrated development program raising several million dollars, you will need at least five development staff members. If you want to raise only $500,000, you probably can do that with two staff members. I typically use a ratio of about $250,000 per staff person; the more you want to raise, the greater the number of staff (just multiply that number).

Let's explore what a development department looks like, how it relates to other departments, how it is different yet similar to other services, and how much time and resources are needed to build a fully equipped fundraising program—essentially, the roles that others (the CFO, the board, program directors, and volunteers) play as adjunct members of your development team:

1. Select a name for your department that reflects the status and honor it deserves: call it the Donor Development Department or better yet, the Office of Philanthropy. Bottom line: It is the development of donors we are talking about here.

2. In today's sophisticated, highly organized world, a development department requires the same kind of infrastructure that other client-service departments need: marketing, communications, finance, record-keeping, technology, professional staffing, and human resources. Just as another department provides direct services, so does the development department: They service the needs and the interests of donors with information, education, counseling, and follow-up through a case management system, which requires policies, procedures, and processes.

3. To be sure, the development department can generate the highest profit ratio of all the other departments (excluding some high-margin nonprofit services like radiology or concert ticket sales.). For every 25 cents invested in a comprehensive integrated development program, you should expect an overall return of 75 cents.

4. The development department needs to be at the top of the organization, working directly with the executive director, the board of directors, and the other department directors—equal in status, purpose, and allocation of resources. If the development department functions only as a subordinate service to other departments (to raise money for them), fundraising

will never have the clout and the connections it needs to be really successful.

5. Finally, the professional development officer you hire must know how to plan, design, implement, manage, and evaluate the development office. As executive director, you should not have to worry about the details; if you do, you have the wrong development professional.

As executive director, here's what you do need to know and *do*.

Define Relationships   Since development is a strategically driven internal and external function, it must be at the right hand of the executive director. In other words, it operates as an extension of your leadership to expand the number and size of philanthropic gifts via high-priority relationships. The development head reports directly to you and no one else.

But remember no matter how many professional fundraisers you have on staff, the largest and most influential donors will still want a relationship with you. I learned this lesson well as executive director of the St. Paul Children's Hospital Foundation. My staff's job was to make it possible for me to spend at least 80 percent of my time closing gifts while they spend 80 percent of their time opening gifts. The other 20 percent of my time was spent managing the foundation and linking donors with board members and the hospital administrator.

It's not that donors need to spend all their time with you; they just want to feel they know you because, in part, it is your leadership they are investing in. This means, of course, that ultimately you are responsible for the department's success or failure, but it is not your job to run the department.

Establish Expectations   As executive director, it is your role to establish expectations. The development staff needs from you a clear delineation of the role of the development department in achieving the organization's vision, mission, strategies, goals, and objectives. You should expect your development staff to put together the following:

Expectations Checklist

• Job descriptions that are updated regularly to remain relevant to the growth of your development department.

• A development strategic plan that is tied specifically to each organizational strategic goal (short-term, mid-term, and long-term), measured by dollars, numbers, and percentages.

- Written work plans for each fundraising activity with detailed outcomes, deadlines, and methods linked to achieve each goal.
- Detailed staff member assignments, with accountability for objectives and outcomes.
- An organization chart that clearly shows relationship connections with the board, with donors, and with other departments.
- A department budget that includes an estimate of revenue and expense, by line item (annual gifts, major gifts, special purpose gifts, capital gifts, grants, sponsorships, other) *and* by fundraising project (personal solicitation, events, telephone, and mail).

Link with Marketing   Development depends on market research and public communications. In fact, fundraising cannot be successful without these input and output systems.

Marketing provides the research necessary to identify and segment constituency groups with the right messages; public relations provides the communication vehicles to send out those targeted messages. It is easy to see that marketing and public relations could stand alone, without development. But fundraising without both in place will cause your fundraiser to focus on tasks rather than relationships.

Since this alignment between departments is so crucial, as executive director you will want to be forthright and strategic in dealing with it. Don't leave the individual departments to figure it out (or, should I say, tough it out).

If you have a larger organization, with separate PR and marketing departments, they should expend at least 40 percent of their time working collaboratively with the development department. If you have a smaller organization, you may want to combine marketing, public relations, and development into one department. In doing so, remember the downside: Marketing (focus groups) and public relations (newsletters) tend to be tactical and easier to check off the list than development, which is a continuous process of building relationships (they never end). When the three functions are combined, you will have to guard against making development a step-child. (Often the reason for not reaching goals is that time is usurped elsewhere.)

Provide Office Space   Development staff need the usual resources to do their jobs, and an important resource is physical space to work and space to meet. Development staff should spend the majority of their time *with* people, not at their desks doing prospect research (unless, of course, they are prospect researchers).

The office space does not have to be the place where they meet donors, but it should be a space where they are close to other department heads and to the frontline delivery of philanthropically supported services. As an example, it would be better for a development office for a hospital to be in the hospital basement (albeit not a visual sign of importance or prestige) than located off-site across town.

Development officers need to be in the midst of the work that is supported by philanthropy. Fundraisers' primary toolkit is the case for support, and if they are not immersed in day-to-day observations of their case, they will not be as knowledgeable or passionate. Remember, the case is the fundraiser's elevator speech, their script, their portfolio, and their cadre of investment opportunities. Without exposure on a regular basis, fundraisers tend to slip into the static repetition of need, and this results in a dumbed-down message that just floats out there, without settling on a donor's doorstep.

Purchase Technology   Technology is as critical as it is for a surgeon who is doing the latest knee replacement surgery. The more sophisticated the equipment, the faster and more precise the procedure, and ultimately, the greater the satisfaction of the patient. If development officers are working off 3-by-5 cards, their time efficiency will be seriously reduced because of the redundancy of sorting, rating, ranking, and tracking donor relationships. If we can expedite data collection, processing, sorting, and outputting, fundraisers will be more focused and more effective.

Whatever you need to spend on a new, comprehensive donor data processing system, I can assure you it will be worth it. If it takes two weeks for a check from a donor to clear the mail room, processing, and finance and eventually show up on a report for development, 14 days has gone by without a first response. Industry standards call for a thank you (first response) in 24 hours after the receipt of the transaction (be it cash, check, or charge).

Link Financial Systems   Your organization's accountants will say that there must be a separation of church and state when it comes to gift receipting, but if the development staff does not see the gift, much information is lost in the pipeline. For instance, when someone writes a check, that check contains several levels of information, far beyond the amount and the account holder. Handwriting can be very telling, as it seems to get wobbly with age; a note on the left side may be a signal that someone is interested in designating or in just "helping where the need is greatest"; the account name indicates whose funds these are beyond the signer (is this gift from a couple or a single?) and maybe this check is coming from a trust or a custodial account (indicating the type of wealth).

I am not suggesting that the finance staff won't see these subtle and important elements, but fundraisers are trained to look for signals that they can inquire about when making the thank you phone call (today, when it is received, not a week later when processed).

There needs to be a balance between donor responsiveness and financial rules. This is best achieved when the development and finance department work together to design and implement the processes, the procedures, and the policies for gift receipting.

Financial systems have to be very sophisticated today, given the increase in donor designators. Our financial accounting systems must be able to track designated gifts coming in and going out. If a donor writes "Cancer Fund" on the check or the transmittal card, there needs to be a bookkeeping process to make sure this gift is transferred as income to the Cancer Fund, not to some larger operating fund. In the same way the revenue went to the Cancer Fund, so does the expense of fundraising for that gift (which may simply be an average cost of 20 percent transferred as income to the development department account). If an organization does not have such a fund accounting system, nor wish to establish one, it will find itself facing an ethical and legal dilemma under Charitable Trust Law.

It is the professional development officer's legal and ethical duty to ensure that every gift received is expended exactly as the donor intended: not generally, but specifically.

Encourage Internal Relationships   Only the executive director can encourage the forging of a colloquial and interdependent relationship between the development department and the other departments (where philanthropy is needed). Left alone to navigate internal relationships laterally will only limit the development staff's ability to do their job.

When fundraisers have a close working relationship with agency directors, the two end up teaming, creating a much stronger rationale for why donors should make a gift to individual agency programs.

As insiders, staff recognize that it takes funding to deliver services (from an accounting view and a management view), but the donor's view needs to be more about why contributed dollars are needed (as differentiated from other revenue). This is the essence of a strong case. Are donor dollars needed to leverage other grants? Are donor dollars needed to cover something that is not budgeted but needed? Are donor dollars needed to cover a shortfall in the budget? Are donor dollars needed for a piece of operating equipment or a particular item? The largest and more important question to be ready to answer comes from the donor: if the donor doesn't fund a particular agency program, what will happen?

Working side by side with all the program directors gives the development staff the opportunity to offer a portfolio of needs to the various donor types, ensuring that donors select a program they are most interested in.

There are times when one or more programs will be more popular to donors than others. Hard to believe, I know, but raising money for child abuse services is not as popular a cause as you might think. Raising money to protect children from being abused is easier. These kinds of human reactions to problems versus solutions are quite normal in the world of fundraising.

The development director's job is to balance the tensions and the demands between agency staff, board members, volunteers, and donors for *their* favorite programs.

Value Volunteerism Volunteerism is a principal tenet of fundraising; it is probably the most important human dynamic associated with the art and science of fundraising. This point was first articulated by Hank Rosso when he insisted that volunteerism tends to come first and financial support second, and research supports this.

There is an element of volunteering for an organization that brings a donor into the family in a way that giving a financial gift does not, producing a little magic. Being a volunteer gives one a realistic view of the good, the bad, and the ugly, leaving the volunteer with the insight of reality that simply writing a check does not.

The fundraising department should promote opportunities for volunteerism throughout the organization, but generally, the volunteer program is separate from the fundraising department.

I have often said to executive directors: If you don't have a formal volunteer program, with a variety of volunteer opportunities, get one. The benefit of having citizens involved in your organization, other than giving or being on your board, is critical to a philanthropic culture.

Often, we think that volunteerism is for fundraising, the idea of recruiting people to raise money. We are not as interested in volunteers who work on the other side of our business model (delivering services). The fact is that when volunteers have been on the service delivery side, they make better volunteers on the fundraising side! If volunteers are not your advocates in the community, you might as well turn in your 501(c)(3) status.

Conversely, I am not in favor of recruiting volunteers who are interested in service but not gifting. The best volunteer jobs (on the front line) belong to those (first) who have demonstrated that they are already interested (having given money). When we give money, we do so from the point of view that we care deeply about something. What better way to screen the really interested volunteer? Why recruit someone who has never made a gift? Why recruit someone to your board who has *not* been a longtime donor? You might be thinking, which comes first?

Frankly, I am not sure, but I do know this: not to consider the implication of giving away your best jobs to someone may convince them to go elsewhere to give of their time and talent. Research tells us that volunteers give proportionately higher amounts than those donors who do not volunteer.

Here are the questions you should pose:

Volunteer Program Checklist

- Do we have a volunteer program that leads to stronger gift giving?
- Do we have a donor giving program that might benefit from a unique volunteer ingredient?
- Is our volunteer program about incentives and rewards or just a volunteer program because we can't hire staff to do what volunteers can do?
- Do we want volunteers because we need them or they need us?
- Do we recruit what we are looking for or take anyone because we are going through the motions?
- Do we view volunteerism equal to or less important than money?

Minimize Tensions   The development department uses the same basic management principles practiced in other fields: analysis, planning, execution, control, and evaluation. But fundraising, as both a management function and a leadership dynamic, presents some challenges not found in other professions.

Fundraising is about multilevel relationships with board members, administration, volunteers, staff, vendors, prospects, and donors. Fundraising is functionally demanding, and those functions, communications, marketing, project development, fiscal administration, and information systems must be integrated. Fundraising operates in an environment of complexity, change, and potential conflict.

Fundraising has an unusual position within your organization; it has wide responsibility but limited authority. Just look at the functional relationships. The development director reports to the executive director, but they relate to and are dependent on people at every level (the board member above you, as well as program staff and volunteers below you). The fundraiser must mentor up and mentor down, follow and lead at the same time.

Fundraisers are expected to inform, involve, and include staff and volunteers, both vertically and horizontally. Add the relationship span to the oversight responsibility of functional management tasks, and fundraisers have significant challenges, with limited power and decision-making authority. This situation calls for engagement and empowerment competency, a communications proficiency, a change agent capability, and a professional stance.

To make things even more challenging, fundraising is replete with potential conflicts of interest: between donor and organization, the donor and the fundraiser, and the fundraiser and the organization, as well as among the fundraiser, the donor, and the organization. Mediating between parties is alleged to be the most difficult challenge the fundraiser must navigate.

Honesty, integrity, and keeping promises are key to resolving conflicts, as is understanding that an organization's and donors' invisible boundaries turn into barbed-wire fences when people begin to cross them.

Fundraisers need to have far more expertise than most managers and leaders, implementing and adapting to fit the circumstances of an ever-changing environment. It is not enough to be versed in and attentive to the organizational environment (people, plans, systems, tasks, goals).

It is crucial that your fundraiser be sensitive to new forces and to circumstances affecting *your* organization and to have the ability to create and direct change to address new conditions. To act as a change agent requires a keen understanding of organizational behavior and group dynamics. Intervention techniques include interpersonal communications, consensus building, teamwork, conflict resolution, and productivity improvement.

TEAMWORK

Key to Unleashing Energy and Talent

> Of all the factors that contribute to sustained success in fundraising, none may be more important than creating a cohesive and effective development team.
>
> —Hank Rosso

Getting the right people on the fundraising bus is especially challenging today, given our competitive marketplace for high-caliber talent, exhibiting a passion for your cause and a fit for your culture. Yesterday's teams were small by comparison to today's fundraising teams. Everybody wants to be on a high-powered team so they can expand their horizons and leverage their expertise. The old axiom that more is better is certainly true in today's fundraising business model.

The concept of teamwork is derived from the notion that everyone has something valuable to offer and that a collective effort is more empowering, enabling, effective, and satisfying than individual work that is hierarchically arranged (gone is the word *subordinate*).

Teamwork is the key to unlocking the energies and talents within an organization, stimulated by those from outside the organization (as in volunteers, board members, donors, and community leaders). The success of sustainable teams comes from a commitment to the value of the team connection, leadership within the team, open communications, and a shared vision.

The most important benefit of team building may be the practice of empowerment, making each team member stronger, and the whole being greater than the sum of its parts.

A *development team* is an organized group of people with defined roles and responsibilities and established goals and objectives. This development team *shares* the decision making, the implementation, the assessment, the evaluation, and the changes along the way. The development team fosters collaboration, develops cooperative goals, seeks integrative solutions, and builds trusting relationships.

The size of the development team ranges from more than one to a small group. As a start, you want two teams.

1. **Development Leadership Team.** This team serves as the think tank for the organization's philanthropy initiative. It oversees the development of fundraising strategies, plans, evaluations, and goal setting (and may meet quarterly). Typically the members include the executive director, board chair, board development committee chair, development director, chief financial officer, and chief program officer.

2. **Development Staff Team.** This team is comprised entirely of development staff members. It serves as the implementation team for all aspects of fundraising, managing the day-to-day operations. Typically, a staff is comprised of a development director, associate director, annual giving director, major gifts officer, donor relations manager, and database manager.

In the nonprofit sector, there is one comment that consistently elicits mixed reactions and strong opinions: "Let's hire a fundraiser, so we won't have to do it!" I'm no exception. This comment provokes me to speak out in defense of the philanthropic process as a partnership between people, not just a money machine. I might go so far as to recommend to my colleagues that they not take a fundraising position in an organization where others have mindfully washed their hands of it.

Let's look at the key players, their reactions, and their opinions:

1. **Executive Directors.** When they want to be rid of the responsibility for fundraising, it's because they see it as begging rather than investing and they think, why be involved if it's not fun or it's lowly? This negative

image devalues the meaning of fundraising and its potential. However, executives who involve citizens and community leaders in other aspects of their organization will likely see philanthropic fundraising as a worthy endeavor and the means to the end (namely, achieving your mission).

When executive directors are part of the development team, they give fundraising the leadership the community expects from a charity of choice.

2. **Board Members.** When they want someone else to do the fundraising, it's because they don't fully understand their role in the fundraising process. In their defense, most weren't told they would have to ask others for money when they were recruited. If board members happen to be experienced in fundraising, they will want to hire a development professional to help them be even more successful.

   When board members are part of the development team, they give fundraising the voluntary credibility it needs.

3. **Program Directors.** When they are quick to jump at the suggestion of hiring someone else to do the fundraising, it's because they are uncomfortable raising their own salaries. Besides, fundraising might take time away from the more important direct service work—a more worthy endeavor, they think. However, when program directors have worked as part of the development team, they are pleasantly surprised by the influence they have in how much is raised for their own programs. Who better to give personal testimony about the impact of contributed dollars than the program staff who are closest to the recipients?

   When program staff are part of the development team, they give fundraising the charitable focus the mission deserves.

4. **Volunteers.** When they suggest hiring a development professional to do the entire fundraising, it's because they are not currently receiving the right amount of appreciation and right kind of recognition from the staff they deal with. But more often than not, volunteers are the greatest advocates for hiring a professional fundraiser, without giving up what they do. They know that such a person will help them to do an even better job by providing the infrastructure as well as the sophisticated expertise they lack.

   When volunteers are part of the development process, they give fundraising the grassroots value that keeps commercialization from taking over.

As you might imagine, it is the development professional who is most likely to cringe at the comment that fundraising is his or her job, alone. Field experience over the past century has demonstrated quite the opposite: Teamwork, we know, is a tenet of successful fund development.

How, then, did so many otherwise sensible people arrive at the notion that if they hired a fundraiser, they would not have to be involved? This kind of attitude is, in part, the direct result of fundraising's professionalization. As the development profession became more advanced in theory and practice, fundraisers become more knowledgeable and capable; as the techniques became more complex and specialized, the development professional appeared to be the one person best equipped to do the job.

Besides, he or she was getting paid to do just that! A contradiction evolved. As fundraisers demonstrated their expertise, they inadvertently sent the wrong message that others were not needed. There are some critical misunderstandings here about:

- The value of interdisciplinary teamwork.
- The impact of personal involvement.
- The exact role of the development professional and who *is* the best one to ask for a gift.

There are also a good many myths associated with talking about and asking for money. Set aside these misunderstandings and the myths. Bottom line: Fundraising is everybody's job. A team of folks can do more, and do it better, than any one person alone.

When development directors promote fundraising as a team effort in which everyone shares the struggles and the triumphs, philanthropic responses will exceed everyone's expectations.

Before offering suggestions about how to involve others in fundraising, let's clarify this—the number one reason people shy away from getting involved in fundraising: fear of disappointment.

In the comment, "Let's hire a fundraiser, so we won't have to do it," the key word is *it*. I believe *it* refers to the uncomfortable act of asking for money. *It* does not refer to the more comfortable aspects of cultivating or recognizing donors.

Consequently, the best way to make fundraising everybody's job is to involve, engage, educate, inspire, and recognize others for being a part of the entire process. Only then can we move them to the hardest and most rewarding part of fundraising: asking someone else to make a gift.

Fundraising is everybody's job. But it's not a new idea. The teamwork concept was the ideology behind organized philanthropy in the United States when it began in the mid–1800s. Sounds a little Tocquevillean, doesn't it?

PLAN FOR FUND DEVELOPMENT PROGRAM

Articulation of Metrics and Methods

> A development plan leads to focused action. It harnesses your charity's vision and creates momentum, but it also forces you to draw out the steps to make it happen—real tasks, with real deadlines, carried out by specific people on your team.
>
> —Carol Rylander

Do you need a separate strategic development plan? Absolutely. Can your new development director deliver one in less than three months after being hired? No.

The development plan will need an allotment of six to nine months for the assessment, the planning, and the writing. A written development plan is an extension of the organization's three- to five-year strategic plan, which must come first.

Let's start with *why* you need a written development plan and *how* your organization will benefit from one. Your strategic development plan is an extension of your organization's larger strategic plan. It supports all the organizational goals and objectives.

A written strategic development plan (an integrated development plan) is your fundraising road map, with ideas shaped by research and intuition. It serves as a base for approval, periodic review, and assessment of progress by the executive director, staff, and volunteers.

As a point of clarification, a strategic development plan is different than an annual development work plan; the first is the smaller high-level directional plan that will be approved by the board of directors and serve as the guide for everyone involved in fundraising. The second, the work plan, is a written internal document that provides the details associated with each aspect of the development department and staffing.

Without a plan, there is no reference point to determine the best route when tough choices have to be made. There are at least seven reasons to have a written plan in place:

1. Forces us to examine the past and the present and to anticipate the future.
2. Disciplines us to think strategically, to achieve potential, and to maximize resources.
3. Involves others whom we depend on for fundraising success.
4. Anchors our strategies in ways that others can understand and appreciate.
5. Provides benchmarks that allow us to measure, analyze, and evaluate.
6. Gives credence to fundraising as a management function.
7. Predicts our outcomes, while anticipating our infrastructure needs.

The development director should draft development plans with input from the executive director, the board of directors, the leadership team, and other development staff and volunteers. The strategic development plan will range from 5 to 15 pages, and the individual work plans (combined) are likely to be 30 to 50 pages.

Written plans encourage well-informed decision making, which results in realistic goals. The development plan prerequisites include the following. It must:

- Be designed to support the organization's strategic goals and objectives (shows how philanthropy supports the strategic plan, over the same period of time).
- Includes the same elements of analysis and planning as the organization's strategic plan (shows historic patterns of giving and projects future trends).
- Be rooted in unique research of donor needs, interests, and capacity (just like a market assessment for the programs).
- Include all stakeholders in the putting together, most importantly donors and agency department heads (using retreats, planning sessions, etc.).

Who else needs to be involved in putting together the fundraising plan? If fundraising is everyone's job then everyone ought to be involved at least in the planning and evaluation.

One constituent group is key to planning: the Board of Directors. Your fundraising program will be only as good as your board's investment and involvement in it. Your job is to see that the board leads fundraising planning rather than just participating in it.

Another constituent group is your program directors, whose projects require revenue from philanthropy. Their participation in the planning process adds many dimensions: firsthand knowledge of the case for support, secondary knowledge of the other programs, needs for philanthropic support, and awareness that *they* need to be involved in fundraising or they won't get as much money as they could.

What is the best way to do planning, and how often? Ironically, most have experienced all-day or weekend retreats, only to walk away with more questions than when they started. This proves a point: The very nature of planning is more organic than rigid because the planning process opens up more discussions about different avenues to explore than originally anticipated. The benefit of group dynamics is its unpredictable nature and the likelihood that more heads focused on a topic produce more and better options.

Thus, a retreat is generally the beginning of a planning process, not the end. Be prepared to spend another 8 to 12 months after the retreat to pull together the numerous projects within the plan, held together by goals, objectives, methods, tactics, and outcomes.

How often do you need a formal planning session like a retreat? My opinion is every single year, but planning should be a process that is incorporated into every meeting throughout the year, at the staff and board level. Fifteen minutes spent on planning, at every meeting, makes the inevitable retreat more effective.

As executive director, your focus should be on only two levels: 1) that a plan is written, approved, and implemented; and 2) that key aspects of the plan are evaluated, by you. The following information includes:

- COMPONENTS of the Plan: Individual Parts, Assembled, and Linked
- EVALUATION of the Plan: Measures to Reduce Risk and Increase Effectiveness

COMPONENTS OF THE PLAN

The Individual Parts, Assembled, and Linked

> The power and the efficacy of the total development plan are in bringing to bear the essential elements for long-term fundraising success.
>
> —Timothy L. Seiler

A written development plan includes a variety of components or sections to show the integration and interdependence of strategies and tactics, combining the art and science of fundraising. The following components are needed:

1. **Philanthropy Mission.** What is the role that philanthropy plays? Is it the primary source of revenue for your organization, or is it a funding source for projects that would not otherwise exist? Your philanthropy mission or purpose needs to be written and published as a way to demonstrate that philanthropy has a unique role to play and that contributions will be stewarded in an appropriate way.

2. **Situation Analysis.** Every good plan includes a succinct analysis of the situation, summarizing the state of philanthropy for your particular organization, including a historical perspective from which to gauge fundraising potential going forward.

   This section includes statements about the strengths, weaknesses, threats, and opportunities—what was, is now, and could be. The situation analysis reminds everyone how philanthropy came to be an essential part of your organization and how the mission was and is financed by donors. When staff and volunteers can clearly see the vision for philanthropy, they better understand how to get there. The situation analysis formulates the strategic initiatives, provides a backdrop for goal setting, and clarifies assumptions.

3. **Strategic Initiatives.** A development plan's strategies are directly correlated to the organization's strategic plan; therefore, they need to be written accordingly (similar language, style, and projected outcomes). This section is based on the 30,000-foot view of the development program; strategic goals are written to embrace all other goals, so they tend to be high level and long-term. For instance, strategic goals are quite broad, such as "reduce dependency on government grants," "increase awareness of the organization's charitable mission," and "build the case for a future capital-endowment campaign."

   Each strategic initiative has specific high-level goals and objectives that or linked to individual fundraising plans within the document.

4. **Case for Support.** A *case for support* is a statement that defends the organization's purpose for raising funds. It is the written rationale for philanthropic support and an expression of the cause that inspires and empowers staff and volunteers to ask others for money. It is the reason donors will be inclined to give.

   For instance, a case for a social service agency might read like this:

   > Currently, there are over 100,000 people in our community who have lost their jobs during the recession; more than 20 million have also lost their homes due to foreclosures. This unfortunate situation has pushed shelters, food shelves, and emergency assistance beyond our capacity. For the next three years, as our economy recovers and employment improves, the XYZ organization will strive to raise more funds to ensure that those affected have help in finding new jobs, getting assistance to find stable housing, and receive counseling to ensure they are able to cope with the demands placed on them. Our community's stability is dependent on their health and welfare. Our goal is to raise an additional $1 million this year, on top of the $3 million raised in previous years from generous and compassionate donors.

5. **Constituency Potential.** This section of the written plan contains the estimated size, number, and frequency of anticipated philanthropic gifts. The goal of this section is to describe who gives now and who could give in the future, in quantifiable and qualifiable terms.

   Each constituency category or segment must be analyzed separately and then collectively. Reasonable and achievable goals do not manifest themselves in isolation. We can't establish a financial goal based on our need to raise money: We must assess *who* will give *what*.

When assessing potential, we only have three methods of fundraising: new acquisition, renewal, and gift increases, and those delineators have industry-wide benchmarks, reducing the guesswork of projecting contribution probabilities. In this section, we rely on several time-honored principles:

- Use the traditional gift range chart, which shows that 80 percent of the donors represent 20 percent of the contributed income, while 20 percent of the donors represent 80 percent of gift income.
- Use the constituency circle which maps donors, documenting who has the best relationship with the organization, concurrent with who can give the most. This tool ensures that time is spent on those with the greatest return.
- Use the giving history of current donors, so you can segment them into high-potential groups based on their linkage, their interests, their length of giving, their frequency of giving, and their ability to give.

In this section constituents are prioritized based on their current giving and projections for their future giving.

6. **Campaigns.** This section of the development plan contains the various components of an integrated fundraising approach and separate plans for each of them.

   At the highest level, it contains methods and vehicles for annual giving, major gift giving, a capital campaign, and planned giving. Each of the methods has strategies, goals, objectives, methods, outcomes, and performance measures. You may also want to spell out the staff or volunteer roles, budgets, and timelines for each campaign.

7. **Budget.** This section includes a comprehensive revenue and expense budget, with backup detail reserved for a file drawer. Three line items are needed for a basic campaign budget:

- Revenue from all sources and campaigns
- Expenses tied to those campaigns
- Percentage of revenue to cost (ROI) for each campaign

   After assembling all these figures, you can add last year's figures, and/or variances in line items. As the executive director, you are primarily concerned with how much you need to raise, how much you need to spend, and what your profit is. Leave the rest of the details to the development director and staff. It is their job to analyze every campaign, against other campaigns, and to add or eliminate methods and tactics based on their effectiveness and efficiency.

If, as the executive director, you have to get into the detail of the fundraising budget beyond the ROI, you have the wrong development director.

8. **Addendum.** There are many other components of a full-blown development plan, designed to spell out the various roles and responsibilities of development staff and fundraising volunteers. As executive director, this level of planning and implementation is far beyond your scope of responsibility, but if you don't see evidence that planning has been done on the following, ask for it.

EVALUATION OF PLAN

Measures to Reduce Risk and Increase Effectiveness

Three principles of budgeting are advocated. First, nonprofits must recognize that the fundraising program is a profit center, not just another cost center. Second, budgeting for fundraising should be based on recognition that each solicitation program, method, and technique used is a separate financial enterprise. Third, budgeting is both a planning and management function.

—James M. Greenfield

Fundraising is a dynamic, strategic, problem-solving process that requires the use of management practices, including analysis, planning, execution, and evaluation.

By way of background, all *management* functions include tasks, relationships, and an ethical stance:

- *Task* functions include doing the research and writing the plan, initiating and coordinating all the activities, diagnosing problems and finding solutions, and monitoring and evaluating accomplishments. Fundraising is functionally demanding because of the need to integrate other functions: communications, marketing, program development, fiscal administration, and information systems.

- *Relationship* functions include maintenance of the staff and volunteer groups, encouraging and rewarding individual team members, setting standards of behavior and reasonable expectations, achieving goals, and minimizing risks. There are challenges in fundraising not found in other professions, since fundraising is involved extensively in multilevel relationships with board members, administration, volunteers, staff, vendors, prospects, and donors.

- *Ethical* management is also critical to the fundraising process. Philanthropic fundraising depends on a value-based orientation, without which it will succumb to a mere commercial activity.

To evaluate fundraising performance, you want to review all functions so that you, your staff, and your board are supported by a solid infrastructure and professionalism.

Management principles require systems, policies, and procedures that will guide the implementation of your written development plan to a successful conclusion. Call it infrastructure, or call it resources.

As executive director, you want to review each management aspect to ensure that it is being attended to as a regular and ongoing part of the fund development program. Running an *integrated development program* requires a constant evaluation and adjustment of processes, including everything from how we ask for a gift to how we receive a gift.

Systems   Time must be allocated to doing research on our effectiveness and our efficiencies. You need to know the real cost and the real return of your direct mail program, your special events, your telethon, your holiday appeal, your major gift program, and so on. For instance, you will spend proportionately more on direct mail than on personal solicitation, but you might be spending too much or too little to get the intended or potential results. On average, I like to track ROI on a quarterly basis, so that changes can be made quickly if necessary.

Counting money isn't the only evaluative measure of effectiveness or efficiency. Are your donor numbers going up? Is your average gift size increasing? Do you have an 80-20 distribution of numbers and dollars? Are you overly dependent on foundation grants? Do you need to grow your individual gifting effort?

You also need to examine the systems side of fundraising. Are donors' gifts processed in 24 hours? Are your thank-you letters out the door in 24 to 36 hours? Are you communicating with donors at least four to six times a year?

If inclined, you can measure your effectiveness with like organizations by participating in an online survey, the Fundraising Effectiveness Survey. It is a web-based questionnaire that collects fundraising data from participating nonprofit organizations beginning with data from 2004–2005. The survey enables participating groups to measure and compare their fundraising gain and loss ratios from year to year and to compare their performance to similar organizations. Participants can use this industry data, which the Association of Fundraising Professionals offers free, to make better-informed, growth-oriented budget decisions to boost donor revenue.

The Fundraising Effectiveness Project (FEP) was launched by AFP and the Center for Nonprofits and Philanthropy at the Urban Institute in 2006 to help nonprofit organizations measure, compare, and maximize their annual giving methods of fundraising.

Technology   The day of index cards has gone with the mimeograph machines, replaced by sophisticated technology designed just for fundraising. Today, we have many choices of vendors and software for small fundraising programs, including project management, but when you have a large donor base (10,000 donors or more), there are only a few vendors who can handle the intricacies of a large database linked to gift processing. You can research the vendors by subscribing to the *Chronicle of Philanthropy*, which produces an annual report on who's who in the world of fundraising technology services.

Regardless of the size of your donor base, you will need the essential computerized infrastructure elements for:

1. Donor and prospect research
2. Database management
3. Gift processing
4. Fiscal reporting
5. Donor gift tracking

To determine if you have the right amount of resources, you can do a simple calculation: Divide your total expenses by your total income to get your fundraising cost. On average, your cost of fundraising should not exceed 25 percent. If it is much lower, you may not be spending enough.

It costs money to raise money, and if you are not providing the necessary resources, you are probably leaving money on the table.

Staffing   Do we have enough and the right staff? There are a couple of industry-accepted benchmarks used to determine how many staff you need, and one of them is based on how much money you are raising. It is said that you need one full-time employee (FTE) for every $250,000 to $500,000 in revenue.

Of course, there are qualifiers for every estimate like this: How skilled are your staff, how old is your fundraising program, and what type of fundraising campaigns are you using?

Annual giving programs need more staff and generate proportionately less revenue than a major gift program would. For instance, an annual giving manager can handle 4,000 donors, but a major gift officer can handle only 250, based on the relationship requirements.

The best way to know if you have the right number of staff is to compare your staff/income/expenses to other similar nonprofits. The next best way to evaluate is to do a time-management study to assess the effectiveness and efficiency of individual staff members, as a comparison with other staff members.

How do we hold staff accountable? It goes without saying that every staff member needs a job description, but it is even more important that it be updated every year. Fundraising, as a job, tends to be more dynamic than static, and each position is a moving target, growing wider and deeper over time. When you first hire fundraisers, you can't expect them to handle a wide scope of responsibilities until they establish relationships with other staff, volunteers, and donors. This takes time.

Job descriptions not only need to be regularly updated but also must include very specific and measurable goals, upon which each employee is measured.

- Number of dollars raised
- Number or type of donors generated
- Number of donor calls
- Amount of time spent cultivating donors
- Effectiveness of communications
- Relationships with others

Fiscal As important as it is for the development staff to see the gifts when they come in, it is more important that gifts are processed in a way that meets accounting standards and reporting policies.

You need at least one staff member (in the fundraising department) to process gift information, log donor information, acknowledge the gifts, and run reports. This person should have control over the information, which is to say that others (unless trained and capable) should not make changes to this information. Data must be 100 percent accurate, not only for fiscal reporting but also for donor relations. A mistake in a gift receipt entry could be as detrimental as a mistake in the spelling of a donor's name.

While the receiving and receipting of the gifts is done by the development department, the finance department must ensure that accounting and allocation processes meet industry standards. A good working relationship between development and finance is needed because of the overlap of processing and the ultimate distribution of the funds based on donor intent.

Budgets are fundraising's best management tools to monitor performance, measure results, and manage the process. The fund development program is a profit center, not a cost center. Yet, the costs, if not monitored, will diminish your profits and, worse, your credibility in using donor dollars. You will want to account for and report the use of both the spent portion on fundraising overhead and the invested portion on delivery of charitable programs and services. The following list provides some reporting tools:

- Cost per dollar raised
- ROI of each fundraising method
- Program performance against goals

- Allocations of funds raised
- Results of funds used

SUMMARY

This chapter has discussed how fund development is a much larger business strategy than is generally understood. It is a function that must be organized as a department to serve a specific clientele (donors), replete with all the infrastructure requirements to steward both mission and money. Fund development must be integrated into the entire organization and have equal status with all other programs and departments, as well as sufficient resources to be able to produce the anticipated "profits."

The next chapter guides you through the process of developing relationships that will be sustainable for the long term. Best practices fall into many categories: Relationship social exchange, alignment, cultivation, and management.

REFERENCES

ACFRE website at www.afpnet.org/Professional/?navItemNumber=504.

Bremner, R. H. 1988. *American Philanthropy*, 2nd ed. Chicago: University of Chicago Press.

Broce, T. E. 1986. *Fundraising: The Guide to Raising Money from Private Sources*, 2d ed. Norman: University of Oklahoma Press.

Burk, Penelope. Cygnus Applied Research. www.cygresearch.com.

Burlingame, D. F., ed. 1997. *Critical Issues in Fund Raising*. New York: John Wiley & Sons.

Burlingame, D. F., & L. J. Hulse, eds. 1991. *Taking Fundraising Seriously: Advancing the Profession and Practice of Raising Money*. San Francisco, CA: Jossey-Bass.

Carlson, M., & M. Donahoe. 2003. *The Executive Directors' Survival Guide: Thriving as a Nonprofit Leader*. San Francisco, CA: Jossey-Bass.

CFRE website at www.cfre.org.

Cutlip, S. M. 1965. *Fundraising in the United States: Its Role in the American Philanthropy*. New Brunswick, NJ: Rutgers University Press.

Duronio, A., & E. R. Temple. 1997. *Fund Raisers: Their Careers, Stories, Concerns, and Accomplishments*. San Francisco, CA: Jossey-Bass.

Hall, H., People Skills No Longer Sufficient for Fundraisers to Thrive, The Chronicle fo Philanthropy, April 4, 2010.

Lindahl, W. E. 2010. *Principles of Fundraising: Theory and Practice*. Sudbury, MA: Jones and Barlett.

Lysakowski, L. 2007. *The Development Plan (Nonprofit Essentials)*. Hoboken, NJ: John Wiley & Sons.

Mixer, J. R. 1993. *Principles of Professional Fundraising: Useful Foundations for Successful Practice*. San Francisco, CA: Jossey-Bass.

Payton, R. L. 1988. *Philanthropy: Voluntary Action for the Public Good*. New York: Macmillan.

Rosso, H. A., & Associates. 2003. *Achieving Excellence in Fundraising*. San Francisco, CA: John Wiley & Sons.

See http://www.afpnet.org/Audiences/ReportsResearchDetail.cfm?ItemNumber=3113.

Seltzer, M. S. 1987. *Securing Your Organization's Future: A Complete Guide to Fundraising Strategies*. New York: The Foundation Center.

Van Til, J., and Associates. 1990. *Critical Issues in American Philanthropy: Strengthening Theory and Practice*. San Francisco, CA: Jossey-Bass.

Wagner, L. 2005. *Leading Up: Transformational Leadership for Fund Raisers*. Hoboken, NJ: John Wiley & Sons.

Williams, K. A. 1998, 2004. *Donor Focused Strategies for Annual Giving*. Sudbury, MA: Jones & Bartlett.

Relationship Concepts

SOCIAL EXCHANGE, ALIGNMENT, CULTIVATION, AND MANAGEMENT

This chapter focuses on the development of relationship concepts because they are so critical to the execution of fundraising. A donor's view of a relationship is, however, quite different than an organization's or a fundraiser's view. For a donor, a relationship is not created, it is earned. It results from the synchronicity of mutual values, not artificially contrived, but authentically evolved. It cannot be predicted, but is predicated on opportunities found. This perspective is called donor-focused; a two-way exchange, not a one-way transaction.

INTRODUCTION

Fundraising is based on the premise that people are willing to invest in your mission; it is not based on your need for additional revenue. If you don't need or want their investment, you can say "no, thank you." But a "yes, thank you," necessitates a reciprocal relationship between you and the donor.

Establishing a relationship with a donor does not happen by itself.

As in all relationships, there must be an environment of mutual goodwill, based on an appreciation of each other's similarities and differences, needs and interests. Strong relationships develop when there is openness, respect, honesty, patience, commitment, and give-and-take from both parties.

Relationships are mutual exchanges of shared values, developed through effective, balanced interpersonal communications, which over time increase in frequency, complexity, and intensity.

As in all partnerships, the desire to be in, or to work on, a relationship is not necessarily equal or 50-50. One person may naturally give more than another; one may have fewer needs. Relationships ebb and flow in a multitude of ways but remain strong when both parties' needs and interests are met. Relationships require a mutual understanding that needs are constantly changing but mutuality is a continuous pursuit.

Dominance by one party, however, diminishes the essence of a partnership; without that relationship exchange will not take place.

The unique challenge for donors and nonprofit organizations alike is simply to maintain *balance* in the relationships, even under the pressure of self-interest (from either party).

Relationships are undermined when organizations try to convince their donors to support something outside their interest under the pressure that the organization's needs are paramount. Conversely, relationships are undermined when donors insist on giving to a program that does not need philanthropic support or leads to mission creep.

Your role as executive director is to ensure that all relationships are balanced and beneficial, managed in a way that establishes an ethical, moral, and synergistic partnership with each and every donor, for the long term.

Your responsibility is to say "no" if the intended purpose for a gift is not on your strategic agenda and to be gracious when a prospective donor says "no" because he or she doesn't like the project you are proposing. When you and your organization are able to establish a relationship with someone inclined to support your mission's value, your interaction with them must be strategic and mutually beneficial.

This chapter addresses how the elements of the social exchange and marketing relationship theory play out in fundraising and describes how donor *moves* occur by design, and over time.

The following sections describe how a marketing perspective improves constituency analysis, links that knowledge to create matches, utilizes cultivation techniques to deepen the relationship, and applies techniques to bring a donor into and up the giving pyramid. This chapter also contains field and academic research on donor segments who have the highest potential, including those with high net worth, women with capacity, and Baby Boomers whose time is now.

Chapter 4 covers:

- SOCIAL EXCHANGE in Relationships: Move From Transactions to Transformations

- ALIGNMENT in Relationships: Constituency Analysis Uncovers Patterns

- CULTIVATION of Relationships: Strategies to Build Long-Term Relationships

- MANAGEMENT of Relationships: Techniques to Expand the Donor Base

SOCIAL EXCHANGE IN RELATIONSHIPS

Move From Transactions to Transformations

> Relationship fundraising is an approach that centers on the unique and special relationship between a nonprofit and each supporter. Its overriding consideration is to care for and develop that bond and to do nothing that might damage or jeopardize it. Every activity is therefore geared toward making sure donors know they are important, valued, and considered, which has the effect of maximizing funds per donor in the long term.
>
> —Ken Burnett

Philanthropic behavior is stimulated by values. We know that people do not support organizations whose values they do not connect with. The level of connectivity, or the match between a donor's values and your organization's values, influences the intensity of their actions to give, to volunteer, to associate, to be reciprocal.

In Chapter 1, the importance of stated values, both personal and professional, was discussed. To reiterate, to attract high-level and long-term donor investments, your organization must clearly define and articulate your value to the community.

As Kay Sprinkel Grace has so eloquently articulated, there is an interrelationship of philanthropy, development, and fundraising; all based on values. Philanthropy is inspired by values; donor development uncovers shared values; fundraising provides people with opportunities to act on their values.

Theories and practices that integrate this values exchange concept are substantiated by an understanding of marketing theory, the application of reciprocity, and the intentional information gathering that shapes your segmentation and targeting efforts. Three aspects are explored here:

- MARKETING: Social Exchange Based on Shared Values
- MOTIVATIONS: Evaluation of Constituency Potential
- CONSTITUENTS: Focus on Highest Potential Prospects

MARKETING

Social Exchange Based on Shared Values

> Marketing is an organizational function and a set of processes for creating communicating and delivering value to customers, and for managing customer relationships in ways that benefit the organization and its stakeholders.
>
> —American Marketing Association

The notion behind a balanced relationship is explained in *social exchange theory* or in *relationship marketing*.

Social exchange theory evolved from psychology, sociology, and economics to explain human behavior based on self-interest and achievement of personal goals. This premise theorizes that people make choices that maximize rewards and minimize costs. They then base the likeliness of developing a relationship with someone on the perceived outcomes.

Relationship marketing is predicated on the benefits of donor retention and a donor's ultimate value to an organization.

In the past, fundraising relied on transfer- and transaction-based marketing. Each and every year, donors were asked to give, and a series of one-time transactions took place. Relationship marketing changes the fundraising approach from a series of one-time transactions to a focus on cumulative donor value and the exchange of shared values.

Because marketing is a business methodology, it is an orderly process that can be applied to fundraising by utilizing the following strategies:

1. **Donor Focus.** Marketing has changed the way our world thinks and behaves. As we moved from a product-oriented society to a consumer-driven society, savvy business minds turned to the principles of marketing to guide the way.

   Since the mid-1980s, the for-profit sector has literally reengineered its business strategies from selling the customer what was produced to producing what the customer wants. The business sector views marketing as the way to gain a competitive edge, to proactively direct the growth of business.

   The nonprofit sector has been less enthusiastic and not as quick to adopt a marketing philosophy, resisting the idea because marketing didn't fit their type of business. The terminology used in marketing—products, price, promotion, and place—seems foreign to those in the nonprofit sector who use words like *clients, services, subsidies,* and *sliding fees.*

   Since marketing often gets confused with selling, it has been rejected by some in the nonprofit sector as manipulative. Others, who mistakenly see marketing as promotion, do not realize that it is really a constituency relationship-building approach (as in CRM, or constituency relationships management).

   Resistance to marketing also comes when professional staff see themselves as the experts, particularly when it comes to designing and delivering programs that serve recipients. When cultural views dictate that the organization knows best what the customer, client, patient, or student needs or wants, it is difficult for them to shift to a marketing exchange perspective where they ask their customers what they want or need.

2. **Managed Process.** Fundraising requires a constituency point of view, hence all the references to donor-focus. Relationships require an exchange between needs and interests, making relationship marketing and the social exchange concept a logical fit with fundraising.

Until recently, nonprofit practitioners who were interested in applying marketing techniques to their nonprofit organizations found very few resources to help them. Today, workshops, books, and journal articles enthusiastically promote the use of marketing in response to the ever-increasing competitive environment.

Today, the use of marketing exchange principles has become a widely accepted way of determining which nonprofit programs or services to initiate, to promote, and to eliminate.

To survive and succeed, organizations must know their markets; attract sufficient resources; convert these resources into appropriate products, services and ideas; and effectively distribute them to various constituencies.

No where is marketing theory more appropriate and natural than in fundraising because it places the donor in a prominent partner position with your organization, rather than a supplier of money (like an ATM). It provides a dignified approach, making fundraising more about receiving than getting, more of an exchange than a transaction, and more of a relationship with the giver than with the giver's money.

When we apply marketing principles to fundraising, it becomes a systematic managed process of matching donors' interests with organizational needs. It strategically targets high-potential markets, rather than the masses.

As executive director, you will need to endorse marketing as a philosophy, not a promotional tactic. It is your role to champion marketing as a strategic and cultural perspective that identifies people's needs and, in turn, designs programs and products to fit those needs.

When applied to your core services and fundraising, a marketing approach can make the difference in driving customers to you or to someone else. A marketing perspective can change your fundraising orientation from a begging or a selling mode to one that is truly donor focused. And marketing is, more important, a sound business approach that is based on information rather than intuition.

3. **Social Exchange.** The exchange concept can best be illustrated by a balance scale with donors on one side and beneficiaries on the other side. See Exhibit 4.1. The center pole represents the organizational structure,

Donor
Affiliation
Affinity
Affirmation

Beneficiary
Acknowledgment
Appreciation
Acceptance

EXHIBIT 4.1 **DONOR-BENEFICIARY VALUES-EXCHANGE CONCEPTS**

positioning itself to balance both sides of the exchange equation. The cross bar represents the two-way communications and linkages that are formed as a result of relationship development, shared values, and voluntary reciprocity.

A marketing perspective in fundraising acknowledges that donors want to get something in return for their charitable and philanthropic contributions, albeit intangibles like appropriate recognition, timely reports, invitations to insider events, and being asked for their feedback and advice.

To donors, those intangibles are the products they are receiving for their purchase. Without them, donor satisfaction is reduced—akin to purchasing a new shirt and then getting home to discover it was made out of newspaper and could be worn only once (you didn't get your money's worth).

In the consumer world, they call this post-purchase dissonance. Without some form of affirmation or some benefit, donors will have the same degree of dissonance about their gifting decisions. Affirmation comes in the form of immediate thank-you calls or notes, personalized reports of where the gift was applied, and follow-ups to confirm that the gift was appreciated and made a difference.

Not only does a marketing perspective encourage the design of more effective strategies, but it forces us to reexamine fundraising methods: assessing the benefits of mass market appeals, impersonal so-called personalized computer-generated letters, repetitive telemarketing calls, and labor-intensive special events.

Marketing encourages greater emphasis on personal relationships built through informal telephone conversations, personal visits, handwritten notes, and social occasions that bond donors as members of the organization's family. Marketing enables us to put the emphasis where it belongs: on the donors who give, not on the goods received.

MARKETING Strategies

- Marketplace analysis and psychographic research
- Market and audience segmentation
- Targeting those with the highest potential
- Organizational positioning with distinct characteristics
- Integrated marketing, communications, and development plan
- Targeted and matched case messages and methods
- Demonstrated benefits to the donor

MOTIVATIONS

Evaluation of Constituency Profile

> To survive and succeed, organizations must know their markets; attract sufficient resources; convert these resources into appropriate products, services and ideas; and effectively distribute them to various constituencies.
>
> —Phillip Kotler and Alan Andreason

Hopefully, your organization already has a distinctive constituency *profile*, defined by those who benefit from what your organization does, either *directly* (in the case of a hospital patient who wants to say thank you for the great medical care they received) or *indirectly* (if they are successful business owners and want to provide scholarships for poor kids from their hometown).

Your current donor base is incredibly important, in that it offers a demographic and psychographic perspective of not only who gives, but who *will* give. Any new donor will be but a mirror reflection of your current donors. So, the more you know about who gives *now*, the more productive you will be in identifying and cultivating new donors.

What Should We Look For In Our Donor Base?   A time-honored practice of fundraising, is called *constituency analysis*. It is a comprehensive look at your prospects' and donors' demographics, psychographics, giving patterns, and linkages to predict and project who might give, how much, and for what.

With careful analysis of your giving records, you will have a reasonably accurate idea of the inclination and the capacity of your defined constituency (current and potential).

Since this analysis uncovers the subtleties of donor behavior that are unique to your particular organization, it helps you decide how much time and effort you want to expend, on what, and with whom. In fact, it is even possible to estimate and predict the market saturation point for the number of donors you might be able to attract, now and in the near future.

As executive director, you want to insist that analysis of your constituency is more that an occasional thing; it should be a constant process and, at the least, utilize sophisticated mapping techniques to ensure that estimates are comprehensive and reliable.

If you don't have the internal expertise to do sophisticated constituency analysis, then hire an expert to do it for you.

Going deeply into the details of your existing donor records will illuminate donor segments under the surface that hold enormous potential for future gifts.

How Can We Estimate Our Donor Potential?   As executive director, you want answers to all the following questions. Your development staff should be able to answer some, but others will require outside fundraising counsel.

CONSTITUENCY Questions

- Who currently gives?
- How many give, why, when, how, and in what amount?
- Do we know enough about them to be able to segment by their demographics and psychographics?
- How many more (like them) might be caused to give?
- How much money can we raise, and what is our saturation point?
- Given our constituency profile, which fundraising methods will be most appropriate?
- What should our donor base look like five years from now?

As implied earlier, ability to raise money is not a given; some types of organizations stand a better chance of raising money because of their mission popularity, their other funding sources, and their number of natural constituents.

Larger organizations have natural constituencies (education and religious organizations) who are already linked and interested, so their ability to raise money is easier and greater.

Smaller agencies who don't have built-in or built-up constituencies have a much harder time raising money, including those that are old, but new at fundraising or those that deal with tough issues (incarceration, abuse, mental health).

Public sentiment has everything to do with fundraising potential.

What Is My Marketplace Potential?   An analysis of your *constituency ability* can help you discover both the good and the bad; regardless of what you find, at least you have the best gauge of how much or how little to invest in your development program.

A recent study of a small but highly respected YWCA in North Carolina predicted they could generate up to $1 million per year from individual gifts and foundation grants, but not much more. That study included a comprehensive constituency analysis, as well as a review of like organizations across the country with comparable deliverable services. The study was able to project the growth in the number of new donors, as well as estimate future retention and upgrade rates. The only thing that would increase their donor base would be an expansion of services at their present location or an expansion to adjacent geographic locations. More services and broader reach equate to more donor potential.

Another study of a large children's home society in the Midwest uncovered a significant number of loyal but neglected donors. Examination of their very large and very old donor base revealed more than 1,000 women over the age of 60 who had been making small gifts, every year, for more than 20 years. The gift size of these double-decade donors kept them under the radar. This constituency analysis led to the creation of a new legacy society to formally acknowledge their loyalty and open the door for dialogue about other gifts. Within one year after initiating the legacy society, several women revealed they had already made provisions in their wills for this organization, and several others were considering other types of planned gifts. More contact and appropriate recognition inspired additional and larger gifts.

A study for a large statewide child and family service in the South that had been in existence for nearly 100 years and was delivering a wide variety of social services and high-need residential programs was very disappointing. In spite of its important services and its statewide reach, this agency had become dependent on government grants and had basically ignored every opportunity to generate philanthropic grants and gifts. After so many years on the government dole, very few citizens saw this agency as a charity; most thought the agency a department of the state's child and family services division. The study concluded that the cost and effort to start a fundraising program would not be a good investment: It was too late, a very big price to pay for ignoring the importance of community involvement via philanthropy. Overdependence on one revenue source results in a perception of "no need."

If only a few hundred people want to adopt your organization, it would not be wise to staff a development program because your expenses (estimated at $75,000 for salary, benefits, and expenses per employee) would generate insufficient revenue (estimated at $50,000 total from 200 donors or grantors).

However, if you are an institution of higher learning and you have 30,000 alumni, history tells us that you could expect at least 23 to 32 percent of alumni will be predisposed to give back, ensuring a reasonable rate of return on your investment.

A comprehensive constituency analysis will also tell you how long it will take to achieve your goals (be it one year or six) and determine what portion of the budget can and should be funded via philanthropy, be it 2, 48, or 90 percent.

CONSTITUENTS

Focus on High Potential Prospects

> Donors of transformational gifts not only wish to support organizations that are addressing issues important to them, they often want to become deeply engaged through board membership or other involvements.
>
> —Kay Sprinkle Grace and Alan L. Wendroff

The goal of all the marketing theories and donor-focused practices outlined in this chapter is to identify the highest-potential prospects and encourage them to select your organization for their most meaningful gifts.

Discernment will be necessary. You cannot develop the ideal relationship with every single donor; you will not have the time, the resources, or even the desire.

You need to focus on those donors where you have the greatest potential, and that is not always measured in dollars.

There are donors who can influence others but might not have huge capacity themselves. There are donors who have given to your organization for a decade or more, and their lifetime value exceeds someone who has given only once. There are donors who will give only once, but that once is good enough.

Knowing your potential will dictate your focus; this is integral to your fundraising strategy. You may decide to focus primarily on Baby Boomers who have another 20-plus years to support your organization. You may decide to focus on women, whose assets and giving inclinations are greater than men's. You may decide to build a strong major gift base and focus on high net worth, both earned and inherited. Your organization may have a foundation of spiritual values, and you might want to focus on people who have similar beliefs.

The point is, if you can't determine a focus, your fundraising program will be all over the board and accomplish nothing more than a little of *this* and a little of *that*.

Relationship building with certain markets requires segmented and targeted approaches. The more you know about each of them, the easier it will be for you to determine what you need to do first.

Your highest-potential donors fall into four categories:

Your Board One measure of a successful organization is the extent to which its board members understand their governance and their legal, moral, and ethical roles and responsibilities. Another measure is how involved they are in the organization's fundraising.

Consider the original premise for the philanthropic sector: a gathering of people who by association could accomplish what one person could not. Consider, too, that when philanthropy emerged, it did not involve intimidation. People *voluntarily* stepped forward for what they believed in, and their reward was self-satisfaction, not financial remuneration.

Board members cannot be coerced into fundraising. They can, however, enthusiastically embrace fundraising on their own terms, when they realize that they bring unique expertise, objective advocacy, and community credibility that is needed to achieve your mission in ways that professional staff cannot.

To gauge the level of board engagement, you need to assess their performance against their fundraising responsibilities.

Given the board's moral and legal responsibilities to be involved in fundraising, there are specific job duties that have to be pointed out to them. Your job as executive director is to know what is required and then help your board self-assess whether they are doing what is needed and expected.

The following questions will help you assess your board's performance. A survey or a formal board assessment process will help everyone get to the same page.

Donors: Do they make their own gifts first? Regardless of the size of the gift, a board member must make the organization they serve one of their top charities. Anything less (a token gift) reduces their board participation and, worse, adversely influences the performance of other board members. When you let one board member off the hook, you let them all off. One hundred percent board giving is a mandate, and so is the requirement of a meaningful gift. A token gift does as much damage (psychologically to the culture) as *no* gift.

A caveat: It is unwise to recruit board members who are not already donors. Board membership should be a reward for past support, not an incentive to give just because you are now on the board. Sharing what every board member gives (with everyone else) clarifies expectations and establishes norms.

Goal Setters: Do they establish and endorse the plan, the case, the campaigns, and goals? Institutional planning is the purview of the board and executive director. It is also a privilege to be able to craft the overall plan, establish goals, and shape the case for support. Being involved in all those decisions is the stimulus that board members need to get serious about the fundraising results. Inheriting yesterday's plan is a disengagement strategy, for sure.

A caveat: Forget the rule that strategic plans are revised or updated every five years. You need to update that plan every single year to keep it relevant. Remind your board members that planning is a process, not a retreat.

Donor Openers: Do they introduce others, cultivate, and solicit them? Board members can affirm their own giving by saying to their friends: "Join with me in supporting this great organization." To do this effectively and with ease, they need a little help from you. They need business cards with their names, materials they can leave behind, training on what to say, and complimentary tickets so they invite high-potential prospects to join them at your next event.

A caveat: Board members need to know explicitly what is expected of them. Give them a list of hard goals, present report cards every quarter, and reward them appropriately for reaching their individual and collective goals. Peer pressure can be a good thing.

Advocates: Do they represent your organization in the community? When board members reach out into the community wearing your organization's name badge, they influence the opinions of others far beyond what you can do. Talking about their passion for your mission and what your organization accomplishes has more impact than talking only about the needs of the community. Equipping them with facts, figures, and measureable outcomes can turn them into likable zealots.

A caveat: Advocacy overtly influences opinion; it is not just courteous conversation. It is the promotional endorsement of your organization's leadership position in the community. It's your job to teach board members how to brag.

Stewards: Do they ensure accountability to donors? Stewardship has many faces and facets, including thanking donors, being accountable for contributed funds, establishing policies, and evaluating the board's performance relative to fundraising. When board members are transparent in talking about your organization, they help to garner the public trust that is so critical to fundraising.

A caveat: It is common for board members to focus more on financial reports than on most other areas of governance. Your job is to cause them to be equally as interested in the care and feeding of their donors (no donors, no money). How about putting the financial report last on the agenda?

Recruiters: Do they recruit other board members who want to fundraise? No one knows better than current board members how important it is to have board members with clout and connections. One of the most important roles of a board member is to replace oneself with someone even better suited for the job. Satisfied board members take on this responsibility without asking; if they don't, you can be sure they weren't suited to be on the board in the first place.

A caveat: Never ever allow your nominating committee to put forward the names of people who are climbing the ladder. If they are not already up the ladder, you don't want them on your board. Help your board members to set the bar high when it comes to recruiting.

Invite board prospects to get involved in fundraising, beyond making their own contribution.

Board Fundraising Suggestions

- Ask their employer to match their gifts
- Identify cases that would attract other donors
- Suggest names for the prospect list
- Mail information to known qualified prospects
- Host an information session at your home or work
- Invite a prospect or donor to lunch
- Introduce friends who are prospects to staff
- Participate in a fundraising event
- Make personal thank-you calls and write thank-you notes

High-Net-Worth Individuals   The amount of new research on wealth donors is more expansive than any other constituent group. This verifies that major gifts from individuals are a significant strategy for most nonprofit organizations.

Experience and some research suggest that wealth, in and of itself, is not a predictor or motivator of philanthropy. Rather, it is a belief that private contributions and nongovernmental organizations (charities) are integral to the American way of life (Odendahl 1990).

That being said, those with wealth to distribute will always be the fundraiser's primary target. With more wealth being generated in the past decade, with social needs rising, with the maturation of nonprofit organizations—the opportunities for raising money from high-net-worth individuals is huge.

Grace and Wendroff, authors of *High Impact Philanthropy,* suggest we have entered a new age of philanthropy with an outpouring of what they call *transformational* gifts that have a *high-impact.*

Transformational gifts are large, major gifts—the ones that have the capacity to alter how organizations do business. They are "inclusive investment of the donor's values made in organizations whose values the donor shares . . . the resultant values exchange results in high impact philanthropy" (p. 16).

Transformational high-impact gifts always constitute the upper portion of your giving pyramid, reaching or exceeding the 80/20 rule. It goes without saying that you the executive director need to spend most of your time with these donors.

In recent years, more research has been done on high-net-worth donors, helping delineate who they are and how they behave.

Many studies have affirmed that high-net-worth donors do have distinctions that are invaluable to the fundraiser. The *new* high-net-worth individual is more likely to have earned his money than to have inherited it. And *he* may be a *she* who has built her own entrepreneurial business from her basement or her laptop.

These twenty-first-century donors seldom wait to be solicited (and they are hard to find, because they still drive their old cars); they, instead, research and select organizations that are capable of delivering high impact. This new breed of donors treat philanthropy like a financial investment. Their goal is not a tax deduction but a social benefit generator. A first gift could have six figures, and it may be a test of your reciprocity and responsibility.

The best research on high-net-worth donors comes from the Bank of America studies in concert with the Center on Philanthropy, all available online.

Another study of wealthy male donors (Prince and File 1994) developed a framework called *The Seven Faces of Philanthropy*. It placed affluent donors into one of seven distinct segments based on needs, motivations, and benefits. Each personality type represented a characteristic and distinctive approach to philanthropy, a set of typical attitudes and beliefs, a range of considerations, a process of evaluation, and a style of involvement with nonprofit organizations. They are called the Communitarians, the Devouts, the Investors, the Socialites, the Altruists, the Repayers, and the Dynasts.

In another study and book, *Women, Wealth & Giving*, Damen and McCuistion examined giving habits of women Boomers. They pointed out the differences between women who earned their own money and those who did not; self-generated incomes allowed female donors be more reflective, independent, and generous with their philanthropy.

HIGH-NET-WORTH Suggestions

- Use statistical and measurable outcomes.
- Be project specific; prove community need.
- Do not assume they will support you.
- Allow them to be the decision makers.
- Demonstrate business savvy.
- Exhibit innovative leadership.
- Clarify their philanthropic values.

Baby Boomers   The supposition that certain generational groups have higher potential than others is not new, but generational differences have become more obvious and more interesting.

The Great Generation, once our largest loyal group of donors, is diminishing in size, being replaced by Baby Boomers, who have very different behaviors as a result of when they were born and raised. For many charities, Baby Boomers now represent as much as 75 percent of their total donor base.

Boomers represent the largest single sustained growth of the population in American history (77 million). They are expected to become the most generous givers and have more time to do volunteer activities as they approach retirement. Boomers are far more likely to be college educated, with more discretionary income. According to a recent study, Boomers now contribute more to charities and causes than the previous generation. A third of them plan to increase their contributions in the next five years.

They are more results oriented. They want to see clear, measurable, tangible results of their gifts and the work of the organization. They will not be comfortable with simply writing a check without seeing how the community actually benefits.

Boomers have less brand loyalty. They shop around and test organizations much like they would shop around for a new bank. To win them over as donors, organizations must prove themselves and cultivate involvement. They tend to favor small, local organizations over large, national ones, as well as different types of charities. Boomers do not give as much to religious causes as the previous generation did.

Still, they resemble older Americans in the way they divide their donations (health, education, social needs, disaster relief, arts and culture, advocacy and political groups). But Boomers are more likely to support organizations that help needy Americans.

BOOMERS Suggestions

- Respect their schedules.
- Treat them as colleagues.
- Develop opportunities that really matter.
- Remember that volunteering is optional.
- Make sure you are organized and professional.
- Reach boomers through their peers.

Women   Other than research on high-net-worth donors, no other constituency group has attracted more interest in the past 20 years than women.

Facts substantiate the level of enthusiasm for women as a high-potential group that every organization needs not only to include, but also to strategically focus on:

- Of the nation's top wealth holders, 43 percent are women (more than 1.5 million).
- Women own 40.2 percent of privately held U.S. businesses.
- Women will control more than 60 percent of U.S. wealth.
- Of all philanthropic giving decisions, 84 percent are made by women.

What motivates women to give? Several themes have emerged that answer this question. First, women like to be agents of change. As such, they tend to support innovative projects rather than the status quo, and they may take a longer time before making what for them is a significant gift. Volunteer involvement is key to their engagement, coming before their financial support.

Second, women retain a personal interest in how their donation is used; they expect the charity to be accountable to them for how their money is being spent. They want to have some control over their donations. Women see their gift as an ongoing relationship with the charity. They feel they have established a personal connection and want the charity to keep it alive by sharing information.

Third, women may not wish to appear to give more than their peer group. Older women are sometimes diffident about public recognition because it will make them stand out from the group. However, younger women may expect public recognition. Women like to feel they belong to a group, a team that is making the world a better place. This may explain why women like to work on special events.

Fourth, women's giving is often dependent on their age group. Older women may defer giving decisions to their husbands or accountants. Women who have earned their money have fewer problems deciding on their own about making a major commitment.

WOMEN Donor Suggestions

- Approach them on a personal level.
- Meet their desire to have a social impact.
- Be prepared to answer a lot of questions.
- Involve them, and ask for a small gift first.
- Introduce them to other women donors.
- Remember that recognition is not an incentive.
- Offer them cases they can relate to.

ALIGNMENT OF RELATIONSHIPS

Constituency Analysis Uncovers Patterns

> Having researched the needs of donors, fundraisers should be able to group donor preferences together in such a way as to make it profitable to meet them, while ensuring that all donors feel that their individual needs have been met.
> —Adrian Sargeant and Elaine Jay

When fundraisers apply marketing principles, fundraising becomes a systematic and managed process that allows us to develop a compelling case and message, and to select the appropriate methods to create a match.

How do the concepts of relationship marketing and social exchange change the way we look at our donor base? They mandate that we discover and uncover, connect shared values, and cause inclinations to be acted on in intentional ways.

An exchange perspective *demands* that we use research to understand why people want to give to us and gain insight into why people do what they do.

It requires us to ask why donors choose to affiliate with us rather than someone else. What causes them to have an affinity for our mission, leaders, programs, and clients? What unique characteristics does our organization have, according to our donors?

The more research we gather, the more we know how to meet the needs and interests of individual constituents and how to build lifelong relationships. The knowledge we gain through qualifying research informs our segmentation of donors into smaller and similar groups, enabling us to target more effective messages that will optimally cause a trusting relationship that will elicit meaningful exchanges.

This knowledge ensures a donor focus and aligns it with our organization's mission and vision. Three steps are needed:

- RESEARCH: Identify Donors With Shared Values
- SEGMENTATION: Organize Similar Donors Into Smaller Groups
- TARGETING: Rate, Rank, and Match Donors With Cases

The art of creating and nurturing exchange relationships with individuals who have an affinity or linkage with our organization is referred to as *constituency building, constituency development,* or *constituency relationship management* (CRM).

The key to building constituencies, cultivating them, and retaining them is linking people to people and connecting interests to issues. The old adage of "people don't give to causes . . . people give to people, with causes" remains as true today as it was when organized fundraising began more than 130 plus years ago.

Using a marketing perspective to build relationships begins with qualifying *questions* and ends with donor-focused *strategies.*

MARKETING Principles

1. Research and Analyze Prospects and Donors
   How, what, and when do they give?
   Who are they (demographics)?
   What do they think, need, and want (psychographics)?

2. Segment Prospects and Donors
   What external motivators elicit a response (influences)?
   How can they be segmented into smaller similar groups?
   How many, small or large?

3. Target Prospects and Donors
   Which groups have the greatest potential?
   What methods should we use for each of them?
   What happens to the others with less potential?

RESEARCH

Identify Donors With Linkage and Interests

> Research is as close as the real world comes to owning a crystal ball. You ignore research at your organization's peril.
>
> —Tom Ahern and Simone Joyaux

Philanthropic motivations are complex and varied. Social scientists have searched for answers about why people give and why they don't, so we have a pretty good idea and a growing list.

As fundraising has become more sophisticated, we have been digging a little deeper into the donor psyche, asking not only the basic motivational questions but also what makes people respond differently to different situations.

Why do certain donors give to our organization and not others? What are we doing, or what can we do, that will strengthen the relationship?

The need to better understand our donors' motivations is especially pressing, given today's environment of intense competition and uncertain economy. It is ineffective to spend time and money on appeals to those who are unlikely responders. A better understanding of donor motivations makes it possible for us to carry out fundraising tasks more effectively and efficiently.

The place to start is your donor base. The more you know about what motivates *your* particular donors to give, to give again, to give more, or not to give, the more you can advance your personalized approaches with new prospective donors.

Key research questions to ask about *each* donor:

- What caused our donors to make their first gift to our organization?
- What did they expect as a result of having made a gift?
- Were they satisfied with what happened with that gift?
- What program or project interests them most, going forward?
- Who and what influence their giving?
- In what ways do donors benefit from being associated with us?
- How do our donors want to be communicated with?

With research about your donors, your philanthropic exchange process will be vastly improved, donor fatigue will be tempered, and resources will not be wasted.

Your job as executive director is to insist that your staff spend at least 20 percent of their time on constituency research. Without your approval and your insistence on allocating time to research, staff will resort to making assumptions about what donors might want or do, which could prove costly, because they may not target the right prospects or build the right relationships.

Research is the systematic acquisition and recording of important information on current and prospective donors. The goal of research is to identify shared values between the organization and prospects to build and maintain the exchange relationship.

Constituency analysis must be cumulative and ongoing, adding pieces of information as they become available, leading to additional searches for specific information. Obviously, a computerized storage and sorting system is key to extracting the right kind of information when needed to evaluate and manage a donor's relationship with your organization.

There are many research tools to use; the three most popular ones are LIA analysis, database and electronic research, donor surveys, and focus groups.

LIA Analysis   One of the most obvious questions about your organization's constituencies is: How do we *qualify individual prospects and donors* to determine high potential? A relatively easy way, particularly when supported by other research, is LIA: linkage, interest, and ability.

Although people have individual, complex, and varied motivations for their philanthropic behavior, the LIA formula focuses on the three primary experiential indicators observed by fundraisers over the years: linkage, interest, and ability. This time-honored LIA principle has represented the easiest method to quickly assess the readiness of someone to make a philanthropic gift.

People's *linkage* with other people not only affords access but also brings credibility from someone they know. Connecting with others influences the way values are shared and deepened.

For instance, if a donor is a close friend of the current board president, they have a social relationships link. A donor who is a former client or student of your institution has a beneficiary-relationship link. A donor who is also a volunteer at your organization has an affiliation-relationship link. The stronger the link with or through someone, the greater the inclination to give because of deepening shared values.

People's *interest* is shaped by their life experiences and values, which in turn give clues about what they are willing to fund. Being able to express oneself through giving is personal and powerful.

For example, we all have special interests that play out in our philanthropic giving. Our values might cause us to support institutions and causes that address children's issues. A donor with an affinity for children will not just give to any children's charity but select those that address certain familiar issues, such as children's rights, medical care, child care, school achievement, athletics, or safety. Very few charities address all of those issues, so the donor will select those that get closest.

When you know what the donor's key values and interests are, you can rank them accordingly or help deepen their interest with more information and more involvement in your organization.

People's *ability* or capacity to give is often tied to life situations or timing. While sometimes limited to financial situations, people's perception of what they want to fund and how much, is influenced by their linkage and interest, not just their financial ability or status.

For instance, donors who rank high in the linkage and interest areas may actually come looking for you because they know exactly what they want to accomplish. As donors get older, they become even more selective in their giving, causing them to reduce the number of charities they give to while increasing the size of the gift. If their earnings increase or their expenses decrease, they will be motivated to give to those who properly stewarded their past gifts. For donors with high linkage and high interest, a wish list is advisable because you cannot be sure what their real financial status is. Their ability is a figure in their minds, not yours.

You could devise a rating or ranking chart to assign a numerical value to each of the LIA values and come up with a list of the highest to lowest donor prospects.

Database Scan   One of the best ways to look at who might give is to look at who currently gives. There is a saying that your new donors are just like your old donors.

Carefully and regularly examine your current donor base to see what it might reveal statistically about donor giving patterns or about donor characteristics.

Your donor profile (whether it is primarily women and couples over the age of 50 or highly successful graduates who own their own businesses) will give you all the clues you need.

A donor profile is not necessarily limited to one or two types of donors—in fact, there are probably many types—but there will be dominance in similarities. For instance, an opera company is likely to attract donors who are middle to high income, educated, musically trained children, annual subscribers, and the children or grandchildren of opera buffs.

As executive director, you want to insist that your development staff and your database are capable of extracting enough information to be able to do some profiling.

To develop a giving pattern profile, you must examine all giving records by source, date, amount, recency, and frequency (how many, how often).

DONOR DATABASE Checklist

- How many are new donors?
- How many are renewing at the same level?
- How many are renewing at higher levels, over time?
- How many donors are making more than one gift a year?
- What percentage of donors are flat givers?
- What is different about each donor? What is the same?
- Is retention of donors within industry standards?
- If solicitation strategies are different, what are the response rates for each type?

To develop a constituent personality profile, you would have to examine their demographics, their psychographics, and their motivating elicitors. (If such data is not available, you will need it going forward so that you can apply marketing principles to your fundraising program.)

Research tells us that each person in your database has an ultimate gift potential. For some, that may be zero; for others, it may be to give every year and stay flat; for others, it could be a major or planned gift. The last category is typically about 15 percent of your donor list.

Hot lists include:

- Donors with at least one gift of $250 to $999 in the past year and a $1,000+ annual giving capacity
- Lapsed donors who have given $1,000 gifts but not within the past 18 months

- Donors with two or more gifts of $100 to $999 in the past three years with $1,000+ annual giving capacity
- Prospects with $10,000+ giving capacity and an identified affiliation with your organization

As you look at your donor list to identify your best prospects for major gifts, it is important to invest in reliable prospect research, which effectively allows you to mine the data using a customer modeling service. Modeling helps develop donor profiles by incorporating information on wealth indicators (real estate, stock holdings, etc.). Data mining and predictive modeling are proven methods for the identification of your best potential donors.

Screen all records by looking at RFM: recency, frequency, and money. These three indicators provide insight into your donors' giving history and help predict their future giving patterns.

By outsourcing your donor file to a firm with the ability to discern major gift potential, your research will really pay off. You provide an electronic copy of your database, and they append additional data fields compiled from the best sources of individual household and aggregated data available. Their analysis provides deep insights into the characteristics that distinguish donors from non-donors and major giving prospects from planned giving prospects. They use these data sources to construct models that address your specific fundraising objectives. With the models complete, your prospects are then analyzed against these models and assigned scores based on how closely their attributes resemble those of each model. Finally, the resulting scores for the models that you've chosen to develop will enable you to identify the best prospects in your file.

Exhibit 4.2 is an output showing the number of prospects and their likelihood to make a major gift at different levels.

EXHIBIT 4.2 PROBABILITY RATING OF PROSPECTIVE MAJOR DONORS

	Gift Range $5,000–$10,000	Gift Range $10,001–$25,000	Gift Range $25,001–$50,000	Gift Range $50,001–$100,000	Gift Range $100,000+
Major Gift (Excellent)	741	166	133	80	43
Major Gift (Very Good)	378	56	49	11	2
Major Gift (Good)	76	5	4	2	1

Donor Surveys Donor surveys and focus groups often do more than the high-cost, time-consuming research done individually on donors. Surveys and focus groups collect information, not from one, but many donors, giving comparative analysis on perceptions, behaviors, and opinions. As such, they give us statistically relevant samples, representative of the much larger numbers of donors.

Surveys and focus groups, functioning as feedback systems, take a limited amount of time, give us pertinent data, and are relatively easy to undertake, inexpensive, and even enjoyable.

As in all research, there is a science to preparing an instrument that doesn't influence the answers or skew the data. In the case of donor surveys (be they written or scripted), you need someone with expertise to help clarify what you need to know, construct the survey questions, and guide you toward the number you need for statistical significance.

Surveys are the preferred choice when you need immediate feedback from a wide variety of donor types. It is best to use a mail or e-mail survey to gather data from a large number (over 1,000) when you have numerous questions. If your list is qualified and your instrument professionally crafted, it's not unusual to generate a 30 to 40 percent response rate. Mail and e-mail surveys are extremely effective, in part, because they are less intrusive to the donors.

Telephone surveys are the preferred choice when you want sample research from a modest number of donors (under 100, with a 75 percent reach), and when your questions are more complex or sensitive. A telephone survey utilizes fewer, more open-ended, subjective questions; a mail survey collects answers that are more quantifiable.

Surveying your donors helps to identify your typical donors (gender, income, education, values, and lifestyles). Surveys allow you to explore how satisfied your donors are with your fundraising program or with one particular campaign. A survey can pose questions about solicitation methods, donor recognition, and volunteer experiences. You can even inquire about your organization's status as compared with other charities by asking: "Please share with us your top three charities" or "Where do we rank in your list of favorite charities?"

Focus Groups   Behind every prospect or donor are sometimes simple, sometimes complex philanthropic motivations, which are themselves constantly affected by changing external influences.

Hence the purpose of a focus group is to gain both objective and subjective insights into what's going on out there. Concurrently, we want to elicit our donors' concerns, provide an opportunity for suggestions, and determine the key elements affecting how others might be encouraged to give.

There is no better method of involving people who are influential to your organization than to invite them to participate in an opinion focus group. In one room, in about one hour, you gather 8 to 10 people in the know and in return for their input, you will receive cards and calls from them thanking you!

A focus group is an exploration process, unstructured except for a few predetermined questions. As such, it is one of the best ways to get at underlying perceptions and attitudes. Ideally, a trained facilitator (not employees from your organization who think they know how to facilitate) provides the assurance of objectivity in leading the discussion. Participants are selected, not simply based on their familiarity with your organization, but on their diverse views and community involvement.

You will need to personally invite 10 to 15 donors to assemble a focus group of 8 to 10. Due to the number and nuances associated with the comments, you need to have a note taker so the facilitator can concentrate on the process. The following questions are typical:

1.   What influenced you to get involved with this organization?
2.   What prompted you to make the first or your largest gift?
3.   What do you see as the fundraising strengths of this organization?
4.   What challenges exist in our seeking philanthropic support?
5.   If you were the organization's CEO, what would you focus on?
6.   What would it take to get you to be more involved?

One of the most effective ways to look at an organization is from the eyes and ears of the donors, and this is just the perspective that well-executed surveys and focus groups provide.

The information you gather will prove essential for strategic planning and visions. Moreover, your development department will find the feedback invaluable and often inspirational. You can be sure it will stimulate new ideas and create energy for positive change.

And there is one more beneficial aspect, which few other research methods achieve. This is the engagement it draws from friends of the organization. By seeking their advice, their input, their concerns, and their aspirations, you will be involving them deeply in your organization, and in all likelihood they will become some of your staunchest, most generous donors in the future.

SEGMENTATION

Organize Similar Donors Into Groups

> Hidden inside any database are opportunities to raise more money, if only you could dig them out; "Segmentation" is your pick and shovel.
> —Tom Ahern and Simone Joyaux

Segmentation of constituencies will rely on what you are able to find out through research about your existing and potential donors. The more you discover, the greater your segmentation potential.

For instance, if your research reveals that Great Generation donors give higher average gifts than your Baby Boomers, you should segment the Boomers into a separate group. We know from research that Boomers are not institutional supporters: Instead, they are interested in giving to programs and projects, and therefore we need to present our case differently. We also know from research that women and men give differently, and they must be cultivated differently. But having just one segmented group of women is not enough; you will need segments for different generations.

Donor segmentation is a mandate in today's sophisticated fundraising environment. Segmentation is the identification and assignment of donors into small groups with similar behaviors, demographics, psychographics, and giving potential. Once segmented, communications can be tailored to influence philanthropic motivations from the different groups in different ways.

The extent to which your organization is able to segment your constituency base is reliant on how many resources you have: staff, computerized systems, research expertise, and time. Not all organizations are able to do as much segmentation as fundraising experts recommend, but studies show that doing so increases their base of support in both number of donors and increased gift sizes.

As executive director, you must insist that your staff not only research donors but also identify characteristics to segment them into high-potential groups. Ask your staff to tell you what criteria they used to establish each segment; ask what their plans are for cultivation and messaging; ask about their tracking devices to evaluate results.

Each organization will have to approach segmentation differently, based on who their prospects and donors are, how they behave, and what their needs and interests are.

The most frequently used determinant of segmentation is *level of giving,* followed by the *frequency of giving.* For instance, it is relatively easy to segment donors into giving levels of under $50, between $50 and $100, between $100 and $500, between $500 and $1,000, and so on.

It is equally easy to segment by frequency of giving: first-time donors, renewed donors by number of years, upgraded donors by years, and so on. Both level and frequency can be combined into segments and the time of year added: $50 first-time donors who made a gift last year in November, $100 donors who have lapsed during the past three years, and so on.

Marketing specialists point to advantages of segmenting by *age group.* Research has demonstrated that older generations make purchasing decisions differently than younger generations (check versus debit card). So the obvious segmentations will be Great Generation, Baby Boomers, Gen Xers, and Gen Yers.

You could group your donors into *demographic* segments (age, education, geography, family size, income, giving history, and types of gifts) Eventually, you will learn enough about them to be able to segment by *psychographics* (values, attitudes, and lifestyles, including spiritual beliefs). Over time, you will gather enough information to be able to segment them by multiple indicators (women, not married, over 65, repeat gift giving, gifts over $1,000).

The goal of successful segmentation is to start simple and become more sophisticated as donor information increases. Remember, all donor information must be recorded in a donor file so it is used appropriately.

Once you have determined how many groups you want to concentrate on, it's very easy to establish targeting parameters.

TARGETING

Rate, Rank, and Match Donors With Cases

> The same message will not work with every audience . . . Targeting helps you solve the problem of finding needles in a haystack.
> —Tom Ahern and Simone Joyaux

The concept of targeting and matching rests with deciding which of the many constituency segments you want to target or focus on.

You can't focus on all of them. You need to select the highest present-day performers, those with the greatest impact for the long term, or even those who might be major donors in the future. The goal of targeting is spending quality time and effort on quality prospects, using quality tactics and quality communications. Targeting improves effectiveness and efficiency because it keeps the focus on those with the greatest potential and puts the rest on auto-pilot.

The concept of matching the right case with the right constituent is simple in theory and at times, but challenging in practice. The more you know about both your cases and your constituents, the easier it is to put the two together, after which you can construct your approaches, your campaigns, and your communications.

Matching is a process that takes intuition, logic, and creativity to cause an exchange to occur between the donor and the recipient organization. A match exists when the need for funds matches the interest of the donor.

Ideally, you will have more than one potential match for each individual donor or donor segment. You must anticipate that the donor may wish to support one project over another and prefers choices.

Our goal is to assist donors by providing factual information that guides them toward a wise decision. Designated giving is integral to the matching concept.

Matching implies trust, entails flexibility, dictates the sharing of power, and accomplishes the philanthropic exchange.

Let's review a few concepts that are pertinent to achieving a successful philanthropic exchange.

- The relationship process is essentially the match between values and goals. The variations and variables are limitless.
- The manner in which a match occurs is ideally by plan, but in reality it is more prone to circumstance.
- Given that fundraising tends to be more art than science, there are many paths to the same outcome. Ambiguities, uncertainties, and judgmental requirements come into play.

As executive director and an agent of philanthropy, you will have to rely on whatever donor research you have. You need to trust your intuition to lead you to the best decisions. You must proceed (with a solicitation) in spite of risk because of the potential benefit.

Maintain an optimistic view, no matter what the outcome, and embrace the fact that matching takes more effort and creativity than raising funds by playing the mass marketing game.

In pursuing matches, you must also accept that donors are entitled to support causes that interest them, and that when appropriate we have to tailor our institutional needs to fit those interests. Be ever mindful of the need to assist donors by providing unbiased information that guides them toward a wise decision. Designated giving is integral to the matching concept.

Matching implies trust, entails flexibility, dictates sharing power, and accomplishes the philanthropic exchange. It goes beyond linking a donor's interest with an organization's program. It also matches the donor's financial capacity with a budgetary element, the timing of a donor's gift with an organization's fiscal year, the type of gift with the type of solicitation, and the amount of effort put toward the relationship with the anticipated potential.

Matching is marketing with four steps:

1. Collecting information from the donor (constituency research).
2. Developing a mission-driven, donor-focused product (case for support).
3. Offering the product at the right time, place, price, and person (selection of solicitation method).
4. Ensuring that the product delivers the benefits offered (stewardship practices).

Communications theory tells us that a match is viable when perceived as such by those being matched, rather than by the matchmaker. If both parties believe their needs are addressed, met, or exceeded, the match is achieved (as in two-way communications when the encoder and decoder send and receive the same messages on the same channel).

Simply put, the giver and the receiver are then in sync. It should be noted that early perceptions at the beginning of a relationship, when satisfaction is high or low, may be different from later ones. However, positive and frequent interactions will nurture the relationship, increasing the perception of satisfaction over time.

The old way of raising funds—the demand-pull methods, in which the organization appealed for funds on demand and pulled in donors who would support it—is passé. Technology has made it possible for donors to seek and gain access to information about charities on their own. They are creating their own demand, initiating their own pull. Interactivity is the new paradigm.

There are many implications for the fundraising process as the matching or exchange concept is fully incorporated into the time-honored solicitation process. Matching takes more information, more time, and more resources.

If you have taken sufficient time researching your prospective donors and have carefully matched them with compelling cases, determining what method to use to solicit them will be a no-brainer. Those decisions will be obvious. See Exhibits 4.3 and 4.4.

EXHIBIT 4.3 **EXAMPLE #1: TARGETING/MATCHING OF CASES, CONSTITUENTS, AND COMMUNICATIONS**

Constituency Segments	Cases	Communications
Foundations	Summer camp Day & residential	Letters from children Phone conversations Lunch with director Formal proposal
Local businesses	Homeless shelter	Visits Fact sheet Evidence of outcomes
Family foundations	New jobs program collaboration	Presentation Facts Details of training Benefits to community
Women's groups	Holiday assistance program	Photos How it works Volunteer opportunities

EXHIBIT 4.4	EXAMPLE #2: TARGETING/MATCHING OF CASES, CONSTITUENTS, AND COMMUNICATIONS

Constituency Donors	Cases	Communications
Ray Glass	Boys & Girls Club	Tour Statistics (fact sheet) Written/verbal ask
Bob Meek	Christmas program	Phone call Ask letter Follow-up
Robert Henderson	Transitional living program	Phone call In-person visit Tour
George Hendricks	Boys & Girls Club	Phone call Attend graduation Written proposal
Helen Novak Former foster child 70 plus	Children's Village	Benefits of IRA gift Lunch & tour Artwork thank you from child resident
Church Missions Board Rural agricultural area	Hispanic ministry	PowerPoint Summary of solutions Wish list Testimonials
Mr. & Mrs. Knight 5th-generation Orange Grove	Transitional housing endowment	Home visit w/officer Benefits of endowment Legacy now for later Annual report

CULTIVATION IN RELATIONSHIPS

Strategies To Build Long-Term Relationships

> Through an ongoing process of exchange, interaction, and genuine choice, donors begin to feel that they are important to the organization and have an important role to play, in return, by supporting the organization's programs.
> —Adrian Sargeant and Elaine Jay

As a process of interactions, relationship building is not left to change. Fundraisers go to great lengths to manage each donor, by strategizing what their next move will be.

In the industry, this is called "donor cultivation." Kim Klein distinguishes it from selling or stalking, saying: "Cultivation is where you treat the donor like a whole person."

Cultivation is what you do to build the loyalty and commitment of the donors to the organization.

The following models are used to illustrate the reciprocity or exchange movement that occurs in building relationships between donors and charitable organizations.

- DONOR PYRAMID: Donor Movement and Monetary Distribution
- CULTIVATION CYCLE: Process to Engage Donors Toward Mission Affinity
- MOVES MANAGEMENT: Relationship System Involves Multiple Contacts

DONOR PYRAMID

Donor Movement and Monetary Distribution

> The primary value of the Donor Pyramid is in demonstrating the interrelatedness of all the components of the integrated development plan. Effective fundraising recognizes that the component are interdependent and manages the process of developing the components as mutually reinforcing.
>
> —Timothy L. Seiler

The relationship pyramid is the best visual known to describe the conceptual stages of increased involvement as donors move up to a higher level of interest and, hopefully, giving. It is used to describe how interests, needs, and desires grow upward in direct proportion to the ways in which the organization informs and involves them.

As donors move from annual giving decisions to major giving decisions, they require more influences, inputs, and rational justification. At the top of the giving pyramid (as in Maslow's theory), the philanthropic partnership is fully realized: Donors have achieved their aspirations, and the organization has fulfilled its mission (implied). See Exhibit 4.5.

I would be remiss not to point out that this pyramid is a more figurative example of relationship development, than a literal one. The steps are not always sequential, nor are they all encompassing.

Relationships don't follow a fine line; they are more fluid and not always predictable. Still the concept of moving from a decision to make a first gift to a charity to the ultimate decision to make that charity one of your favorites follows a logical path of affiliation and affinity.

The time-honored pyramid model helps explain how large numbers of small donors enter the pyramid at the bottom, and as they increase giving, they move up the pyramid. Eventually, a few donors become major donors, forming the tip of the pyramid. This constitutes the 80/20 rule of donor giving: 80 percent of the regular donors give 20 percent of the dollars, while 20 percent of the major donors give 80 percent of the dollars.

The pyramid portrays the interlinking concepts of prospect research, leading to donor acquisition, encouraging donor renewal, and materializing in donor upgrading, sequential steps used to create a donor giving pyramid.

These seem like simple concepts on the surface, but their applications are complex. The day-to-day cultivation of activities and motivational nuances associated with helping donors move from one level of giving up to the next is not a simple process, nor can it be left to chance.

Experience demonstrates that a donor's upward movement takes place only when there is a well-managed relationship process in place. Such a process is referred to as *cultivation moves,* which facilitate exchanges between a donor and your organization, growing in intensity over time. Cultivation moves are designed to increase a donor's affinity for your mission.

As executive director, you need to know that cultivation moves are not one-sided, employed by professional staff alone. They are strategic activities, employed at each stage of the relationship, that also involve key volunteers and other organizational leaders. They are developed as external elicitors of internal donor motivations or as exchanges. They are not attempts to convince people to do something they are not inclined to do. They are, instead, authentic outreaches of expressions of gratitude for a donor's benevolence. Cultivation moves embody the following assumptions:

1. Relationships as partnerships are developed through effective, balanced interpersonal communications that, over time, increase in frequency, complexity, and intensity.

2. Strong relationships develop when there is openness, respect, honesty, patience, commitment, and give-and-take from both parties.

3. Ongoing relationships depend on mutual goodwill and an appreciation of each other's similarities and differences, needs and interests.

How much of your time and energy should be devoted to the management of cultivation moves? For the answers, picture an inverted pyramid laid on top of the relationship pyramid. It would suggest you must allocate the most time and energy with donors who are at the top, giving the least effort to donor relationships at the bottom (unless research suggests high potential).

We can apply these relationship principles to our development program in a few ways, including:

- Today, with relatively little effort, we could identify our top 50 donors and determine where they are in the process. We can record their giving history, primary contact, and relationship stage in our database.

- Tomorrow, we can articulate how we intend to cultivate each of these key relationships as a managed case. The process continues with the identification of the staff person who will oversee each case and each move, who else should be involved, and when and how certain techniques should be applied.

- By the end of the week, we can print out that list and tape it to our desks or our wall, to ensure that our top donors get our primary attention every day, not just when we make time at the end of year to ask for another gift!

- Next week, we could begin scheduling meetings with staff and volunteers whose involvement is key to a particular donor. This helps keep the relationship-building process front and center, not only for the development department but also for the entire organization.

- Next month, the idea of creating an individualized plan for each donor has encouraged us to look at this particular relationship as unique, moving us from stereotypes of donors as similar.

The Donor Relationship Pyramid

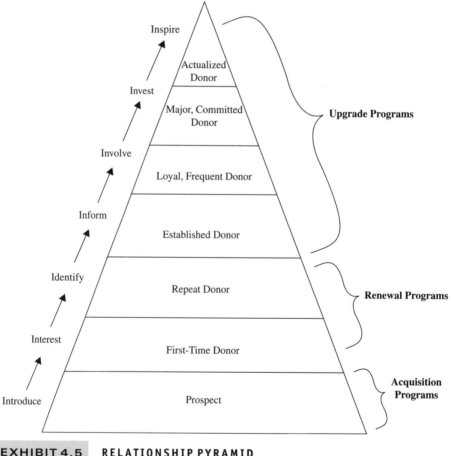

EXHIBIT 4.5   RELATIONSHIP PYRAMID

CULTIVATION CYCLE

Process to Engage Donors Toward Mission Affinity

> Cultivation is a two-way street. It is the series of steps you take with each person to learn as much as you can about him, and he in turn needs to know as much as he can about your organization.
>
> —Laura Fredricks

The second model is used to describe the cultivation and commitment process to manage the donor-organization relationship. It is a more dynamic, fluid, synergistic model. Its conceptual framework is a ball of energy that describes the attraction between a donor and an organization, moving from an outer surface incrementally toward the center.

The cultivation and commitment cycle describes how donors pass through a series of cultivation steps designed to increase their commitment to the mission over time or, in the absence of satisfaction, are spun off. As the donor is cultivated and grows more committed, the connectors grow stronger, the exchanges are more frequent, the interactions build in quantity and quality, and the satisfaction multiplies.

Over time, a synergy develops that brings the donor and the organization's mission into sync. In the absence of positive synergy, donors may decide to leave because their experiences were unsatisfactory, their interests have changed, and/or their needs were not met. Others may come into your system to replace them. The goal is to add more donors to the cycle over time and to build a larger, stronger, more sustainable donor constituency that is propelled forward by the infusion of energy gained.

The cultivation and commitment cycle shows the donative relationship stages—the sequence of moves that donors make to form an exchange relationship and the corresponding moves that the organization makes to facilitate the philanthropic partnership. See Exhibit 4.5.

They are the following:

1. **Prospect: Introduction Stage.** Information has been collected about the prospect that indicates a relationship might be developed. The organization introduces the prospect to its charitable mission, using appropriate communication methods: in person, by phone, by mail.

   The introduction stage may include three steps: presentation of the organization's mission (a newsletter), a cultivation activity (invitation to a benefit event), and a direct solicitation (an annual appeal).

   This stage may start with donors who introduce themselves to the organization by visiting the website, researching your mission, asking questions of others, and possibly sending you an unsolicited gift.

2. **First-Time Relationship: Interest Stage.** Having made a first gift, the donor has indicated some level of interest in the organization's mission. Of greater importance is the affirmation donors receive that their gift was needed and will be used appropriately.

   The organization's interest is expressed by the way the donor is thanked, recognized, and resolicited. The communications now shift from why support is needed to what a difference the donor's gift has made.

   The organization now needs to collect additional information about the donor and begin to explore areas of mutual interest, shared values, and future support.

3. **Repeat Relationship: Identify Stage.** Interest should now be growing, as the donor decides whether to make repeat gifts, as if unsolicited. There should be a desire on the part of both parties to learn a little more about each other and to make more frequent contacts and to identify mutual values.

   The organization might make contact by mail or telephone to thank the donor in a more personalized way. The donor may now be initiating contact in other ways: by attending special events, supporting a particular program, or having a discussion with a volunteer or a board member about their investments.

   Exchanges are growing and increasing: Observations are taking place, information is being processed, questions are being asked, and opinions about the relationship are forming. The communications shift from what *I* can do to what *we* can do.

4. **Established Relationship: Information Stage.** Having initiated personal contact, communications turn to sharing more detailed and personal information about the donor's interests and the organization's specified or special project needs. Personalized invitations are made to donors that call for a response—an offer to tour the facility, attend a luncheon, join a giving club, or participate on a volunteer committee.

   By now, the donor has likely revealed interest in particular areas (or something about themselves that would lead to an area of obvious interest). Dialogue will be more open, with questions about the mutual interests, stronger rationale as gift decisions grow in size.

   The donor's expectations and needs are being met, and the organization is evaluating the benefit of further investment of time and effort in the relationship. Agreement about the relationship is established, and if in sync, the contacts are increased.

5. **Loyal, Frequent Relationship: Involvement Stage.** At this stage, both parties are actively involved in the relationship exchange, voluntarily. Common interest is apparent; pride of association is obvious. Interpersonal communications are occurring on a regular basis. Exchanges are open and challenging. The donor wants to be involved in activities that demand more time and talent, such as committee work or board membership. The level of giving is substantial and relatively stable.

   The organization wants the donor's involvement in leadership aspects: as a volunteer fundraiser, advocate, and community representative. The donor is receiving information that is typically reserved for insiders, attending events designed for the organization's best friends, and having a personal relationship with the organization's leaders. At this point, the donor is beginning to consider the relationship as long-term and may even consider the possibility of a legacy gift, in addition to lifetime gifts.

6. **Major, Committed Relationship: Donor Investment Stage.** By now, the organization and the donor have a significant investment in each other as partners. Time, talent, and treasure have been received; appreciation, recognition, and stewardship have been given.

   The exchange has reached an important level; involvement is at its highest. The donor may be involved in decision making that affects not only how the organization delivers services, but also where the organization is going in the future. The donor may be a trustee and a leader in a major capital campaign.

   The organization values the donor's counsel, input, and leadership. Given the high level of investment in the organization's mission, this is the time when tensions may arise around roles, relationships, and directions. Reciprocity is needed, so the relationship can reach its final stage with trust and appreciation.

7. **Actualized Relationship: Inspiration Stage.** At this stage, the relationship is stable and predictable. Both parties are focused on the mission over the money and are engaged in a true partnership.

   Given the accomplishments, inspiration takes over, setting the stage for a donor to realize his or her lifetime aspirations and the organization's focus on what can be done, rather than what can't be.

MOVES MANAGEMENT

Relationship System Involving Multiple Contacts

> The moves concept focuses major gift fundraising on changing people's attitudes so they want to give. To do this, we take a series of initiatives or moves to develop each prospect's awareness of, knowledge of, interest in, involvement with, and commitment to the institution and its mission.
>
> —David Dunlop

Many years ago, a couple of successful fundraisers (G.T. "Buck" Smith and David Dunlop at Cornell University) devised a term and a process called Moves Management. *(Moves Management is a registered trademark of The Institute for Charitable Giving, Chicago.)*

Moves Management is the set of processes nonprofits use to develop constituent relationships and move them toward higher-level giving. But simply adopting a moves management strategy is not enough; it needs to be supported by tools that help you identify and foster personal relationships that are essential to giving.

As a conceptual framework, this process keeps track of every communication between the donor and the organizations while strategizing which "moves" will be most beneficial to deepening a relationship that will translate into a philanthropic exchange.

But this process was not just an attempt to track activities; it was designed as a management and cultivation strategy that involves a team of staff/volunteers in the "moves" process. Each donor is assigned several key individuals to develop the relationship with a prospective donor. By assigning one member of the team, at a time, to send the donor a note; at another time, another member of the team will invite them to an event—all part of the strategy to ensure that the "right person" is eventually the one who asks for the gift.

Moves Management requires an organizational buy-in to be effective, given the high number of cultivations occurring among many staff members and volunteers. Obviously, the process needs to have a core moves team to provide the strategic assignment of donors/prospects and to limit the number to those with the highest potential.

In Moves Management there is not a deadline; although everything is documented, it is all about building the relationship.

Here's what each MOVE in the donor file keeps track of:

MOVES MANAGEMENT Donor File Contents

1. What is the name of the donor?
2. Where did the meeting or event take place?

---

3. On what date and at what time?

4. Who was present at the meeting or event (prospect, staff, volunteers, others)?

5. What information did you convey during the visit or event?

6. What happened during the meeting or event (comments, concerns, objections, questions)?

7. What materials did you distribute or leave behind, if any?

8. What is the next step?

9. Who will perform the next step?

10. When is the next step to be performed?

The depth and progress of your donor relationships can be significantly impacted by the effectiveness and efficiency of CRM (constituency relationships management), a technology tool that works with your database to track each activity and to identify prospects with higher potential for giving and for greater involvement (be it larger gifts, a planned gift, willingness to solicit others, participation on your board, introducing you to other potential givers).

According to nonprofit fundraising software company Convio, "Having the ability to consistently identify and cultivate the most promising prospects enables your staff to nurture relationships in a way that's tactful, timely and efficient."

By giving you a full picture of their involvement, their communications preferences, and their relationship values, links, and patterns, CRM software helps you connect more completely with donors. It is an automated process that delivers meaningful reports for measurable goals.

Connecting and cultivating, each donor requires different activities to develop a relationship:

- If a prospective major donor gives online, you should have that information sent to you electronically the same day. And it should be processed that day.

- If one of your development staff speaks to a high-profile donor or a board member you work closely with, you want that information immediately, and certainly for the next time you see them.

- If a major donor signs up to attend a special event, and you are going to have lunch with them next week, you need to be able to acknowledge this.

- If a major prospect or donor signs up to volunteer in one of your programs, your program director needs to let you know, as well as letting the development staff know.

- If a major donor or a board member is listed on Facebook or other social media sites, your CRM can inform you of this so you can friend them and extend your relationship online.

In terms of prospecting, a CRM system collects information about your constituents so you can see all the ways they are engaged with your organization, whether it is e-mail subscriptions or personal communications; their demographics; and their financial capability. Not only can a CRM track giving history, but it will also store wealth-screening information and ranking. It can tell you who has the most contacts, the greatest number or size of gifts, and even who has visited your website most often. The number of touches a donor has with your organization is a clue as to how interested they are and wish to be going forward.

For instance, you can:

- Track all moves between a donor and you to increase the effectiveness of future interactions.

- Identify the right prospects, and make note of who the best contact is.

- Assign specific tasks to different staff members to help keep a donor moving through the stages.

- Set goals and benchmarks and produce meaningful reports that are tied to measurable goals.

MANAGEMENT OF RELATIONSHIPS

Techniques To Expand the Donor Base

> There are several dimensions to asking for a gift: an exploration of the psychology of asking for money, the identification and cultivation of the prospects who will be asked, and the solicitation itself which connects your goals and mission to the values of the prospective donor.
>
> —The Fund Raising School

Fundraising has four methods: donor acquisition, donor renewal, donor upgrading, and donor over-above gifting—commonly referred to as *moves* or *methods*. These methods encompass a series of managed steps that form relationships by helping donors increase their giving levels. Akin to a simple version of Maslow's theory, the donor can move ahead, stay in one place, or retract to a lower level of giving.

The level of giving often correlates with the level of commitment to the organization, but not always.

Someone with limited financial ability may stay at the same giving level (say, $1,000) for 20 years because of financial reasons, not commitment reasons. Someone else could make a two-year repeat gift of $5,000 and never make another gift, yet continue to think of themselves as one of your best donors. The four methods include:

- ACQUISTION: Identify and Invite Donors to Give
- RENEWAL: Encourage Donors to Repeat Behavior
- UPGRADE: Build Donor Loyalty and Attachment
- OVER-ABOVE: Final Steps in Donor Managment

MANAGEMENT Methods

ACQUISITION

Build the Base of Support (Identify and Invite)

- Identify and solicit donors
- Initiate an exchange relationship
- Raise unrestricted gifts and restricted grants
- Identify and involve volunteers

RENEWAL

Strengthen Base of Support (Inform, Involve, and Interest)
- Renew donor support annually
- Communicate with and inform donors about their gifts
- Give donors choices to give
- Build donor loyalty
- Recognize and reward donors

UPGRADE

Increase the Base of Support (Invest and Inspire)
- Cultivate donors to higher giving levels
- Form lasting two-way relationships
- Expand giving options
- Determine donors' preferences for designations
- Involve donors as volunteer leaders

OVER-ABOVE

Seek Gifts for Special Purposes (Challenge and Champion)
- Identify donors with special circumstances
- Cultivate donors who are transformational givers
- Provide donors with naming opportunities
- Identify major, capital, and planned gift donors
- Offer special projects for large single gifts

ACQUISITION

Identify and Invite Donors to Give

> Donor acquisition is critical to the health and growth of any nonprofit. Every organization loses donors through attrition each year and needs to replace them. But, if you intend to grow in your ability to serve, you will need to grow the number of donors supporting your work well beyond those lost through attrition
>
> —Doug Shaw

A donor acquisition program is generally directed at a large group of prospects with the hopes that a few of them will respond with a gift.

In many ways, the larger donor acquisition processes work like a child's beach sand toy; sand is scooped in the sifter, allowing small particles to pass through while capturing the larger ones, along with a few pebbles and seashells. It takes a lot of patience and effort to locate a few perfect-size treasures. With experience, the great professional fundraisers become a little more discerning and discriminating about where to do their sifting.

In recent years, donor acquisition has become more selective, reducing the pool of prospects with advanced technology screening. The point is that acquisition works with many prospects, a few, and even one at a time.

In practice, successful donor acquisition is more than a process to gain new donors; it is the process of selectively acquiring high-potential donors. A sophisticated, selective acquisition program targets the most qualified prospects: those who have the potential to become fully engaged and invested in your organization over time.

The goal of donor acquisition is to increase your organization's base of support, not to generate an immediate profit. Initially, the cost of acquiring new donors may be as high as $1.50 for every $1.00 received, but that expense becomes an investment when it is recovered many times over through renewals. Each subsequent renewal is less costly to implement, generating greater net returns with each repeat gift.

A donor acquisition program has four steps: identification, cultivation, solicitation, and appreciation. These steps are repeated in the renewal and the upgrade process with donors who are then prospects for repeat and larger gifts.

1. **Prospect Identification.** Prospect research, focus groups, and volunteer rating and ranking sessions help uncover prospects with the highest potential.

   The development team does almost all prospect identification; some of the best leads come from program staff and board volunteers. As representatives of the organizations, they are the first to hear: "Oh, you are involved in that organization. . . . I think they are doing a wonderful job" or "I had such a great experience there."

These comments are really signals of interest; essentially, these speakers have identified themselves as prospects.

When we establish a process to collect names of people who say things like this, we are building our prospect base, where they can be incorporated into our acquisition process. A sign of a philanthropic culture is when our program staff and board members proudly collect and submit names to the development program on a regular basis because they have been out talking about the organization they represent.

There are other methods, of course: holding special events and adding those names to our solicitation lists, exchanging donors' lists with other organizations, asking board members to send in their holiday card list, and adding anyone who walks in your door (guest list) to your prospect list.

2. **Prospect Cultivation.** Cultivation is a method of making prospects *aware* of the need for philanthropy-funded services to the community. Awareness actually begins when a prospect is first introduced to the cause, either through someone who is already involved, attendance at an event, or communications from the organization's marketing department or perhaps from the service area they have had contact with. Awareness has to be built (this is cultivation) with high-quality, frequent, informal and formal communications.

The obvious goal of planned cultivation is to improve the chances of an acquisition by preparing the prospect for a solicitation. During cultivation, information is exchanged that helps the prospect better understand the organization's mission and case while delving into what the prospect might be interested in. According to Mixer, "The prospects' cognitive interest in an agency's clients or service ranks as a fundamental prerequisite in the process of building awareness" (1995).

Once prospects are adequately qualified (we know their needs and interests), their attributes become the focus of the cultivation process (for example, an expressed interest in helping youth, reducing violence, high school or college graduation).

Cultivation activities are key to bringing people together for the purpose of stimulating greater awareness that others are making contributions to the organization: newsletters, tours, luncheons, presentations, and websites.

Nothing works as well as on-site events where prospects can meet the organization's leaders, socialize with other donors, and learn firsthand from a program expert about the needs of the organization and about the role that philanthropy plays.

The more relevant the information you give out, the more compelling the case; the more urgent the need, the more responsive the prospect.

3. **Prospect Solicitation.** For clarification purposes, the word *solicitation* means the process of inviting someone to consider making a gift; *acquisition* is the organization's way of saying the solicitation was successful. In reality, the organization controls only the solicitation process; donors determine if they want to be acquired.

Stories are told about donors who say, "I don't want to be asked, I just want to give." What they are probably saying is "I don't want to feel like you are pressuring me to give; I want to give when the asking feels good." There is a delicate balance between asking (solicitation) and the giving (acquisition).

A prospect solicitation–donor acquisition initiative is very complex; approaches and the variables change based on persons, timing, and place. The success of a donor acquisition program is correlated directly with the following factors:

- Quality of the prospect (research on motivational indicators)
- Quality of your case (as selected for each prospect)
- Influence of the solicitor or vehicle (right person, right ask)
- Image, mission, and vision (your institutional readiness)

Not all prospects become donors the first time they are solicited; some never become donors. The key is to solicit all qualified prospects at least three times to ensure that they are hearing the request. Every qualified prospect should have the privilege of saying yes or no. It would be a disservice not to solicit those who appear to be capable and interested. However, the success or failure of donor acquisition rests to a large extent on how prospects are qualified.

Each annual campaign has individualized acquisition goals. For example, a college's annual fund campaign may include only one strategy: "acquire 300 alumni as new donors at the $1,000 level from the 2008 graduation class." Another strategy could be "acquire 50 new donors at the $500 level from parents of current students." A social service agency may embark on a special purpose campaign to "acquire 250 new donors who have an interest in children, at the $25 level." An arts organization may use a strategy to "acquire 20 new event donors at the $1,000 level who have been attending performances regularly for the past three years."

4. **Prospect Appreciation.** When you go to sign those solicitation letters, please remember you are privileged to be doing the thanking. And no boilerplate, please.

A computerized thank-you letter is not a personal communication. Donors know the difference between a personal thank you and a computer-generated one (and the latter is but trash). If we want to retain our first-time donors, we must allocate sufficient time and resources to the acknowledgment process. It is the first-time thank you and follow-up reporting that affirms the donor's decision to give and sets the stage for additional gifts.

For all donors, an official letter from you, the executive director, is the most sought-after thank you, sometimes along with a personal phone call from one of your board members.

ACQUISITION Checklist

- Your donor acquisition program should not waste resources soliciting nonresponders, low responders, or people who have little in common with your organization or little evidence of interest in your mission.

- Experience has proven that nothing is gained by frequent acquisition of small or one-time donors who make token gifts without intentional investment. If the first gift was not meaningful from the donor's perspective, there will not be a second gift; raising one-time gifts is not cost effective.

- The idea is to solicit only qualified prospects, to acquire high-potential donors, and to encourage others to support other favorite charities, wherever they may be.

Questions to Ask

- What are our acquisition rates for each campaign?
- How many new donors from each campaign?
- What is their average gift size?
- What is our total cost and net (ROI)?

ACQUISITION Benchmarks

- 30 to 50 percent if highly qualified LIA and asked personally by a peer
- 25 percent if highly qualified LIA and asked by the organization
- 5 to 10 percent if marginally qualified LIA and asked impersonally
- 1 to 2 percent if qualified and approached through direct mail or cold call

RENEWAL

Encourage Donors to Repeat Behavior

> Through an ongoing process of exchange, interaction, and genuine choice, donors begin to feel that they are important to the organization and have an important role to play, in return, by supporting organization's programs.
>
> —Adrian Sargeant & Elaine Jay

While the acquisition effort can be compared to sifting for treasures, the renewal effort can be compared to planting seeds. The gardener spends a little money to purchase perennial seeds, cultivates the soil before planting, arranges the seeds carefully in the flower bed, and fertilizes and waters them. Having made the original investment, the gardener needs only to take care of the flowers until they bloom. The following spring, the perennials reappear, ready to bloom again.

Donor renewal is a resolicitation program that will be directed annually at about 75 percent of your donor base. Donor renewal rates rise as the frequency of giving grows. Also, donor renewals will be higher if the donors' needs have been met and they are fully satisfied with their experience.

We often say that renewal begins the day after the first gift was received, meaning that donor satisfaction doesn't wait one year until we ask again; it begins when we thank and acknowledge the first gift, hopefully within 24 to 36 hours.

Of course, it takes more than a thank-you call or letter to keep a donor content for an entire 12 months; other communications help to cement the beginning of a relationship by creating information flows. Typical donor communications include invitations to events, newsletters, annual reports, updates on the use of their gifts, and personal outreach by someone they know.

Within the renewal donor group are many subgroups that need not only your attention but also a different approach:

- Your core group (reliable, every-year donors)
- Your frequent donors (give several times a year)
- Your growth group (upgrade on their own)
- Your influence group (invite their friends to join them)

Renewal Steps   A renewal program is designed very differently and managed separately from the acquisition efforts. Renewal, too, is an objective, not a program in and of itself, with subgoals for each renewal aspect of each annual campaign. For instance, a campaign run every year at the same time would use:

- A different appeal for acquiring donors
- A slightly different appeal for first-year renewing donors

- A significantly different appeal for third-year renewing donors
- A highly personalized appeal for mid-level and major donors

For different groups, it is inappropriate to send the same generic appeal. Not taking the time to write a personal letter or make a personal phone call to an established or major donor is taking the donor and philanthropy for granted in the worst possible way—it is like telling the donor that he or she is not special or really needed.

Renewal and acquisition do have some similarities. Both articulate the case in rational and emotional ways. Both use the same techniques: personal phone and mail solicitation. Both are targeted for a particular group of people. Yet renewals differ in four ways: segmentation, personalization, techniques, and information.

1. **Segmentation.** Once a prospect has become a donor, your marketing strategy changes. Research is much easier with donors, and even more critical. Donors (unlike prospects) are quite accessible and willing to give information about themselves and others. With information about donors' particular interests, we are better able to make the appropriate distinctions and to segment them into smaller constituent groups. Once segmented, the most appropriate solicitation strategies and techniques can be determined, which can vary from group to group.

2. **Personalization.** Renewal is not the time to batch donors; it is the time to treat each donor as an individual who is special to the organization. As compared to prospects, it is much easier to personalize communications to donors. First of all, when donors made their initial gift, they gave you an enormous amount of information about them: their preferred names, the person who sent or signed the check, what they wanted to fund, the type of solicitation they will respond to, and their level of interest.

   With subsequent communications and especially at renewal time, there are many ways to personalize the messages. It may be the right time to use the first names of both solicitor and donor. The renewal appeal should be personalized to make note of the donor's previous gift (size and designation) and its use (what happened as a result). Other personalized information can be added, such as a reference to a previous phone call, a visit or tour, survey comments, or attendance at a special event.

3. **Techniques.** As donors move up the giving pyramid, so do the techniques. If the acquisition occurred by direct mail, renew with a personal

letter. If acquired by personal letter, renew with a letter and a follow-up phone call. If acquired by personal letter and call, renew with a personal visit; if acquired by personal visit, renew with a personal tour, lunch, or meeting.

4. **Information.** The actual renewal may be done in one visit, one call, or one letter, but the activities leading up to and following the renewal set the stage for other yes responses. The renewal process is designed to achieve a series of communication goals: interest, inform, involve, invest, and inspire.

RENEWAL Checklist

- A renewal of one previous donor is more cost-effective than an acquisition of two new donors! But you have to allow (and insist on) more staff time, increased personalization, and greater steward-ship with renewal donors. A strong renewal program is key to major gifts.

- Renewals are very different from acquisitions. In acquisitions, we ask prospects to give to a need that exists. In renewals, we tell donors "your gift addressed a need in the following ways. . . ." Renewal letters and phone calls focus on the results: They have outcomes, outputs, testimonials, and a request to give again because of the re-sults (not the need).

- Because 70 to 80 percent of your donor base will be renewals, be sure your staff spends 80 percent of their time here.

Questions to Ask

- What is our retention rate (what percentage of donors renew)?
- What is our average gift size (for each renewed segment)?
- What is the ROI on each fundraising method for each segment?

RENEWAL Benchmarks

- 70 to 80 percent of your donors will need renewal
- 80 to 90 percent will renew, if giving has become a tradition for them
- 60 to 70 percent will renew if they are relatively new donors (three to five times)
- 50 percent of first-time donors will renew
- 60 to 75 percent ROI on overall renewal program

UPGRADE

Building Donor Loyalty and Attachment

> At the heart of the relationship approach to fundraising is the concept of lifetime value . . . when fundraisers have a sense of how much a given donor will be worth to them over the full duration of their relationship, they can develop communication programs that reflect the value, and tailor the offering to that donor according . . .
>
> —Adrian Sargeant and Elaine Jay

The third objective in annual giving is to invite donors to become more involved in the organization by making larger and more frequent contributions. This objective, like renewal, can be accomplished better with a little more effort, making it a higher priority in the integrated development plan.

At times, we see donors moving themselves, without our asking, because of something that triggers their motivations. This could be caused by having more to give, a decision to concentrate on a few charities, or wanting to be part of a special initiative.

If they do not move up on their own, our job is to cause donors to consider doing so by using motivational elicitors (a compelling case that shows how a larger gift could have a much greater impact). We can also induce the bottom-to-top movement concept by offering incentives and rewards such as gift clubs, recognition items, publicity, and even volunteer opportunities.

When someone moves up to a higher giving level, they tend to stay there, in the same way that other donors stay at their own levels.

An upgrade in the size of the gift moves donors further up the giving pyramid, allowing them to become more involved with the organization, providing them with more opportunities to give and more options to give to, and sharing with them the organization's accomplishments and its future directions.

As a strategy, donors are best invited to upgrade a gift in the early stages of renewal, when they are first becoming involved and are enthused about what they can do. Upgrading is not as successful once a donor's gift level is firmly embedded at a certain amount or level.

Upgrade Steps   A donor upgrade program is best designed as an individual strategy for each qualified donor, implemented immediately after the first or second gift. The thank-you letter should include a courtesy suggestion to participate in yet another way, maybe a tribute gift or a holiday gift. Throughout the year, every donor should receive newsletters or mailings with appeal envelopes to remind them that you are looking for contributions year round, not just once a year.

Our goal is to upgrade with larger-size gifts and/or more frequent gifts and to acknowledge this increased level of giving with more tailored communications and involvement opportunities.

As is obvious, upgrading is not a mass marketing strategy; it is an individualized and tailored approach for your high-potential donors, with many complexities. At least 15 percent of your donors should be upgrading each year.

Techniques like gift clubs, challenge grants, giving choices, payment options, and tangible recognition items are excellent elicitors to encourage donors to give more. A word of caution: Some donors give more as a result of the psychosocial benefits they receive (gathering with others). Most, however, make larger gifts based on the strength and relevance of the case and the feeling of being needed.

UPGRADE Checklist

- When we fail to invite donors to upgrade their gifts, it is like saying: "Your gift is nice, not critical." Failure to invite donors to make larger gifts is not only a disservice but also an insult to their capacity and your organization's worthiness.

- If donors have satisfactory experiences from their first gift and the ones that follow, they are naturally inclined to give more when the case merits it and when the solicitation articulates it.

- Please don't wait until a capital campaign to upgrade a donor's giving level; upgrading is intended to be a gradual increase over time.

Questions to Ask

- What percentage of our donors upgraded last year? The year before?
- How does that compare to national statistics and benchmarks?
- What are we doing to improve that rate?
- Who among that group of upgrade donors could move to a major gift level?

UPGRADE Benchmarks

- Annual donors over two years need to be upgraded.
- 25 percent is a typical upgrade rate from direct mail or phone.
- 50 percent is a typical upgrade rate from face-to-face.
- 50 percent will upgrade with a special project that appeals to them.
- 25 to 30 percent rate is typical on an overall upgrade program.

OVER-ABOVE

The Final Step in Donor Management

> Organizations seeking to retain donors need to give adequate consideration both to enhancing service quality and to building commitment.
>
> —Adrian Sargeant and Elaine Jay

The fourth objective of the giving program is to figure out who your over-above donors are, because you will need to target them differently. Essentially these are what the industry refers to as "loyal" donors whose lifetime value (LTV) is significant.

Typically, they are not really "annual donors," not by our definition and not by theirs. But they still think of themselves as donors, nevertheless, and expect to be treated as such. This poses a dilemma, because our large annual giving programs tend to become mechanical with renewal letters. If a donor doesn't respond to a renewal appeal (or several), we drop them from our lists (or put them in a lapsed file folder).

Forgetting about over-above donors doesn't bode well with them.

A recent study done by Penelope Burk suggests that if they are not treated as well when they are not giving (as in lapsed) as they are when they are giving (as in active), they will be reluctant to continue their relationship with you.

Who are the over-above donors?

They are the ones who not only give regular annual gifts, they give extra gifts—maybe to the holiday campaign or when they have a little extra money in the bank. Sometimes we can identify why but, more often, only the donor knows the reason that provoked a gift. I have observed donors who made a $1,000 gift one year and, several years later, as if out of the blue, made a $10,000 gift. Keeping them in your sights is important, but asking too often could backfire for donors in this category, since their giving decisions may be extremely private or anonymous.

Donors who give frequent or substantial memorial or honor gifts fall into this category. They are generally giving because of their connection with someone close to them; philanthropy is a second thought (a benefit, not the incentive). Their primary goal is keep a memory alive, which eventually leads to consideration of a legacy gift.

There is yet another group of donors who make gifts occasionally but do not intend for them to be annual gifts. They have special reasons, maybe an inheritance, a holiday bonus, or a stock sale profit. They are not thinking about giving it regularly; they are dealing in the moment, making the gift without further commitment.

OVER-ABOVE Checklist

- When an over-above donor makes a gift (first time or additional times), do not make the mistake and think it is going to be an annual repeatable gift for general operating.

- This type of donor has no intention of making special gifts every year. Their motivation is just as described; the donor is making a giving decision that is extraordinary (and to them, annual giving may be ordinary). This donor needs to be treated as a member of the organizational family, regardless of whether he or she is currently giving.

- If you put them on the regular solicitation list, they could be offended. If you forget about them, they will be even more offended. They need their own category, given their enormous motivation and potential for significant gifts.

- I worked with a donor who sent his first gift of $1,000 in response to a holiday mailing. His next gift, two years later, was $34,000. Several years later, he called me and told me he had just transferred a sizable amount in stock to my organization. When I inquired what the value was, he said, "$1,275,000." When I inquired about his intentions (where he wanted it to go), he said, "I don't know; let's talk about that when we have time!" This donor was not an annual donor by definition, but the annual giving program is home to many types of gifts. The way we treat our donors at their first gift is influential for future gifts.

Questions to Ask

- What percentage of our donors give for special reasons?
- How are we tracking these donors?
- How do we solicit and steward them differently?
- What is the total revenue from this group?

OVER-ABOVE Benchmarks

- 10 percent of your donors will need special attention.
- 50 to 80 percent will give again at some point.
- 50 percent are candidates for a special project or legacy gift.
- 90 percent ROI since most will self-determine their giving.

Summary

This chapter brought all the philosophical, theoretical, and practical elements of relationship-building in fundraising together. It applied the sensitivities and sensibilities that are integral to respectful relationships. So often, fundraising is seen as doing something to or for a donor, when, in reality, as staff, we are never in charge or in control of the outcome. We can only hope to be of some help to donors as they work through their own very private exploration of what they want to say about themselves when they act in philanthropic ways.

References

Ahern, T., & Joyaux, S., 2008. *Keep Your Donors: The Guide to Better Communications and Stronger Relationships*. Hoboken, NJ: John Wiley & Sons.

Brest, P., & H. Harvey. 2008. *Money Well Spent: A Strategic Plan for Smart Philanthropy*. New York: Bloomberg.

Burk, P. 2012. The Cygnus Donor Survey; Where Philanthropy is Headed in 2012 (US Edition). www.cygresearch.com/publications/orderReport.php.

Burnett, K. 2002. *Relationship Fundraising: A Donor-Based Approach to the Business of Raising Money*. San Francisco, CA: Jossey-Bass.

Center on Philanthropy, in conjunction with the Bank of America studies. www.philan thropy.iupui.edu/high-net-worth-studies.

Crutchfield, L. R., J. V. Kania, & M. R. Kramer. 2011. *Do More Than Give: The Six Practices of Donors Who Change the World*. San Francisco, CA: Jossey-Bass.

Damen, M. M., & McCuistion, N. N. 2010. *Women, Wealth & Giving: The Virtuous Legacy of the Boom Generation*. Hoboken, NJ: John Wiley & Sons.

Dunlop, David. "Moves Management: The Science of Fundraising." White paper. www .prosperfundraising.com/pdf/moves_management.pdf.

Fredricks, L. 2010. *The Ask: How to Ask for Support for Your Nonprofit Cause, Creative Project, or Business Venture*. Hoboken, NJ: Jossey-Bass.

Frumkin, P. 2006. *Strategic Giving: The Art and Science of Philanthropy*. Chicago: University of Chicago Press.

Grace, K. S. 2008. *Over Goal: What You Must Know to Excel at Fundraising Today*. Medfield, MA: Emerson & Church.

Grace, K. S., & Wendroff, A. L. 2001. *High Impact Philanthropy: Now Donors, Boards, and Nonprofit Organizations Can Transform Communities*. New York: John Wiley and Sons.

Graham, C. 1992. *Keep the Money Coming: A Step-by-Step Strategic Guide to Annual Fundraising*. Sarasota, FL: Pineapple Press.

Grave, K. S., 1997. *Beyond Fundraising: New Strategies for Nonprofit Innovation and Investment*. New York: John Wiley & Sons.

Klein, K., *Donor Cultivation: What It Is and What It Is Not: Grassroots Fundraising Journal*. www.grassrootsfundraising.org.

Kotler, P., & Andreasen, A. 1987. *Strategic Marketing for Nonprofit Organizations*, Englewood Cliffs, NJ: Prentice-Hall, Inc.

Mixer, J. R. 1995. *Principles of Professional Fundraising: Useful Foundations for Successful Practice*. San Francisco, CA: Jossey-Bass.

Odendahl, T. 1990. *Charity begins at home: Generosity and self-interest among the philanthropic elite.* New York: Basic Books.

Prince, R.A., & File, K. M. 1994. *The Seven Faces of Philanthropy: A New Approach to Cultivating Major Donors.* San Francisco, CA: Jossey-Bass.

Sargeant, D., & Jay, E. 2004. *Building Donor Loyalty: The Fundraiser's Guide to Increasing Lifetime Value.* San Francisco, CA: Jossey-Bass.

Seymour, H. J. 1994. *Designs for Fundraising: Principles, Patterns, Techniques.* 2nd ed. Rockville, Maryland: Fundraising Institute.

Wilson, T. D. 2008. *Winning Gifts: Make Your Donors Feel Like Winners.* Hoboken, NJ: John Wiley & Sons.

Solicitation Concepts

CASE, CAMPAIGNS, COMMUNICATIONS, AND GOALS

This last chapter dives deeper into the best solicitation practices utilized by the most successful fund development programs in the country. Best practices are not nicely configured in black-and-white, replicable formulas; they are some do's and don'ts, a few maybes and shoulds, but no formulaic absolutes. By now it has probably become apparent that best practices do not stand alone, but move instead in tandem. If one goes missing, the integrated development process falls apart.

INTRODUCTION

What do you need to know about soliciting donors, as the executive director?

First, you should know what is *proven* and also what is *practical*. You need to know what is *particular* to your type of nonprofit. You should insist on certain *processes* and *procedures* to accomplish essential *principles*. You need to insist on tested *proformas*.

Last but not least, as the executive director, you need to evaluate your staff's *performance* by using evidence-based metrics and benchmarks, so you are not wasting your time doing what you hired someone else to do.

Your staff's job is to use your time effectively and to make sure you see the right people, open doors to new partnerships, and set the stage for growth in the number and size of donors' gifts.

Your job? In a nutshell, to inspire your development staff to design a fully *integrated development program*; so they can call on you as appropriate and as needed. Your job is to champion your mission and inspire board members, community leaders, donors, and staff to follow.

As executive director, it is your job to insist that your development staff put into place best practices via an integrated development program that incorporates the four basic fundraising theories: *annual* gifts, *major* gifts, *capital* gifts, and *legacy* gifts. Together, these theories utilize methods that address three aspects of giving: *why, what,* and *how.*

Additionally, you want to be sure your staff utilizes principles and techniques that have been field-tested over time. These include, but are not limited to, the donor pyramid, the constituency circle, the LIA concept, the case for support, the ladder of effectiveness, and the social exchange concept. All these principles are codified and supported by practitioner application and substantiation.

Finally, as executive director, you want to internally scrutinize every aspect of fundraising, so your approaches have the highest level of integrity externally.

This chapter covers what the executive director needs to know to be able to assess where to apply inspiration, when to make certain demands, what to hold others accountable for, when you need to step up and exhibit leadership, where to best apply resources, and finally, how to minimize your risks.

This chapter helps you put together all the components of a successful integrated development program.

Chapter 5 covers:

- CASE to Solicit Gifts: Critical Elements of a Case for Support
- CAMPAIGNS to Solicit Gifts: Integration of Fundraising Methods
- COMMUNICATIONS to Solicit Gifts: Motivational Elicitors to Generate a Response
- GOALS to Solicit Gifts: Budgetary Approach to Match Needs and Interests

CASE TO SOLICT GIFTS

Critical Elements of a Case for Support

> Each organization that uses the privilege of soliciting gifts should be prepared to respond to many questions, perhaps unasked and yet implicit in the prospect's mind. Among these are: who are you and why do you exist?
>
> —Eugene R. Tempel

Raising money is not a given or a right. An organization has to earn this privilege from donors by demonstrating they are responsive to community needs, can deliver worthwhile services, and are prudent in their stewardship.

Since donors have the right to say *yes* or *no,* they, in essence, influence your organization's providence. You want to be perfectly posed for this privilege by attaining a high level of institutional readiness.

If you, the executive director, were asked if your organization was well positioned to do fundraising, you would likely say yes, of course it is. But in the world of philanthropy, it's the donors' opinions that count. So, like it or not, you are advised to go through a process that asks them what they think about five readiness components, in order to craft a compelling needs statement or case for support:

- MISSION: Relevance and Achievability of Vision
- LEADERSHIP: Marketplace Position in the Community
- STABILITY: Structurally Sound and Financially Responsible
- READINESS: Institutional Assessment of Worthiness
- CASE: Compelling, Urgent, and Realistic Goal

MISSION

Relevance and Achievability of Vision

Donors want your organization to function like a business but behave like a charity. So your mission and vision need to be very idealistic but also realistic—to them.

The one thing I can tell you with assurance is that donors are fickle and quick to shift their loyalties from one charity to another one that appears more relevant.

Remaining mission and vision *relevant* in today's accelerated and recession-fraught marketplace, is also not easy. It takes ingenuity. It requires an inherent and genuine interest in external trends and issues, a desire to be proactive and change oriented, and being flexible and financially nimble.

If your mission statement has not been updated within the past five years, it probably does not reflect the current environment.

Given the increase in the number of new nonprofits, competition comes in many more forms. In a typical mid-size community, there are probably three outstanding universities, at least two or three homeless shelters, possibly two hospital systems, as many as five performing arts companies, and the list goes on . . . all asking your community for philanthropic consideration.

Your job is to stand out among all the worthy nonprofits and compete for a place on someone's favorite charity list, which may have only five or six slots.

Today's major donors are not only skeptical about how charities function but they also hold nonprofits to the highest standard of public trust and accountability. So you must ask them what they think. Their answers are the ones that count.

One of the best ways to test mission relevance is to ask your donors to describe your organization's mission in one or two sentences. Can they give you a quick or clear sound bite, or do they seem confused by the complexity or even the simplicity of it? Do they say, "I know they do good work, but I'm not sure what all they do," or do they say something like this: "I have seen, firsthand, how young people's lives dramatically changed when they joined the Boys and Girls Club."

Subtle but very revealing: The first response is almost apologetic; the second is intensely prideful. These comments become the litmus test of how clear and compelling your mission or case is to the outside world.

If your mission is outdated and your vision dull, your case will be weak and your ability to facilitate philanthropic exchanges will be diminished. Since philanthropy acts as the conscience of your mission and the catalyst for your vision, you want both to resonate with donors.

LEADERSHIP

Marketplace Position in the Community

Donors gravitate toward organizations that play a major role in the community's philanthropic landscape. They favor successful organizations over those struggling to stay alive. They have greater respect for those that stand out in their field.

To donors, an organization's credibility emanates from the clout of the trustees, the leadership of the executive director, and the competence of program staff.

A formal *institutional readiness assessment* will discover if your organization and your leadership are respected and valued, and if not, why not.

Chapter 1 addressed the need for the executive director to earn the reputation of leader. Boards have to earn respect, too. We constantly hear members of the community make facetious remarks about good boards and weak boards. People applaud (and envy) nonprofits that attract the who's who for their boards. Boards with a reputation for credibility and clout are, quite simply, better able to leverage their influence and raise more money. Donors can see this. But a power board doesn't come about by accident; it comes from a deliberate strategy to recruit independent-minded and highly successful community leaders. The key is to recruit peers who run in the same circles, have similar aspirations, and can trigger healthy competition to raise funds . . . even if they don't know each other before coming to your board.

A weak board, however, appears (and is) disconnected, disparate, and dysfunctional.

If an *institutional readiness assessment* discovers that your board is weak and not strong enough to embark on a major philanthropic initiative, you don't want to be the one to deliver the bad news. It is far better for outside counsel to issue this message!

To donors, an organization's credibility also comes from having highly competent, professional staff. An organization first in its field is the one that attracts program staff who have earned their stripes via academic credentials, pursued cutting-edge projects along the way, and gained regional or national recognition.

A great organization serves as a magnet for accomplished professionals who in turn magnetize resources to move things further along. Donors can see this, too.

Shared leadership, between the board and staff, results in a wide circle of interconnecting links. The larger the leadership circle, the greater the synergy and the greater the fundraising potential. A positive empowered leadership culture attracts donor investment.

By contrast, weak leadership (almost an oxymoron) at one level will affect or contaminate other levels, producing what Max DePree refers to as organizational entropy or disconnected links. The lack of leadership repels donor investment.

STABILITY

Structurally Sound and Financially Responsible

Financial responsibility is a key characteristic of a healthy organization and one that influences philanthropic support.

Donors evaluate organizations by the way they define success and failure and where they place their focus. Some organizations focus on where they have *been,* others on where they *are,* and still others on where they are *going.* Donors favor organizations that are highly focused on where they are going as a direct result of being well-managed and already financially successful.

Just like you, donors prefer giving to achievable outcomes, not shortfalls or gaps. When a number of donors give, other donors follow suit. Success begets success.

A recent scenario proves this long-held point of view: A private university in the Midwest recently received an anonymous gift of $25 million. Upon announcement of that gift, the chief development officer stated: "The calls with additional gifts are coming so fast, I can hardly keep up with the return calls and the thank-you visits. That one large gift opened a floodgate of other large gifts, as if they were waiting in the wings."

On the other side of enthusiasm for giving is over-solicitation and donor saturation. Experience tells us that hoping for gifts or pushing donors to their max results in fundraising drudgery. Weakness begets weakness.

This scenario proves this point: A young pastor was assigned to a church shortly after a failed capital campaign. He was instructed by his supervisors to implement a second capital campaign (a debt-reduction campaign.) But when he approached parishioners with the idea of a second campaign, he encountered huge resistance. He told his supervisor: "Our parishioners are so tired of heavy-handed solicitation calls at their home, they have asked for us to make this second campaign a non-ask . . . they have refused to consider another gift, unless they receive it by mail. They do not want another pressured solicitation; they want the freedom to say "no, I don't want to support a project that was not well-thought out."

Beyond looking at your organization's soundness and financial success, donors also look at how well your programs and services are delivered and whether they are making the necessary systemic changes.

Since Baby Boomers arrived on the donor scene, organizations have been forced to be more transparent. The balance sheet, the audit, and the 990 are only the first level of evaluation by donors; they also expect benchmarks, metrics, vital signs, and report cards of your program outcomes. Outcome measures now include: number of people served, cases carried, number of client graduates, dollars earned, number of grants, net or gross balance sheets, percentages of increases, comparisons with competitors, and national standings and awards.

In the end, an *institutional readiness assessment* will enable your organization to sharpen its focus, establish new priorities, discover opportunities, and connect aspirations with strategies for the best fundraising program possible.

As executive director, you should insist on an *institutional readiness assessment* at least every five years.

READINESS

Institutional Assessment of Worthiness

An assessment of your organization's readiness to solicit gifts is best done by an outside organizational development consultant who specializes in nonprofit fundraising. Someone with fundraising experience and expertise can realistically determine your philanthropic potential; a consultant without that expertise is likely to produce a boilerplate report. Note: While some for-profit consultants insist their experience is transferable to the nonprofit world, it is not, when it comes to fundraising.

A formal assessment is a process that objectively measures your *internal* strengths, weaknesses, opportunities, and threats—pointing out where you need to spend time and resources.

It also examines your organization *externally*, assessing if the greater donor community is inclined to support your type of organization based on *their* attitudes, financial ability, and resonance with mission.

Together, the *internal* and *external* findings form the basis on which the fundraising plans are developed, how strategic fundraising decisions are made, what goals are set, and which fundraising projects are implemented.

A formal assessment process serves as your organization's reality check and should be done every five years. It not only collects the data but also compares responses from the inside with those on the outside, including feedback from your service-provider competitors. The assessment process asks people on the *inside* why they are personally involved in the organization and asks people on the *outside* what would cause them to be involved. This opinion research provides the basis for comparative analysis, which uncovers missed alignments as well as surfacing areas of high potential.

The process of assessing readiness and responsiveness is the same whether you are starting a new fundraising program or reinventing one. It is akin to doing a capital campaign feasibility study (which most are familiar with) and is best done by a consultant with expertise and experience in your particular type of nonprofit. For instance, sophisticated environments like higher education require consultants who specialize in that subsector. Knowledge within a particular subsector is the key to analyzing cultural dimensions and making recommendations that are valid.

Virtually all assessments find redundancies, inefficiencies, and missed opportunities, and they uncover untapped potential for contributions. Professional fundraising consultants are trained to go looking for new ways to raise money and to save money. Thus, the cost of any assessment is likely to be recovered within 12 months of implementing their recommendations.

The following activities uncover a multitude of clues about whether your fundraising program is as good as it could and should be.

- Personal interviews with key staff, board members, volunteers, and donors
- Focus groups with key staff, volunteer leaders, and donors
- Review of the strategic plan and supporting documents
- Analysis of the fundraising program and all the aspects
- A comparative analysis of similar organizations' fundraising revenue and expenses
- An assessment of the staffing and budget of the fundraising program

Optimally, when done every few years, an institutional assessment will renew, revitalize, and reengineer your fundraising services and your staff.

CASE FOR SUPPORT

Compelling, Urgent, and Realistic Goal

If you have a compelling, urgent, and relevant case to present to highly qualified donors, they will say *yes*, if not, this answer will be *no*.

What does the word case mean? Essentially, it is a description of your cause—written or verbal—to get your donors' attention, stimulate their interest, and influence them to make a gift.

Harold Seymour, author of the first fundraising book in 1966, put it so succinctly that he has been quoted in virtually every fundraising book since: "The case is an expression of the cause, or a clear, compelling statement of all the reasons why anyone should consider making a contribution in support of or to advance the cause."

Other authors explain that your case is the way you convince a prospect that your mission is worthy of support.

The term *case for support* is the accepted nomenclature for both your overall umbrella case (how the charitable mission intends to change the world) and for your individual subcases (how the different initiatives, programs, and services will accomplish that mission). Consider that your macro goal is defined by your overarching case for support and that your micro goals are really your objectives (programs and services as articulated in your subcases).

It is reasonable for a small organization to have only one case for support, whereas a large organization could have one large case for support, with more than 25 smaller cases. The way your case is written or presented causes a donor to determine if, and how much, to give.

What is in the Case Statement? It is a written document, brochure, grant request, solicitation script, video, or website statement that describes why your organization needs and deserves gifts and grants from the general public and from grant-making foundations. There are so many variations and versions (subcases) because, in the end, each case statement is tailored for each and every prospective donor.

Case statements are constructed from information gathered from existing files and by asking pertinent questions. I cannot think of anyone better equipped to answer the following questions than you, the executive director.

- Given the organization's financial situation, what is the total need for philanthropy this year?
- Which projects and services comprise that need?
- What amount is needed from philanthropy for each project?
- How much is needed next year and each year beyond?

Who writes the Case Statement and the subcases? The information about the various program goals and objectives must come from the program directors themselves. They are the only ones who can provide the program methods, timelines, and outcomes. They are the resident experts when it comes to defending the community's need for the program, as well as articulating what will be accomplished if funding is available (or, if funding is not available, what will happen).

The actual writing of the various case statements, including the interpretations of them into *donor speak*, is the responsibility of the development staff. Fundraisers are trained to know how to turn a factual document into one that jumps off the page for donors to resonate with; thus, fundraising professionals are often the ones who will be able to project which cases will be most popular and to judge which ones will be hard to raise money for.

How do we measure case relevance?   When a prospective donor reads or hears your case for support, it triggers a response in them to say yes or no. The case is the fundraising elicitor of a donor's motivation to be charitable.

If it has been prepared with the prospective donor in mind, it fulfills a need that the prospective donor has to do something. If not, the case for support falls on deaf ears.

As mentioned earlier, the case is also the elicitor of the size of the gift. If your case is seen as minimal, you are likely to generate a token gift. If your case is seen as compelling and systemic, you are more likely to generate a significant gift.

Best practice demands that we critique, challenge, rate, and rank all of our case statements so we can determine our fundraising priorities.

- Which of our cases are more or less important to the organization?
- Which are more or less important to our donors?
- How have our donors ranked them again other organizations' cases?
- Do we have a case for each donor segment?
- Do we have different cases at different amounts?
- Are our cases competitive, compelling, relevant, and urgent to raise all that we need?

CAMPAIGNS TO SOLICIT GIFTS

Integration of Fundraising Methods

> All parts—annual fund, major gifts, capital campaigns, and planned giving—are interrelated; success cannot be achieved in isolation.
> —Philip L. Brain Jr.

With more than 130 years of fundraising history behind us, and four codified techniques, one might assume a nonprofit organization need only implement

them, one at a time or one after another. The time-honored giving pyramid actually implies such simplicity. Nothing could be further from the truth.

The four techniques—annual, major, capital, and planned giving—are not simple techniques that can stand alone. They are complex development programs, reliant on each other. They require a seamless integration to be effective in today's complex and individualistic marketplace.

To gauge your campaign integration, you need to assess whether all four methods of fundraising are implemented and integrated, and are attracting the most donors and dollars

You might start your assessment by asking for a description of your donor base as compared with a typical giving pyramid. See Exhibit 5.1.

In doing so, you are asking for the number and size of donors, the duration of donor giving, the movement of donors up the giving pyramid, and the allocation of resources to each of the four methods of fundraising outlined on the giving pyramid. By the way, the methods are not constructed haphazardly; they are built sequentially, one upon another, as resources and donors increase.

Although the pyramid seems to imply that donors move in a linear fashion, they do not necessarily.

Within the pyramid are many types of donors (the following list is an example). How many types do you have? What are your plans for them?

- Single donors (one year)
- Repeat donors (give annually, at small levels)
- Occasional donors (give regularly but skip an occasional year)
- Established donors (core group who give generously every year)
- Loyal donors (increase their gift every year or give several times a year)
- Committed major donors (gives a major gift regularly)
- Special donors (give to a large campaign or to endowment)

The donor pyramid represents how donors can begin giving at the first annual level, move up to the major level, eventually participate in a capital campaign, and/or make plans for a legacy gift.

- ANNUAL: Program for Repeat, Loyal Gifts
- MAJOR: Program for Inspired, Impactful Gifts
- CAPITAL: Program for Mega, Named Gifts
- LEGACY: Program for Donors' Last Gifts

Donors give for different reasons, from different sources, for different results, requiring fundraising tactics that offer different campaigns. See Exhibit 5.2.

EXHIBIT 5.2   HOW DONORS GIVE

Different Campaign Methods	Different Sources
Annual Gift Program	Cash Pocketbook
Major Gift Program	Income Checkbook
Capital Gift Program	Savings Stock/Bank Account
Planned Gift Program	Assets Net Worth

Different Reasons	Different Results
Immediate or Short-Term Need	Unrestricted Operating or Programs
Systemic or Longer-Term Project	Designated Projects or Special Needs
Innovative Initiative or Special Campaign	Capital or Institutional Advancement
Memorialize or Leave a Legacy	Interest Area or Endowment

ANNUAL

Program for Repeat, Loyal Giving

> Over the years, it has become apparent that there is a greater need than ever for nonprofit organizations to have a strong and carefully thought-out annual campaign.
>
> —Robert Schwartzberg

Your *annual gift program* is the foundation for all your fundraising processes, practices, procedures, and policies.

More important, this program utilizes the four donor relationship pillars: acquisition, renewal, upgrade, and over-above giving—making it the feeder for major, capital, and planned gifts.

Your job as executive director is to make sure that the *annual gift program* is never obscured by the other methods of fundraising. This program deserves the maximum investment of financial resources and the employment of the brightest and best professional fundraisers.

Annual gifts constitute a *lifeline* to your community because this fundraising method connects your organization with the greatest number and most diverse group of donors.

Not only do these donors form the base of your giving pyramid, but also they form a large network of supporters who extend out into the community. Individually and collectively, they affirm that your organization is a community asset. Their mixture of voices and votes indicates that your organization is inclusive, not just exclusive in the donor world.

When donors first enter your giving pyramid, they are expressing an interest in what you do. With each subsequent year, the annual gift program moves your donors to renew their gifts, causing them to become more involved and more committed. Over time, the annual gift program moves some of your donors to larger gifts, creating a heightened sense of commitment between their own philanthropic goals and your organization's mission and vision.

Akin to a simple version of Maslow's theory (the other motivational pyramid), donors do not always move in a linear fashion up the giving pyramid. The choice of involvement and level is really theirs to make, depending on their stage in life and in giving.

In fact, a donor may choose to move up at any point in time, stay in one place for years or decades, give for a few years and then take a few years off, or retract to a lower level of giving as financial assets increase or decline.

Giving patterns do not always represent the donor's psychological commitment to your mission. For instance, donors with limited financial ability may stay at the same giving level (say $1,000) for 20 years, but their commitment to the organization still grows over time. Other donors could make a two-year repeat gift of $5,000 and not another one, yet continue to think of themselves as your best donors.

These unpredictable giving patterns require an extremely sophisticated donor management program and professional staff who are sensitive to donors' unique motivations and complex situations.

Finally, in the process of giving over time, annual donors become part of your organizational family and turn into connectors and advocates out in the community. Their confidence and commitment to your organization cause others to give. That's what the concept of *lifeline* is about.

Annual gifts constitute a *livelihood* for you because they are your primary source of unrestricted operating revenue, so critical to the delivery of your core services.

Annual gifts represent dollars that are irreplaceable. Because annual donors become more committed and loyal over time, you can reasonably predict their giving behavior. And you can build a budget on that.

Annual campaigns generate both small gifts (under $25) and large gifts (over $10,000) from a few donors (under 100) to many (over 25,000). These gifts constitute between 10 and 90 percent of an organization's budget, depending on the type of organization and the resources allocated to running the annual gift program.

The potential for annual gifts is enormous; there are no limitations to the kind or number of fundraising campaigns that can be run on an annual basis, nor are there time constraints. Gifts can be solicited and received 365 days a year.

Once established, an annual gift program can produce all the individual donors needed for the larger and more ambitious endeavors.

Who Are Annual Gift Donors? Most annual gift programs utilize a multitude of activities and individualized campaigns that acquire, renew, upgrade, and recognize donors who give small to medium-size annual gifts. Included among those are two distinct groups.

Individual Donors (60 to 90 percent of your annual gifts)

- Board members
- Your own employees
- Your organization's volunteers
- Recipients of your services
- Donors who give to similar missions
- Friends and family of your donors

Corporate and Civic Organizations (10 to 20 percent of your annual gifts)

- Businesses whose social platform aligns with your mission
- Their employees who benefit from your services
- Sponsors of programs or projects
- Those with community volunteer programs

How should I assess my annual gift program? Annual giving is unmistakably both art and science. There are a number of tried-and-true annual giving variations, but what works for one organization does not routinely work for another. There are no quick fixes or formulas for success in annual giving, other than hard work, strategic focus, and ample resources.

Each organization's distinctiveness necessitates that its annual program have its own style, look, feel, and tone—one that is easily recognizable and consistent, year after year.

Marketing savvy will set one apart from another. Fortunate is the organization with an entrepreneur staff member in the annual director's seat who will occasionally take the annual giving program apart and put it back together again, breathing life into it in imaginative ways.

As executive director, you need to encourage your development staff to create an annual giving program with a unique personality that mirrors your organization (not the one they came from), your culture, life stage, and resources.

ANNUAL Gift Program Checklist

- Do we understand and research annual donors, their motivations, and their interests?
- Do we segment annual donors into similar, discrete constituent groups?
- Do we communicate the need for gifts to create an exchange with each donor?
- Do we utilize different fundraising vehicles based on the donor segment?
- Do we manage the process for each annual donor to move up the pyramid?
- Do we recognize, communicate, and steward each and every relationship?

MAJOR

Program for Inspired, Impactful Gifts

> The definition of a major gift varies as greatly as the institutions themselves. One thing is certain: major gifts are inspired that have a significant impact on the development program and the institution.
>
> —James. M. Hodge

In fundraising laurels, there is a hypothesis that a donor's real-time potential is 10 times the size of their annual gift. That's the simple reason you need a major gift program. Of course, there are more reasons.

Most major donors start out as annual donors and move up when they see a larger need and/or when their commitment grows more intense (and their financial means permit them to give more). The exception to this is the wealthy donor who is able to make a major gift the first time around.

A major gift program is designed to raise large sums of money from a relatively small percentage of your donor base (about 20 percent). Major donors tend to be highly committed persons of means who will make up the largest percentage of your contributed revenue (about 80 percent).

Not only are major donors your greatest asset internally but also they are your strongest advocates externally. It has been said that major donors feel such an obligation to see things through that they feel compelled to keep on giving, so as to not disappoint you or let you down.

There are several ways to measure the meaning of the word *major*. A major gift is a contribution that has major significance to the donor. Concurrently, it has a major impact in the eyes of the institution, making the donor a major investor.

For some organizations, a major gift is $1,000. For most others, a major gift is $10,000 and up. But if your donors list your organization as one of their top three to five charities, that's major.

The motivations to give a major gift are very personal and even private. When major donors recognize how much they can do to ameliorate a problem or advance a cause, they are eager to give as much as they are able.

Some major donors may give only once; others give regularly (even annually); still others think of each gift as part of a larger gift that accumulates over time. We need to respect all these points of view and various giving patterns and make our major gift program flexible and donor-centric. All major donors require tailored approaches to fit their different needs and interests.

Major donors require solicitations that are more personal than annual gifts. Almost all first-time major gift solicitations (asks) are made in person by someone who is known to that prospective donor, whereas future asks are actually more akin to a thank you, personally reporting on how the last major gift was utilized.

Recognition programs must reflect credit for single major gifts, as well as lifetime giving. It is advisable that recognition levels include the number of years, not just gift amounts, such as a 10-year club.

Because of their size and motivation, major gifts tend to be designated or restricted for programs, services, or projects that are of particular importance to the institution and of special interest to the donor.

Remember, major gifts do not materialize without a strong annualized effort to build donors' interest and commitment to consider giving at the major gift level. Beyond that, when we have built a strong major gift program, our organization will be posed to run a successful major campaign and to become the beneficiaries of both solicited and unsolicited legacy gifts.

Who Are Major Gift Donors?   Generally, major donors are people of means, but it is not always possible to ascertain the extent of them.

We do know that people over the age of 50 control much of the nation's wealth. Research and experience tell us that older adults are also among the most philanthropic. We also know they are going to live longer, making it possible for them to be major donors longer.

Although it is not always possible to determine people's wealth factor, today's high-potential donors are those who are mature individuals with a philanthropic attitude and spirit. These are the folks who will find the resources if they see the need and believe they can make a difference. It may be more important to find out what their over-arching philanthropy goals are, if you are going to help them realize their giving potential. Some of the questions to ask are:

- What is your philanthropic agenda?
- How do you want to make a difference during your lifetime?
- Are you strongly linked to a particular issue or another organization?
- What caused you to give to our organization in the first place?

Additionally, there are private foundations (otherwise known as family foundations or independent foundations) that make large grants that fall into the major gifts category. In the case of a foundation, it is easy to research their linkage, their interests, and their abilities; it is all public information. While foundations can provide a rich resource of philanthropic support, just like individual major donors, they require a very sophisticated solicitation and stewardship process.

What should I look for when assessing my major gift program?   Because of the importance of major donors within our fundraising program, we must employ a relationship management process that ensures each and every donor's needs are met. Coordination of communications is essential to this, as is the ultimate goal of establishing a stronger mutually beneficial relationship.

We do this by using a case management approach or moves management system. This system can be manual or electronically driven, depending on the number of major donors.

Case management of donors occurs when each high-potential donor is assigned to a specific staff member (based on personal style and values orientation) as the primary contact for all interactions with the organization.

The case manager is responsible for writing the management plan and for strategizing and implementing the moves, but will call in others as needed (tour with the executive director, lunch with a program director, phone call by a peer who sits on the board). The case manager oversees every activity, be it a tribute for gifts, a request for information, an invitation to a special event, an address correction, a stock transaction, or a decision to make a bequest.

Your role as executive director is to insist that each donor's status be reviewed regularly, so that this case management system does not become overly institutionalized. Donors are not file folders, and relationships are not ever finished. Each and every major donor relationship requires adaptation within each interaction. We cannot script human dynamics.

MAJOR Gift Program Checklist

- How many major donors do we have, as compared to five years ago?
- How many prospects do we have in our pipeline?
- Do we have a major gift recognition program, with giving levels?
- Are all major donors assigned to a staff member to execute moves management?
- Do we utilize board connections to attract more major donors?

CAPITAL

Program for Mega, Named Donors

The importance of a capital campaign to any institution at a critical moment in its history cannot be understated. Throughout this century, it has been the one public undertaking that exposes the hopes and aspirations of an institution to critical market segments who ultimately are asked to invest the time, energy, and financial support crucial to its quality and, at times, its survival.

—Kent Dove

Mega campaigns, run every 7 to 10 years, are inevitable; we can't avoid them. Most comprehensive strategic planning processes result in the consideration of a major fundraising campaign, be it for capital, a special purpose, or an endowment.

Although we still use the word capital for this type of fundraising, it does not mean "only capital." In fact, you would use this method for all major initiatives.

The capital campaign approach was the first method of fundraising, initiated by our nation's first universities to generate large gifts from people of wealth to pay for what is fondly referred to as bricks and mortar. The campaign method has changed very little since its inception, serving as the rubric for all other campaigns, large and small.

Campaigns fall into three basic types: those that raise only capital, those that raise endowment, and those that are comprehensive (capital, endowment, and program expansion).

Examples of campaign gifts run the gamut:

- A $2 million lead gift for a capital campaign to build a new women's shelter
- A $25 million gift to endow a named scholarship fund at a donor's alma mater to honor a cherished professor
- $250,000 toward the local hospital's heart center campaign to have a room named for the donor's family
- A pledge over five years of $500,000 to help fund the renovation of the historic seats at a local performing arts theater

The campaign method has many distinctions. It always has a large stretch goal, motivating donors to give what may be the largest gift of their lives.

Successful capital campaigns are always volunteer-led, supported underneath by professional staff and a time clock. They have a defined start and finish and, in between, have a series of tightly controlled steps, schedules, report meetings, and deadlines.

There is an enormous reliance on large lead gifts for as much as 15 percent of the total goal, with additional gifts getting smaller toward the end of the campaign. Solicitation is always person to person, working from the top (largest donors) to the bottom (smallest donors).

No other method of fundraising is as visible and vibrant as a campaign, in large part because it:

- Attracts some of the largest gifts that an organization will receive.
- Rewards donors with public recognition and tangible notoriety.
- Provides an opportunity for an organization to move closer to its vision.

It is interesting to note that a donor generally views participation in a campaign as a one-time, over-and-above occurrence (albeit a gift that is pledged over several years).

A capital campaign has many forms: For a hospital, it might build a cardiac center; for a university, it might raise funds for a postgraduate engineering school; for an environmental organization, it might underwrite a student over-night learning center; for an arts museum, it might build a new collection wing; for a social services agency, it might fund a residential treatment facility.

In the world of higher education, capital campaigns seem to mesh together, coming one on top of another. The only thing that seems to change is the number of zeros.

For other organizations, campaigns tend to be a strategy that is more occasional, with the rule of thumb being 5 to 10 years apart. The length of a typical capital campaign is roughly three years (from start to finish), with campaign pledges payable over three to five years.

There are multiple and sequential phases in a traditional campaign, and each one must be followed religiously to ensure a successful conclusion.

Who Are Capital or Campaign Donors? Major donors are motivated by large and major campaigns that are designed to transform or move an organization to the next level of service (via capital expansion, technology upgrades, programmatic innovation, endowments, and so forth).

In fact, so experienced are most major donors that they will ask you when your next campaign is or pose the big question, "What will it take for us to establish national recognition?" They stand ready to make investments via philanthropy that will leverage an organization's stature and impact.

It is not uncommon for a large campaign donor to come out of your annual giving pyramid, but it is just as likely that they will be a first-time donor to your organization—making a capital campaign one of the best acquisition programs you will ever have!

Many have observed a kind of phenomenon with large campaigns that can only be characterized as magical. They seem to attract donors who see the big picture, so campaigns give them a chance to find big solutions to big problems. In fact, some donors can be classified as campaign donors; their philanthropy is triggered by bigger-than-life projects (as opposed to annual projects supported by small annual gifts).

What should I look for when assessing my capital gifts program? It probably goes without saying, but campaigns require careful planning and thoughtful testing. Regardless of their size and scope, every large campaign requires a professional feasibility study, by an expert consultant. A large campaign is not a strategy you want to take on if you cannot be successful; the public fallout from a failed campaign will linger for decades to come.

A thorough feasibility study evaluates both the readiness of the organization to undertake a campaign and the readiness of the community to support it.

The consultant tests this assumption by using interviews with potential supporters, as well as a review of your internal systems and procedures. A key component of the feasibility study is the extent to which your board of directors *gives* and *gets* financial support for your organization and their level of interest in leading a big campaign. Hopefully, there is someone on your board who can and will serve as chair.

A key ingredient of a large campaign is an existing constituency, already involved and supportive. The feasibility study also tests the reaction of leaders and major donor prospects for the proposed project and campaign. It helps address whether the projected goal is achievable, if the project makes sense to donors whose support is needed to make the goal, and if the timeline is reasonable.

CAPITAL Campaign Checklist

- When was our last big campaign, and what did it raise?
- Are our donors ready for another big campaign?
- Are we ready; do we have needs that can be met only through a campaign?
- Is our board the right group of leaders to take on a campaign?
- Is there a campaign window in our community in the next few years?

LEGACY

Program for Donors' Last Gifts

> Once a donor has decided that your organization merits support (with a legacy or planned gift), helping the donor understand the various giving opportunities and how to make the gift in the most advantageous manner becomes the responsibility of the charitable gift planner.
>
> —Dean Regenovich

The industry use of the term *planned gifts* seems so technical that many of us prefer to use the term *legacy giving* to recognize that when donors make decisions to leave something behind, they do so to make a lasting statement.

Granted, the gift has to be planned by using thoughtful financial and estate considerations for the distribution of one's assets, but that is the means to the end. Some financial advisors suggest that planned and legacy gifts should be made to achieve tax savings, but tax benefits are not usually incentives for giving; they are benefits of giving. Only the donor can say for sure.

In recent years, there has been heightened interest in hiring planned giving staff in an attempt to capture a portion of what was touted as the largest intergenerational transfer of wealth. In 1996, estimates by Cornell University economists predicted $10.4 trillion would be transferred. In 1998, the Center on Wealth and Philanthropy predicted a much higher number of $41 trillion.

Unfortunately, the nonprofit sector has yet to see much evidence of this projected transfer, challenging the legitimacy of such predictions. It might be helpful if economists considered the philanthropic influences rather than relying solely on financial indicators.

Nevertheless, legacy giving has become a highly visible and important strategy for fundraising and should not be overlooked or overstated.

Who Are Legacy Gift Donors? Legacy giving is a highly sophisticated form of fundraising because of the complex legal requirements associated with the various gift instruments.

Donors who make legacy gifts are typically older and have a specific charitable goal. Today, bequests make up the largest number of planned gifts and represent the most dollars.

Bequest donors are unique in their own right; they tend to be less known to the organization than other types. More often than not, bequests come from people who have made only a few gifts over the years (some so small you may not even have good records of them).

Bequests also come from people who are modest about their end-of-life giving and don't want you to know that they have your organization in their will until they die. Is that because they might want to change their mind? Who knows?

As an industry, we have very little behavior research to tell us the answers. But we do know that we must make sure people know that we are in the will business, that we need them to help grow our endowments, be they unrestricted or restricted.

Key to attracting bequests is public awareness that you will accept them. So often donors have said to me that they didn't know XYZ organization wanted bequests or had a legacy program. Promotion of your endowments, your named funds, your receipt of bequests, will generate greater donor confidence in entrusting all or a portion of their life-earned assets.

Examples of legacy gifts include:

- A million-dollar bequest, unrestricted, to a local social service agency
- A will provision for 15 percent residual, to a donor's church, where the donor attended services the past 20 years

- A gift of a fully paid life insurance policy, with a face value of $100,000, to a donor's educations institution
- A gift to the local art museum of a donor's collection of a famed artist's original watercolors, valued at $283,000

What should I look for when assessing my legacy gift program? One question you might pose is: How many of the planned gift instruments do we offer or need to offer? You may not want to offer them all, but you need to consider if you will accept them, should a donor decide to give one. They are:

- Wills
- Charitable gift annuities
- Deferred-payment gift annuities
- Pooled income funds
- Charitable remainder unitrusts
- Charitable remainder annuity trusts
- Retained life interest gifts
- Life insurance gifts
- Retirement plans

You also want to assess your staffing and your financial planning acumen for these more sophisticated gifts. Most small and medium-size organizations will not be able to hire a planned gift officer, so they will need to rely on a planned gift committee of volunteers who have expertise in financial planning, nonprofit law, endowment investment, fund accounting, and audit processes.

Last but not least, you will need to be sure you have all the stewardship policies and procedures in place to accept these unique charitable gifts whose allocation process will go on for decades or centuries to come. (More about stewardship systems later in this chapter.)

Along with this come your ethical practices of accepting and utilizing a gift from a donor who has died. It is commonly accepted that end-of-life gifts should not be used today for your general operating budget but used instead for tomorrow, applying the earnings and not the principal for generating operating expenses or a specific program designated by the donor. From an ethical perspective, I have always been of the frame of mind that bequests (particularly the unrestricted ones) must be placed in some kind of endowment account to be used over time because they were accumulated over time.

LEGACY Gift Program Checklist

- What is our organization's history of receiving and generating legacy gifts?
- How many future planned gifts do we know about, and what are the values of those gifts?
- How many prospects are on our list for a legacy gift?
- How do we work differently with these donors versus other donors?
- Do we have all the policies and procedures we need to safeguard these donors and their gifts?

COMMUNICATIONS TO SOLICIT GIFTS

Motivational Elicitors to Generate a Response

> Fund development communications, oral and written, are ultimately about action; if not now, then sometime.
>
> —Tom Ahern and Simone Joyaux

When donors are involved, informed, invested, and inspired in the work of a charitable institution, their interest, commitment, pride, and willingness to do more grows, and they become aficionados of your cause. Even times of trouble can't keep philanthropic aficionados from standing up and supporting their favorite charity.

The gift pyramid has long been used to illustrate the increased level of involvement necessary to build relationships with donors as the fundraising process moves donors up the pyramid. It is unclear precisely where the multiple pyramid adaptations came from, but I prefer a version that uses levels of engagement: *introduce, interest, identify, inform, involve, invest,* and *inspire.* Each level requires communications that are market-driven and donor-focused.

Most nonprofit organizations have a separate, professionally staffed marketing or public relations department that handles all organizational communications, in addition to helping the development program with fundraising collateral.

As executive director, you need know that professional fundraisers generally have expertise in case development and messaging, but they do not have the honed skills of a graphic designer, a professional writer, an advertising specialist, or a professional photographer. Therefore, they need to work in tandem with the marketing department for artistic creation, printing services, media promotion, and the like.

If this collaboration mandate doesn't come from you, or if there is not already an existing team spirit, there will be tension about interdepartmental roles, allocated costs, and established deadlines. And your communication messages will not be donor centered (relationship development), they will be organization centered (image development).

To achieve your communication goals, you should consider the following:

- DONOR-FOCUSED: Creation of a Social Exchange
- METHODS: Solicitation Effectiveness and Efficiency
- STEWARDSHIP: Accountablility for Donors and Dollars

DONOR FOCUSED

Creation of a Social Exchange

The basic purpose of donor-focused engagement and communications is to build relationships that are sustainable, adaptable, resilient, and growing over time. The premise of a donor-focused approach is to ensure that our approaches are constructed on the donor's side of the equation, not just ours.

As executive director, your challenge is to create a culture that views donor-focused communications to be as important, if not more so, than asking for a gift. In other words, acquisition of donors is only as good as the retention of donors. Your priority must be first and foremost on retaining existing donors before you expend time and effort on acquiring new donors.

Let me put it this way: Asking should not exceed 20 percent of your allocated time for fundraising, but donor relationship management will take at least 80 percent of your fundraising time.

This emphasis on donor relationship management (retention) is so critical to the success of your fundraising program that oversight for this activity merits a staff czar to pose questions like:

- What would our donors think if we did this?
- Is this in our donors' best interest?
- How are we doing with donor satisfaction?

Donors give in order to get. They do not want to feel like they are giving their money away; they want to feel like they are investing it and getting something in return that is bigger than their association with you. This is why the emphasis cannot be on the dollars per se or on the money the organization needs. The emphasis must be on the donor's investment itself. As investors, donors want to know how their stock is doing, including:

- Is my charitable investment competitive with other investments?
- Who is investing my money, and what are my gains?
- Is my money getting a good return, and is it being applied wisely?
- Has my stock split, or did someone else buy it. Was the investment a wise one?
- How much did it cost to manage my investment?

Donors naturally feel attached to their gift, they feel entitled to information about its use, and they feel good when there is a return on their investment, when they get something for it.

Like all good investors, donors feel a sense of ownership of the institution and its work.

What Do Donors Think? Having made a thoughtful gift, donors think that everyone in the organization knows about what they did and who they are. Obviously, this is not all that it seems; it would be impossible and impractical for *everyone* to know the donor.

Nor does this mean that donors expect to be placed on a pedestal for what they did; most donors prefer anonymity of a sort. But it is imperative that the right people know, remember, and act on the information they have about their organization's donors. The people who represent the organization—you, your leadership team, the board members, the program directors, the volunteers— should all receive regular reports of donor gifts when they are received, so they are prepared to acknowledge and thank donors when they come into contact with them.

Like other consumer purchases, donors reflect on the wisdom of having made a decision to contribute to charity. They need reassurance that this gift was a good decision. If their decision had an impact, they need to be encouraged to think about making another gift, soon.

What Do Donors Want? When someone is asked to describe his or her favorite charity, the answer usually falls into two response groups:

1. The donor will rationally describe how the organization fulfills its mission in ways that are distinct and meritorious.
2. The donor will emotionally describe his or her relationship and involvement with the organization.

When we understand donors, we discover that they are no different than we are, and we all want the same thing: thanks, thoughtfulness, respect, reminders, information, appreciation, and insider news.

In her classic book, *Keep the Money Coming,* Christine Graham says:

> You owe your prospects respect, kindness, and appreciation. You should be frank and straightforward about the organization's needs when you solicit them, and grateful when they help. You should remember that it is the cause they are supporting, not your personal needs. Anytime you wonder how to deal with a prospect, put yourself in his or her place. How would you want to be treated? You and your prospects and donors are partners, working toward a shared goal. . . . One of the most remarkable aspects of the nonprofit world is the focus on others. Learn to spear that generosity of spirit, which you certainly have for the beneficiary of your work, to your donors and prospects as well. (Graham 1992)

What Will Donors Do?   People have an inherent need and ability to be change agents. When motivated by the right reasons, donors will not only give money, over and over again, but also become your organization's best spokespersons, too. As they become further invested, they give more, and they become more adamant, dedicated, outspoken, and eager to be involved as volunteers. They will do whatever is asked of them to help, but they do need to be asked.

Donors can and should be asked to do the following, and they will almost always exceed your expectations:

- Participate in a focus group
- Fill out a survey
- Work at an event
- Join an advisory committee
- Sign up as a program volunteer
- Bring a friend to an event
- Make or secure an in-kind gift
- Offer expert advice and counsel
- Identify people who need service
- Introduce friends to a board member or the CEO
- Host an information event at their home or business
- Solicit others, after they have made their gift

What Do Donors Need from You?   Communicating effectively requires an understanding of communication principles, techniques, and messages.

The goal of all communications, especially in fundraising, is to elicit a response—an action-oriented one. As in marketing, fundraising communications are designed to influence attitudes and opinions, which then influence decision making. Educating prospects and donors or expanding public awareness about your organization is *not* marketing. Marketing requires a transformational outcome: a favorable exchange relationship between the donor and the organization.

Within the communication-relationship stages, we must determine how much information should be given, when, and what kind. The *how much* is determined in part by the stage of the relationship, the level of the gift, the frequency of giving, and the interest indicated by the donor.

The *when* is determined by how much, after which a schedule is developed to coordinate all communications to ensure there is not too much and to eliminate duplication. Nothing offends a donor more than receiving duplicate mailings, non-personalized letters, or nothing at all. Few donors complain about receiving too much, but their criticism comes when information is not on point or tailored to their interests. The general rule is that the longer, the larger, or the more invested a donor, the more important the quality of the information and its frequency. Donors want the following information:

- Whether the organization is doing what it said it would
- Changes in the organization or its leadership
- News of new programs or ventures
- Results of the program they supported
- The exact use of their gift
- Who was served by their gift, with examples
- What the need is in the future
- Who else is giving and is involved

Once a prospect becomes a donor, it is as if he or she said, "I am interested in your mission; now show me what there is to be interested about." Once a donor goes on your mailing list, it is time to determine the appropriate type and amount of communications, as well as the timing and the sequencing for the following:

- Project reports
- Newsletters
- Event invitations
- Annual reports
- Updates, fact sheets
- Press releases
- Other solicitations
- Invitations to tour
- Invitations to volunteer

Policies are needed to determine how many and how often and to coordinate communications from all the other departments in your organization.

For instance, it might *not* be a good idea to mail a four-color magazine to donors under $100, though doing so may be quite appropriate for others on your mailing list, including some high-potential prospects.

It would *not* be a good idea to send every donor a 30-page annual report; for lower-level donors, it is better to send an annual summary inside a newsletter.

An inexpensive quarterly newsletter should be sent to all donors and to qualified prospects. As a rule, it is *not* wise to mail two items within a few days or even weeks of each other: The subtle message is that the organization does not have its act together or has money to burn, especially if the two could have been combined into one mailing.

As for annual solicitations, it is advisable to send at least two or three solicitations a year for different campaigns or projects (holiday, tribute, special event); donors will decide which projects to support, and not to inform them of those projects is to exclude them from the opportunity of giving and of being *in the know.*

In your communications, do not talk about your organization; talk about the results and the impact you have made. Do not hold up your campaign with a thermometer; show what the gifts are going to do.

- Websites should feature stories about who has been helped and what issues you are working on.

- Newsletters should show where the money came from (donors) and where the money is going (clients).

- Thank-you letters should say exactly how the gift will be used to achieve the mission.

SOLICITATION Material Checklist

Do they invite people to give to others with needs?

The demonstration of human needs is a powerful catalyst to giving and a crucial element of the case for support. The key is to portray that need in a way that others can relate to, using words, phrases, and other stimuli that will help them recall their own situations and elicit feelings of compassion and a belief that their gift will help somebody.

Do you tell people what the result will be, and who benefits?

The concept of making a gift to charity is more complicated than it used to be. Growing skepticism and donor fatigue have created a need for more information—enough to show that programs can respond to problems properly and seize opportunities. People want evidence from outside sources that an organization meets charitable standards. They need to be reassured that their gift will benefit the recipient, the family, the neighborhood, and the community. They want to know precisely what will happen as a result.

Do they explain how much is needed?

More and more donors want to be advised of the big picture, as well as the small details. They want information about the whole budget, the revenue, and expenses. They will compare what you ask them for to what the organization needs and decide the relative impact. They want to know if their gift will make a difference, or not.

Do they give an example, tell a story?

Telling stories is an effective way to create visual images, supported by audio messages. When people can imagine a situation, they are better able to assimilate the information, process it, and react to it. Visual and audio messages are especially useful when the case or problem is outside someone's personal experience. A story told about a specific person in a specific situation can illustrate the case emotionally, because the donor's experience may not.

Do they provide a balance of emotional and rational information?

Most people are able to make decisions when they are given sufficient data, but the data need to be both emotional and rational in the delivery. Psychology tells us that when people make decisions that come from their hearts and their heads, they have less post-decision dissonance. Emotional information comes from examples, quotes, choice of words, and visual enhancements. Rational information comes from statistics, facts, reference points, and clear, succinct language.

Do they convey a sense of urgency?

Urgency is tied to the case or condition being so critical that to delay a response would impose a hardship on those who may not be served. A campaign deadline does not convey a legitimate sense of urgency. Challenge and matching gifts do help, as long as they are time framed and limited to increased or new gifts.

Do they treat people as individuals?

With technological advances in fundraising, it seems that every appeal is computer-personalized in one way or another. The problem is that everybody recognizes this so the effect is lost. Therefore, we must use other methods of personalizing our appeal. First-person language; hand-written salutations, signatures, and notes; tailored case solicitations; and phone calls all help let people know they are more than a computer record.

Use language that gives the donor a feeling of pride, achievement, status, and belonging.

Do they articulate how efficient and effective the effort is?

Not only does the public promote nonprofit ventures with pride as an expression of American philosophy but also it fully expects that a nonprofit will operate in a less costly and more productive manner than government. Donors want to be reassured that their giving decisions are good ones, that their gifts were used in the best possible way, and that they went as far as possible.

Do they demonstrate past success?

Show donors how they can fund solutions, and demonstrate that your organization has capable management, visionary leadership, and past successes. If you have won national acclaim, awards, credentialing, or endorsements, put them out there. Pride of association is one of the strongest motivators for donors to associate with a particular charity. Any attempt to raise money for a financial problem, rather than a program solution, forces the organization to resort to begging and apology.

Do they articulate vision and leadership?

The presence of leadership is a powerful force; it results in a culture that is both value-centered and value-added. Messages that come from known leaders are inspiring and influential. Donors resonate with plans of what can be done, what the organization should be or do, and what part they might play in the grand plan.

Do they use images and tones conducive for each constituency group?

Social behavior research points out that people's attitudes differ if they were born at a different time, raised with different values, and have different experiences. Thus, they must be communicated with through different styles, moods, and methods. For instance, younger, career-oriented women respond to crisper copy and bolder graphics, whereas traditional older women seem to respond better to subdued colors, graphics, and copy. Baby Boomers respond best to straightforward language; older generations respond best to optimistic copy. Almost everyone responds positively to a case that is presented with an upbeat tone, action words, and a creative bent.

Do they ask people to respond and show them why and how?

So many fundraising appeals approach people timidly and with apology. There is no need for apology when the case is worthy of support and no way to invite people's participation except to ask, in a straightforward manner and with pride. Appeals should provide a balance between the reasons to give and the benefits of giving for the exchange concept to be clear. Some donors will want to charge their gift (to get frequent-flyer miles), and others will give more if they can.

METHODS

Solicitation Effectiveness and Efficiency

Many people new to the world of raising money do not realize that there is a great deal of preparation and planning that needs to be done before you can ask for money.
—Laura Fedricks

There are solicitation communications that are personal, personalized, impersonal, and participative and approaches that work in tandem with solicitation techniques in person, by telephone, by mail, and by event. From these come many interpretations and a multitude of combinations.

Successful development programs seldom use one method or one technique for all donors. They use a combination that reflects their constituency's unique characteristics.

An integrated development program includes not one but a series of multifaceted, continuous, positive, asking scenarios that offer donors multiple opportunities and choices to meet their personal giving objectives.

The concept of integration addresses the uniqueness of each donor and acknowledges that everyone has different reasons to give, different patterns of giving, different preferences for communications, and different reactions to solicitation approaches.

As executive director, you should insist on a rationale behind every solicitation method for each donor segment. The selection of which method to use is made easier by the work already done in the planning and strategic analysis stages, using four primary criteria to frame decisions. The selection of which method to use depends on these four variables:

1. Constituency composition: size, ability, interest, access, and previous support
2. Organizational capacity: strength of case, leadership, and technology

3. Financial and human resources: cash flow, staffing, and volunteers

4. Fundraising goals: number of prospects, donors, techniques, and activities

Although a combination of solicitation methods is advised to maximize the potential reach, nothing is constant; the internal and external environments are always undergoing change. Dynamic functions will affect and are affected by changing opinions and attitudes.

The approaches used today may remain viable for several years but could lose their effectiveness over time. New configurations will be necessary as technology is advanced and as younger donors (Gen X and Y) select their preferred methods of communications.

Each solicitation communication method has merit in and of itself, but none is freestanding; therefore, we utilize them in duals and multiples.

For instance, you might send a letter to advise a donor you want to visit with them. Then you would make a phone call to set up an appointment. The appointment would include a face-to-face solicitation. If the donor needed more information, you would follow up with a letter. Finally, if you did not hear back from the prospective donor, you would call on the phone to inquire about his or her decision. In this one scenario, there are four or five personal and personalized communications.

In solicitations, communications have to achieve multiple levels using the exchange concept, which includes the following elements:

COMMUNICATION Checklist

Be Targeted: Fundraising communications must be structured to attract peoples' attention. Given the noisy marketplace, this challenge can be met by making sure the communications are directed and designed for the target market, not a mass market. Copy tone and graphic design play a significant role here.

Be Personal: Communications must be written to focus enough on the prospect's interests to be considered. A personalized approach, as if directed only to the receiver and from someone familiar to them, improves the likelihood that the communication will be read or heard. If the appeal gets into the bill box, it stands a good chance of serious consideration.

Be Competitive: Communications must sustain a test of evaluation against other options. At this point, the evaluation decision may be influenced by the strength of the case, the precision and value of the match, or the influence of others who are involved in the organization.

Be Relevant: Communications must be situationally correct. Timing is everything, and everything must be right—the amount of the ask, the case, and the perceived outcomes. If a personal situation prohibits response at this point, it negates previous steps, and communications need to start over.

Be Direct: Communications must include a call to action and make it easy for the prospect to respond. The message must be compelling and urgent enough to eliminate the option of decision delay. When the response vehicle, card, envelope, and website address offer all the needed information, the prospect has only to check a box.

Be Prompt: After the prospect decides to respond affirmatively, follow-up communications must provide a positive reinforcement for the donor's decision, validating the reasons behind the exchange. These communications must set the stage for future repeat gift decisions.

Today's best practice solicitation communication methods are listed in the following order of effectiveness by The Fundraising School at the Center on Philanthropy at IUPUI. Also see Exhibit 5.1.

SOLICITATION METHODS of Effectiveness

1. FACE TO FACE: A Personal Solicitation Between Two People
2. PERSONAL LETTER: Directly Written To/For One Person
3. PERSONAL TELEPHONE: Call Between Two People
4. TAILORED LETTER/INTERNET: Slightly Tailored Version
5. TAILORED TELEPHONE/PHONATHON: Use of Volunteer Callers
6. DIRECT MAIL OR INTERNET: Mass Letter Solicitation
7. TELEMARKTING: Mass Phone Calls by Paid Callers
8. FUNDRAISING EVENT: Activity for Many People to Attend

---

1. **Face-to-Face.** All high-impact donors deserve face-to-face solicitation strategies, be they large givers, long-term givers, or just loyal friends of the institution.

   Face-to-face is always used in major gifts, capital campaigns, legacy giving, and annual donors for who are special members of the organization's family, including: board members, key staff, high-level volunteers, community leaders, and high-potential prospects and donors.

There may be times when a personal face-to-face solicitation includes several people: a peer, a key expert, and the executive director. In other cases, one person is sufficient (and could be a peer volunteer or a staff member).

This *should* be your organization's primary way of soliciting. You may occasionally ask for a gift in a personal letter or over the phone, but most of your *asks* will be in person, with a highly-qualified prospect. It is unlikely and certainly not wise to make a cold call.

However, you will not be involved in every personal ask. Board members, fundraising volunteers, and, of course, your development staff will share this responsibility, if you are using a sophisticated moves management system.

Approximately 20 percent of your donors should receive an in-person solicitation, if not every year, at least every few years. The cost of generating gifts through in-person solicitation ranges between 10 and 15 percent, depending on the use of volunteers or staff.

2. **Personal Letter.** Letters that are personal and personalized constitute the second most effective method of soliciting a gift. The key word here is *personalized,* which implies the highest form of personalization, not the lowest form.

    The optimal example is a letter on personal letterhead, with the context personalized to that person and that situation. This references your friendship, family matters, your challenges, and your successes; it can't read like a letter to 20 or 20,000 people; it's just to that one person.

    Even if you have more than 1,000 top donors to solicit, each solicitation letter must be written just to them, preferably by the person who will follow up.

    The cost of personalizing letter solicitators will only be around 15 percent (mostly staff time used to prepare them) because of the high response rate (above 80 percent if properly qualified).

3. **Personal Telephone.** The third most effective form of solicitation is a personal phone call. It is similar to a call you might make to a family friend. It references personal information, challenges, mutual interests, and, of course, the philanthropic needs of your organization.

    The more often you call your donors, the less need they will have for personal letters (which take much more time than a phone call). Additionally, the phone gives you the opportunity to get immediate dialogue and feedback.

    The decision to use the telephone (rather than an in-person solicitation) is justified by the following:

1. The two of you regularly talk on the phone.
2. You may be in different cities.
3. You may be doing a follow-up to a recent visit.
4. You may not have been successful in getting an appointment for a personal visit.

The cost of soliciting highly qualified prospects by phone also has a relatively low cost, about 15 to 20 percent.

4. **Tailored Letter or Internet.** The fourth most effective solicitation strategy includes a communication via e-mail or post mail that may not be as personal as you'd like. For this category, we make the assumption that you will write one (or more) stock letters that you then tailor for each constituency segment.

   The concept of tailoring is not to send boilerplate letters and make them look personalized; they really are. This requires more than a name inserted in the salutation and a handwritten signature in blue ink.

   Tailoring requires that the body of the letter makes reference to their donor status ("thank you for your last gift," "good to see you at our recent event," "your gift was used for XYZ") and also references donor interests ("given you and your family's interest in XXX;" "when we last spoke, you mentioned being concerned about YYY:" "your interest in project BBB over the past five years has successfully impacted thousands of recipients"). Additionally, you will want to use tailored letters for upgrading a gift size and/or seeking additional gifts for occasional special projects.

   Tailored letters are best used when you have donors who need a little extra attention or need more information to give more. The group who needs this level of tailoring will represent about 30 percent of your total giving base. In general, I recommend that this group includes all donors who have given a gift over a certain level (say, $1,000), have given for more than five years, are earmarked for a larger gift, or are prospects for a campaign gift, an endowment gift, or a special purpose gift.

   The cost to generate renewal gifts with tailored letters is between 15 and 20 percent with a relatively high response rate.

5. **Tailored Telephone or Volunteer Phonathon.** Telephone solicitation is seldom used for a first ask or a *cold call*. It is best used as a follow up to a letter.

   It is an effective mechanism for gearing up or wrapping up a campaign, after solicitation letters have gone out. A volunteer-led phonathon can create a sense of campaign urgency, which is transmitted to the donors who are quicker to make a pledge than to reply to an appeal letter.

The telephone provides for two-way communications that are obviously more effective than a one-way letter. The phone call will be open the door to future conversations (whether they say yes to a pledge or not).

If your organization has a telephone thank-you call system in place, you will be posed for telephone solicitation calls, because the donor has already talked with you by phone. The cost of utilizing telephone phonathons to solicit donors, will range from 20 to 40 percent, depending on the quality of your callers

6. **Direct Mail or Internet.** After reading about the effectiveness of the personal or tailored solicitation methods, you might wonder why it's necessary to cover the impersonal methods. With a large donor base, it is virtually impossible to have personal contact with every donor. As many as 50 percent of your donors will fall in a category that necessitates some kind of boilerplate letter, be it a form of direct mail, a stock letter, or a mass Internet appeal.

   As we often say, it's all in the numbers. You will spend most of your time with those at the top range of giving and the least amount of time with those at the bottom.

   Direct mail is still an important methodology for acquisition and low-level renewals. Despite the drop in response rates during the past decade, recent research studies indicate that direct mail is still very effective with all age groups, including the highest responders, women over the age of 65.

   Direct mail works especially well during the holidays, given that November and December are prime months for making contributions and that phone calls are less appreciated by donors during the holiday season. The cost to generate gifts using direct mail or impersonal email appeals could be as high as 75 percent for acquisition and as low as 25 percent for renewals.

7. **Telemarketing.** Utilizing the telephone for the masses is certainly less effective than direct or impersonal e-mail, since it tends to be a little invasive for donors who regard their phone (and their home) as their private domain. With the shift to cell phones and the no-call restrictions, it becomes even harder to reach people this way, and thus telemarketing efforts are now used only with constituency segments that have a history of telephone exchanges such as college students calling alumni every year for a class gift or congregation members who call each other to encourage an annual stewardship pledge.

Using the phone to solicit people we don't know personally has become a thing of the past, because of the low reach rates and the growing resistance to making financial commitments over the phone. The cost to generate a gift via impersonal telephone calls could range between 40 and 60 percent, using an outside telemarketing firm.

8. **Special Events and Benefits.** Special events used for fundraising purposes remain a very effective acquisition and cultivation tool with potential for long-term gain *if* the event attendees become regular donors. If they remain only special event donors, then your effectiveness drops because of the high cost associated with special events.

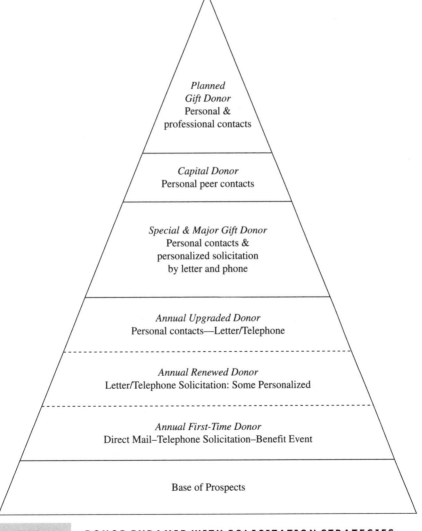

*Planned
Gift Donor*
Personal &
professional contacts

Capital Donor
Personal peer contacts

Special & Major Gift Donor
Personal contacts &
personalized solicitation
by letter and phone

Annual Upgraded Donor
Personal contacts—Letter/Telephone

Annual Renewed Donor
Letter/Telephone Solicitation: Some Personalized

Annual First-Time Donor
Direct Mail–Telephone Solicitation–Benefit Event

Base of Prospects

EXHIBIT 5.3   DONOR PYRAMID WITH SOLICITATION STRATEGIES

People who are attracted to special events are generally looking for the psychosocial benefit of being with others they have something in common with. Events serve to inspire people to get connected to a charity, bring people together to build a sense of community, and generate a large amount of money at one time. The cost of a special event is high, ranging between 40 and 60 percent (maybe even higher), because of the cost of the venue, food, entertainment, invitations, and the like.

Every organization needs at least one major public event to attract new donors into the mix, as well as a few minor events, to create a sense of camaraderie and garner public awareness. Arts and culture organizations are more naturally in the event business; others struggle to keep an event alive for more than a few years. The key to events is to use them to raise friends first and raise money second and then to transfer event donors to annual or major donors in the future.

STEWARDSHIP

Accountability for Donors and Dollars

> Stewardship—the challenge that "to whom much is given, shall much be expected"—is more than a particular program in our fundraising department. In fact, good stewardship is a way of life.
>
> —Paul Pribbenow

The term stewardship, long associated with the religious sector, is now being used in the larger context of nonprofit philanthropy.

The tremendous growth in organized philanthropy, the increase in contributed dollars, the need for sound fiscal management under charitable trust laws, government interest in taxable income, and nonprofit regulations have all contributed to heightened awareness of how contributions are stewarded and accounted for.

The legal, professional, and ethical definitions of stewardship can be found in a growing number of professional codes, professional literature, journal articles, and accounting and financial reporting texts.

Nonprofits are held accountable for what they do and how they do it by virtue of public trust. The public has high expectations of nonprofits, higher than might be imposed on other sectors. In fact, accountability is the public's biggest point of contention; public trust literally depends on it. According to Boris and Odendahl, "In business, profit and the satisfaction of customers may be paramount. In government, public interest and the well-being of the citizen and the state may be the primary objectives. In nonprofits, public interest and the well-being of the clients or ideas served may be the most important."

The public feels entitled to ask the following questions:

- Are nonprofit organizations and the people who work in them doing what they say they do?
- Are they wise and prudent users of resources?
- In all that they do, do they follow strict guidelines, standards, and procedures?
- Are there measures and benchmarks of productivity?
- Are there consequences and penalties if accountability fails?
- Do they expend each dollar and each hour in the best possible way?
- Do they have the public's interest and well-being in mind at all times?

Accountability is the way the public measures what charitable organizations do in three basic areas: charitable purposes, program performance, and donative resources.

State and federal regulatory agencies, national and local charitable governing organizations, and even organizations themselves have policies regarding accountability governance, use of funds, and fundraising practices.

A few things to think about include:

1. What if an organization proclaims its mission is the prevention of teen pregnancy?
    - How would the public hold the organization accountable?
    - What are the criteria for measuring pregnancy counseling services?
    - What are the services measured against? How are the results interpreted?
    - What are the consequences if the organization cannot provide evidence that teen pregnancies were prevented?
2. What if a volunteer agrees to solicit six of his friends who have been identified as high-potential prospects, and he solicits only two of them?
    - How is the volunteer held accountable? By whom?
    - What are the consequences of his inability to fulfill his voluntary responsibility?
3. What if your organization implemented three different fundraising projects last year, but only two of them generated a profit?
    - Does the fundraiser combine the results of the three projects and report to the board that the overall fundraising program was successful?
    - Or does he or she let the donors who supported the failed project know that their money was lost?

It is, unquestionably, the organization's legal responsibility to monitor the receiving, recording, management, allocation, and reporting functions associated with all charitable gifts. The best way for organizations to demonstrate to donors that their contributions are used not only as intended but also with meaningful results, is to keep records of how each and every gift is expended, not just received.

The key is sophisticated fund reporting that provides full disclosure, public reporting, and honest self-evaluation. The objective of financial policies, procedures, processes, and financial statements is to provide information useful for evaluating the effectiveness of the management of resources in achieving the established mission goals. This objective can best be accomplished by using fund accounting, a system where separate records are kept for donations that are given for certain purposes or uses.

Because development professionals are often the liaisons between donors and the organization they represent, they bring a slightly different perspective to the subject of stewardship. Although stewardship requires that a contribution be expended in the way a donor contributes it, there is always room for interpretation. Sometimes a donor makes an informal request to help the children; at times a donor will say to use it where it is needed the most. It is the responsibility of the professional fundraiser to dig a little deeper, to better understand how to steward that donor and the gift.

Stewardship is our virtuous regard for both the human and the financial assets.

1. **Donors.** Of all the stewardship components, donors come first in fundraising. Most of the time, donors give gifts and expect little in return, save appreciation. But we need to give them more, if we expect them to give more.

    When people are highly appreciated, informed about changes, advised of activities, and made aware of their gifts' results, they fill an important part of the organizational family. When donors are listened to and invited to participate in the organization's betterment, they will better understand the depth of your challenges.

    When people are brought into the organization and meet the staff running the programs, they not only feel involved but to some extent privileged. When you introduce them to a person who has benefited from their gift, they sense that your organization is real. These expressions of stewardship heighten a donor's satisfaction.

    Donor recognition policies establish the criteria for recognizing donors at each giving level and determine the various parameters for naming a building, a chair, a program, or a re-endowed fund.

    Interestingly, some donors do not want public recognition; instead, they want a form of private recognition (we see evidence of this with the growing number of anonymous gifts). Public recognition is very popular in large campaigns, and private recognition is generally preferred in legacy gifts.

The Great Generation is more comfortable with tangible recognition items; Baby Boomers consider them wasteful and frivolous, unless they are functional. The days of mugs, calendars, pens, and paperweights are gone.

Private recognition, such as a handwritten note, private luncheon, or bouquet of flowers, is much more personal and greatly appreciated.

2. **Financial.** Stewardship of donor funds has many implications, including how gifts are solicited?. When fundraising is approached with pride over apology (to advance a cause rather than fund a crisis), people are solicited in a respectful way. No pressure is exhibited; no exaggerations are made. Solicitations are transparent, giving full disclosure about who will receive the services, how they are delivered, and what the expected outcomes might be.

Determining what to raise money for has stewardship implications. What are funds solicited for? When both staff and volunteers are involved in selecting the cases and articulating the case for support, their confidence in soliciting gifts will grow. When this happens they can say with conviction that money is needed, where it is needed, why it is needed, and what will happen if a gift is received, they are empowered to be good stewards of the fundraising process and of the funds when they are received.

Of course, stewardship policies are needed to delineate how philanthropic funds are handled after receipt, as well as in future years. Our professional mandate is to formally restrict their use, invest them prudently, and ensure they grow in value over time.

3. **Policies.** Stewardship principles dictate written policies and procedures that transcend leaders and boards, who change with time. Every organization should have a master policy book that question how gift stewardship is handled to safeguard the best interests of all concerned. The following policy categories are recommended:

- Gift Acceptance Policies: Who can accept a gift, with its legal liabilities and moral implications? Who is the contact going forward, to thank and recognize donors and to steward those gifts?
- Gift Type Parameters: What types of gifts are sought and accepted: in-kind gifts; pledges over time; gifts of tangible value such as property, insurance, real estate, art, closely held stock, publicly traded stock? How will these gifts be disposed of (sold, kept, invested, transferred)? What minimum and maximum gift levels are required for planned gifts?

- Gift Restriction Policies: How and when are gifts restricted for program services, endowment, special uses, and capital improvements? What are the minimum and maximum requirements for restricted gifts? How are unrestricted bequests applied?
- Gift Management, Investment Policies: How and where are donor funds invested and managed? Are investment guidelines in place and reviewed annually for marketplace changes? How is fund investment and use reported and to whom?
- Gift Distribution Policies and Procedures: Who decides, beyond donor designations and restrictions, how and when funds are allocated? What happens if funds are designated or restricted for a program that no longer exists? What percentage of the investment earnings will be allocated? Can you tap principal or only earnings?

GOALS TO SOLICIT GIFT

Budgetary Approach to Match Needs and Interests

> Each fundraising endeavor that an organization attempts can and should be assessed in terms of the "financial risk" or the fundraising activity's up-front costs as well projections of staff and volunteer time.
>
> —Bonita M. Bergin

This goal-setting action brings your *constituency ability* into alignment with *case need*, allowing you to set realistic goals for each segment, each case, and each campaign.

To gauge whether your GOALs are realistic and attainable, you must balance the ability with need.

This step is both challenging and opportunistic since it ends with concrete budgetary goals established for each and every fundraising project. It must involve everyone who has responsibility for living with a goal, including your program staff, development staff, board members, and the fundraising volunteers who sit on your development committee.

How Much Do We NEED to Raise? The specific budgetary needs are uncovered in the case development process. Individual programs and projects are identified, budgets developed, and the need for philanthropy determined. The cases will fall into three general need categories:

1. Unrestricted operating support
2. Restricted operating and/or project support
3. Restricted for special purposes

Combined, they represent your organization's entire case for support. Each category has its own case, and within each category are subcases for support. All cases have detailed budgets, goals, objectives, and philanthropic revenue estimates.

How Much Will People GIVE? Your estimates will be based on how much people are already giving (use renewal and upgrade estimates, along with the anticipated number and amount of new acquisitions). Each constituency group is assessed separately to determine its level of interest (on a qualifying scale, say, of 1 to 5) and its financial ability (again, on a qualifying scale based on wealth indicators or philanthropic inclinations).

Some donor groups have a higher average gift size than others, and some have higher retention rates. This information is taken into account when estimates are made. The estimates are also based on the LIA (linkage, interest, and ability scales). Opportunity estimates must be conservative but at the same time made with confidence.

Experience proves that an enthusiastic, positive attitude is the stimulus for exceeding even the most aggressive goals. There is no room for pessimism in fundraising.

How Much Can We RAISE? When matching the case needs and the constituency ability, there are likely to be disparities between what the organization needs and what constituencies can/want to fund. Some programs will be underfunded, and some programs will be overfunded; this is the nature of donor-centered philanthropy.

Donors make contributions to their charity or program of choice, and the gift remains theirs as we accept it and steward it according to donor's intentions. Donors do not always see our world as much as they see their world, so sometimes we need to educate them to give wisely.

For *underfunded* cases, consider the following:

- Find another source of funding to fill the gap.
- Invite your most loyal institutional donors to adopt these programs.
- Incorporate the difficult programs into the unrestricting grouping, where discretion is allowed.
- Initiate a new campaign targeted at only those donors who might be interested (not everyone).
- Cut back the program.

For *overfunded* cases, consider the following:

- Expand the program if the need can be justified.
- Restrict the funds and use them when and as needed.
- Advise donors of the overfunding, pointing out other critical needs.

A few cautions about fundraising goals:

1. **The goals must be *realistic*.** Goals must be based on projections that make sense to both staff and volunteers, and this means they are made on the basis of sound data. It is not realistic to project an increase in annual revenue of more than 5 or 10 percent unless you implement an over-and-above fundraising strategy, like a special major gift campaign. If the needs are greater than the amount you can raise from the various constituency groups (foundations, corporations, individuals, organizations), you must accept that hard reality, set your goal lower than what you need, and find another source of revenue to make up the difference.

2. **The goals must be *achievable*.** If the goals are beyond tested donor capacity, they probably won't be reached, creating frustration and disappointment for both volunteers and staff. Goals that are not achievable send staff looking for jobs elsewhere; no one wants to fail. It is psychologically advantageous to set a lower goal and go over it than to barely meet a goal. So goal setting must be both realistic and idealistic—a very fine line indeed.

3. **The goals must be *challenging*.** Everyone loves a challenge, but if your staff and volunteers are raising more money than you actually need for a specific program, that challenge becomes yours. You need to acknowledge that certain projects may be more important to donors and have to expand a popular program or even retract an unpopular one. Raising money too easily, like not raising enough, can be a disincentive to volunteers.

The ultimate goal is to match your organization's need with the donor's ability. While a single goal for fundraising is key to financial budgeting, a smaller project goal will incentivize volunteers and staff who work on individual campaigns.

For instance, volunteers who chair this year's board campaign can relate to a $115,000 goal in contrast to the total goal of $2.3 million. In the same way, a group of special event volunteers can relate to a $75,000 goal as opposed to the big goal of $2.3 million.

The process used to set fundraising goals ranges from incremental-based budgeting (a percentage over the previous year) to zero-based budgeting (starting from scratch) to plugging the bottom line gap (setting the goal to do that, without knowing what the constituency probability is). Although the last approach is seldom recommended, it may not be possible to start from zero.

Good budgeting is not as difficult as it sometimes appears if the parameters are established. You need to:

- Allocate sufficient time, well ahead of the budget deadline to take all the variables into consideration.
- Involve as many volunteers and staff as practical to allow engagement to result in investment.
- Set fundraising goals only after constituency analysis and needs assessment are done and synchronized.

Financial goals that are balanced, not too high or too low, ensure that the fundraising process is rewarding for all concerned, year after year. When goals are realistic, achievable, and challenging, they will not only be met but also stand a very good chance of being exceeded.

The right goal will motivate volunteers to do all it takes to meet the need and to work a little harder to achieve success. The joy that comes from such an effort is unparalleled, enough to bring them back again next year.

SUMMARY

This chapter wraps up the proposition that executive directors need to lead the fundraising charge, if they want to be among the top philanthropic institutions in the country. Last we detailed how the case, replete with donor-focused communications, is at the heart of our work. When a case is mission-driven it triggers a donor's sensitivities and sensibilities—the heart and the head.

Everything prior to this chapter leads to a pivotal point in the fundraising process. Now it is time to solicit your donors if you have all the other pieces in place—visionary leadership, a philanthropic culture, a sophisticated development program, high-potential constituency, a compelling case, and solicitation tools. If not, do not ask. Some say a "no" is only a "maybe," but I am inclined to say both responses come as a result of not doing our homework . . . I want a "yes" every time.

REFERENCES

Ahern, T., & S. Joyaux. 2008. *Keep Your Donors: The Guide to Better Communications and Stronger Relationships.* Hoboken, NJ: John Wiley & Sons.

Boris, E. T., & T. J. Odendahl. 1990. "Ethical Issues in Fundraising and Philanthropy." In *Critical Issues in American Philanthropy,* edited by J. Van Til, 188–203. San Francisco, CA: Jossey-Bass.

Burnett, K. 2002. *Realtionship Fundraising: A Donor-Based Approach to the Business of Raising Money.* San Francisco, CA. Jossey-Bass.

Chatt, R. P., W. P. Tyan, & B. E. Taylor. 2004. *Governance as Leadership: Reframing the Work of Nonprofit Boards.* Washington, DC: BoardSource.

Cygnus Applied Research. www.cygresearch.com/files/free/US-2011-Cygnus-Donor-Survey_Report-Executive_Summary.pdf.

Dove, J. E. 1988, *Conducting a Successful Capital Campaign: A Comprehensive Fundraising Guide for Nonprofit Organizations.* San Francisco, CA. Jossey-Bass.

Fredricks, L. 2010. *The ASK: Now to Ask for Support for Your Nonprofit Cause, Creative Project, or Business Venture.* San Francisco, CA. Jossey-Bass

Frumkin, P. 2006. *Strategic Giving: The Art and Science of Philanthropy.* Chicago: University of Chicago Press.

Gary, T., & N. Adess. 2008. *Inspired Philanthropy: Your Step-by-Step Guide to Creating a Giving Plan and Leaving a Legacy.* San Francisco, CA: Jossey-Bass.

Grace, K. S. 2005. *Beyond Fundraising: New Strategies for Nonprofit Innovation and Investment,* 2nd ed. Hoboken, NJ: John Wiley & Sons.

Grace, K. S., & A. L. Wendroff. 2001. *High Impact Philanthropy: How Donors, Boards, and Nonprofit Organizations Can Transform Communities.* New York: John Wiley & Sons.

Graham, C. P. 1992. *Keep the Money Coming: A Step by Step Guide to Annual Fundraising.* Sarasota, FL: Pineapple Press.

Howe, F. 1991. *The Board Members' Guide to Fundraising.* San Francisco, CA: Jossey-Bass.

McNamara, C. 2008. *Field Guide to Developing, Operating, and Restoring Your Nonprofit Board.* Minneapolis: Authenticity Consulting.

Mixer, J. R. 1993. *Principles of Professional Fundraising: Useful Foundations for Successful Practice.* San Francisco, CA: Jossey-Bass.

Ragsdale, J. D. 1995. "Quality Communication in Achieving Fundraising Excellence." *New Directions for Philanthropic Fundraising* 10: 17–32. San Francisco: Jossey-Bass.

Rosso, H. A., & Associates. 1991. *Achieving Excellence in Fundraising.* San Francisco, CA: Jossey-Bass.

Rosso, H. A., & Associates. 2003. *Achieving Excellence in Fundraising,* 2nd ed. San Francisco, CA: Jossey-Bass.

Sargeant, A., & E. Jay. 2004. *Building Donor Loyalty: The Fundraiser's Guide to Increasing Lifetime Value.* San Francisco, CA: Jossey-Bass.

Walker, J. I. 2006. *Major Gifts, AFP Nonprofit Essentials.* Hoboken, NJ: John Wiley & Sons.

Wilson, T. D. 2008. *Winning Gifts: Make Your Donors Feel Like Winners.* Hoboken, NJ: John Wiley & Sons.

Zimmerman, R. M., & A. W. Lehman. 2004. *Boards That Love Fundraising: A How-to Guide for Your Board.* San Francisco, CA: Jossey-Bass. http://www.convio.com/our-research/search.jsp?query=research+studies.

About the Author

Karla A. Williams is an organizational consultant with more than 35 years of professional nonprofit experience. She is recognized as a leader in the philanthropic field, an innovator of organizational change models, and a pioneer in the integration of marketing techniques with fundraising strategies.

She is principle of The Williams Group, a North Carolina firm that serves clients across the country; assessing their potential for civic engagement, creating innovative programs and recruiting talented people for key positions. During the past 20 years, she has assisted 230 nonprofit entities including national fundraising associations, large social agencies, community foundations, religious organizations, hospitals, medical clinics, universities, zoological parks, botanical gardens, museums and historic cemeteries.

Prior to consulting, she served as President of the Children's Hospital Foundation of Saint Paul, Communications and Development Director for Children's Home Society of Minnesota, and Executive Director of the Minnesota Zoological Society.

Karla is a frequent keynoter, seminar presenter, workshop instructor and writer on organizational culture, leadership dynamics, and constituency marketing. She serves as faculty director for the new *Leadership Gift School* in Charlotte NC; and adjunct faculty at The Fund Raising School at IUPUI Center for Philanthropy, Center for Nonprofit Management at University of St. Thomas MN, and Saint Mary's University of MN graduate program in Philanthropy.

She holds a B.A. in Nonprofit Management from Metropolitan State University and an M.A. in Philanthropy and Development from Saint Mary's University of MN. She is the author of a best-selling book, *Donor Focused Strategies for Annual Giving.* Karla was twice awarded the Association of Fundraising Professionals (AFP) Fund Raiser of the Year award; from the Charlotte AFP Chapter and the Minnesota AFP Chapter. She recently served as Chair of the national ACFRE Board, responsible for a rigorous certification process for advanced fundraising professionals.

Karla A. Williams, MA, ACFRE
Reinvention & Organizational Consultant
The Williams Group

Index